SOCIOLOGICAL CONSTRAINTS TO INDUSTRIAL DEVELOPMENT IN NORTH EAST INDIA

About the Editors

Dr. B. Datta Ray a pioneer in promoting research in social science in North-east India, during the last three decades, is a Freedom Fighter and a tamropatro holder. He is a former Principal, Women's College, Shillong and has authored and edited a number of publications.

Dr. Prabin Baishya a former Principal of S.B.M.S. College, Sualkuchi, Assam is a well-known economist and a analyst of North East India economics and industrial growth. He is well-known writer and his analysical papers are published in economic Journals and Magazines including *Economic and Political Weekly*.

SOCIOLOGICAL CONSTRAINTS TO INDUSTRIAL DEVELOPMENT IN NORTH EAST INDIA

Edited by

B. DATTA RAY
PRABIN BAISHYA

CONCEPT PUBLISHING COMPANY PVT. LTD.
NEW DELHI-110059

ISBN: 978-81-7022-733-5

Edition 2024

Published and Printed by

Since 1974

Concept Publishing Company Pvt. Ltd.
A/15-16, Commercial Block, Mohan Garden,
New Delhi-110059 (India)
T: 91-11-41101460
E: publishing@conceptpub.com, *W*: www.conceptpub.com

DEDICATED

TO

OUR BELOVED PARENTS

CONTENTS

LIST OF CONTRIBUTORS

Dr. S.K. Agnihotri, Indian Administrative Service, Shillong.

Dr. Prabin Baishya, Former Principal, Sualkuchi College, Sualkuchi, Assam.

Dr. M.C. Behera, Dept. of Tribal Studies, Rono Hill, Arunachal University, Itanagar.

Dr. M. Banerjee, Anthropological Survey of India, Shillong.

Dr. P.R. Bhattacharjee, Dept. of Economics, Assam University, Silchar, Assam-10.

Dr. N.N. Bhattacharyya, Dept. of Geography, Gauhati University, Guwahati-14.

Dr. Sanjib Kr. Borkakoti, Dept. of Economics, A.D.P. College, Nagaon, Assam.

Mr. T. Cajee, Formerly of Indian Administrative Service, Shillong-3.

Mr. Dani Chobin, Dept. of Economics, Arunachal University, Doimukh, Itanagar.

Dr. S. Chakrabarti, Sociological Research Cell, Indian Statistical Institute, Calcutta-700 035.

Dr. D.N. Chakravarty, Formerly Dean, Assam Agricultural University, Jorhat-13.

Dr. Samir K. Das, Dept. of Political Science, Calcutta University, Calcutta-27.

Dr. B.J. Deb, Dept. of Political Science, North Eastern Hill University, Shillong-14.

Dr. Gurudas Das, Dept. of Economics, St. Anthony's College, Shillong.

Dr. P.C. Dey, Dept. of Economics, Manipur University, Imphal-795 003.

Dr. P.C. Dutta, Dept. of Statistics, S.S. College, Hailakandi, Assam.

Dr. A.K. Agarwal, Dept. of Economics, NEHU, Aizawl Campus, Aizawl-Mizoram.

Dr. J.B. Ganguly, Former Vice-chancellor, Tripura University, 4, Minapara Road, Calcutta-40.

Dr. Lipi Ghosh, Dept. of South-East Asia Studies, Calcutta University, Calcutta-19.

Dr. P.J. Goswami, Dept. of Economics, G.C. College, Silchar-Assam.

Dr. M.N. Karna, Dept. of Sociology, North-Eastern Hill University, Shillong-14.

Dr. P.K. Kuri, Dept. of Economics, Arunachal University, Itanagar, Arunachal Pradesh.

Mr. B.B. Kumar, Formerly Principal, Science College, Kohima, Nagaland.

Dr. V.S. Mahajan, 206, Sector 9-6, Chandigarh-17.

Dr. A.K. Maiti, Sociological Research Cell, Indian Statistical Institute, Calcutta-700 035.

Dr. Amitava Mitra, Dept. of Economics, Arunachal University, Doimukh, Itanagar.

Ms. Helina Mantaw, Dept. of Tribal Studies, Rono Hill, Arunachal University, Itanagar.

Dr. B.C. Pradhan, Dept. of Statistics, S.S. College, Hailakandi, Assam.

Dr. B. Panda, Dept. of Economics, I.G. Govt. College, Tezu, Arunachal Pradesh.

Dr. Bibhuti B. Pradhan, Dept. of Commerce, Manipur University, Imphal-3, Manipur.

Dr. N.C. Roy, Dept. of Economics, Arunachal University, Itanagar, Arunachal Pradesh.

Dr. Arunoday Saha, Dept. of Economics, Tripura University, Agartala-4.

Dr. Keya Sengupta, Dept. of Economics, Assam University, Silchar-10.

Dr. A. Rajmani Singh, Dept. of Commerce, Manipur University, Imphal-3, Manipur.

Mr. Anjan Thakur, National Productivity Council, Guwahati.

Mr. S.S. Devbarman, Scholar, Agartala, Tripura.

ACKNOWLEDGEMENTS

Papers included in this volume were presented in the seminar on Sociological Constraints to Industrial Development in North-East India held in 1996 organised by North-East India Council for Social Science Research, Shillong. NEICSSR is grateful to Indian Council of Social Science Research, New Delhi, Industrial Development Bank of India, Bombay and Meghalaya Industrial Development Corporation, Shillong for their generous financial support to undertake, this, study. We sincerely thank Professor R. Radha Krishna, Dr. Ranjit Sinha of ICSSR, Mr. S.K. Srivastava, Indian Administrative Service, Shillong and Mr. Brojen Bora, IDBI for their help. We take this opportunity to thank Mr. Ashok K. Mittal, Concept Publishing Co., New Delhi for undertaking the publication of this volume expeditiously. He has deep understanding of the serious challenges confronting the development of North-East India.

B. DATTA RAY
PRABIN BAISHYA

1

INTRODUCTION

North-East India is struggling with the problems of economic development. The region depends on imports of foodgrains and other products like fish, egg etc. on large scale in spite of vast land mass remaining unutilised in the marshy areas of the plains and particularly in the hills. In the industrial field, the region has only 1.8 per cent of the registered factories and employing less than 2 per cent of the factory workers of the country. Almost every item of mass consumption and every item of conspicuous consumption is imported from the rest of the country. In spite of the region having a long heritage of weaving every metre of mill made textile and every item of hosiery product is imported what is more, most of the few medium and small industries outside the corporate sector are owned and managed by non-local entrepreneurs who had been living in the region for a very long time, and contributing much to economic development of North-East India.

Agriculture is based on traditional low technology, subject to periodic ravages of floods and droughts in the plains while in the hills terrace cultivation through crop diversification on scientific basis is yet to replace shifting cultivation which destroys rich top layer soil and green coverage on a large scale. The household industries using age old technique, failing to bring innovation are gradually decaying due to its failure to cater the new taste of modern consumers. Thus the entire North-East India is caught up in a low productivity and low income syndrome.

The value system of the societies of the different ethnic and cultural groups of North-East India are mostly grounded to fatalism based on continuity and traditions, customs and usages. The potentialities created by modern science and technology are either really known or not readily available or not systematically applied owing to the advice to preserve the tradition and heritage.

The population is growing; markets are expanding and consumerism has caught imagination of the expanding middle class. But what is lacking is work culture. There is an antipathy to undertake new ventures in grain production, animal husbandry, poultry, fishery etc. so also lack of initiative for manufacturing, trade and commerce. The new generation feel that the benefits of planning over the years have been taken away or denied by non-indigenous working people engaged in industry, trade and commerce. There is a widening gulf between the youth and the non-indigenous people engaged in soiling their hands by undertaking new ventures in every field.

The current economic policy since 1991, has left the major initiative for economic development to private sector. Even the infrastructural development responsibility now lies with private initiative. Under this circumstance the genuine growth of local entrepreneurship would very much depend on the radical change in our outlook, the culture component of the people, the sons of the soil.

There is an urgent need to identify the factors responsible for inhibiting the emergence of local entrepreneurship in different sectors among the ethnic groups of North-East India societies. Is the quantum of capital made available since 1950 for industrialisation adequate? Or are the non-economic factors like the traditional soft life-style and the attitude of the bulk of the indigenous people, their surrender to fatalism responsible for this lack of economic development of North-East India? In spite of elaborate steps taken to provide infrastructure and financial incentive, industries have not come up in any significant way. Many a time when it comes to the question of setting up of an industry at a specific location, it becomes a problem as the local people are not ready for it. There is social resistance.

North-East India Council for Social Science Research held a seminar to examine the problem of social constraints to industrial development in North-East India in July 1996.

The papers presented to the seminar analyse the issue in a social perspective based on field data of the contemporary divergent societies in North-East India. The canvas is regional with local commitment to rapid development for the society.

The J.B. Ganguli argues that the expansion of the service sector, disproportionately to the growth of the primary and the secondary sector, indicate that the development that has taken place in the North-Eastern region is largely government-sponsored. He feels that in the present economic environment, development would depend more on the cultivation of the spirit of private enterprise and initiative. He finds that the culture of enterprise is already in evidence in different parts of the North-East, but it has not yet assumed the character of a widespread phenomenon.

M.N. Karna questioned the validity of looking for the constraints to development within the existing social structures in the region. He expects the force of enterprise to emerge from within the North-East societies. He does not see much problem in inculcating a national, scientific and secular outlook in the value system of the tribal societies of the North-Eastern region. Ganguli and Karna advocated a revival of the spirit of community. P. Baishya describes the tribal communities of the North-Eastern region as transitional 'Asiatic Societies'. The impact of modernity has brought in conflicts between generations in these societies. One of the fallouts of this is the growth of extremism and insurgency. He foresees the emergence of indigenous bourgeois in course of time who, he says, would join hands with the immigrant capitalists in the act of exploitation.

A.K. Maiti and S. Chakrabarti argue that in view of the small size of the domestic market, general poverty and seismicity of the region, large scale industrialisation programme would be largely unsuitable here. Analysing data for registered industries, they argue that the exploitation of industrial labour is extremely high. So, among other measures, they urge for steps to increase the share of wages in the value of output.

B.J. Deb mentions the tribal notion of exploitation and in that context attempted to explain the tribal feeling against the outside forces. It (Deb views) is one of the major constraints to industrial development in North-East India.

A. Saha states that the North-Eastern region being a closed economy bounded mostly by foreign countries stands completely isolated. This complete isolation appears to be standing on the way of industrialisation of the region. If industrialisation is to take place in North-East India, that it must be integrated with neighbouring countries to break its isolation. Saha, therefore, advocates opening up of North-East economy to the neighbouring economies of the Asian Tigers of South-East and North-East Asia. This suggestion sparks off a lot of questions. Should industrialisation be thought of only for the sake of industrialisation? If the region is open up to the Asia Tigers, will there be any guarantee that one day it might not be a hinterland of the Multinational corporations? And should we allow the region to be taken over by the Multinationals? If unplanned economic development is allowed to operate in a big way, the question of displacement and rehabilitation of the people has also to be thought of seriously. The befits of the local population should be given priority first, before toying with the idea of opening the North-East India to the multinational companies.

D.N. Chakravarty draws the attention to the problems of agricultural development of North-East India. He pointed out a number of detrimental causes leading to the backwardness in economic and agricultural development. He, therefore, advocated for proper analysis of the socio-cultural and economic factors, as well as also the material and cultural conditions of the people of region. Besides these, he calls for proper assessment of the psychological hold of the people, the different areas of deficiencies of the region and protection of the rights of the people. Necessary incentives to modern use of agriculture should be encouraged for the overall economic development.

S.K. Agnihotri deals with the sociological issues leading to impediments to Industrial Development in North-East India. He cites a number of impediments faced by the region like regional dimension of industrialisation, emphasis on achieving financial targets, non-availability of income generated saving and capital formation, subsistence agriculture, mislocation of industries, land and land tenure system, etc. He also cited four major deficiencies in implementation of industrial projects like absence of systems approach in desicion-making, required quality, competence and motivation of administrative man-power, socio-political environment and deficiency in planning process. He therefore suggests a number of possible ways in wich the society responds to such a situation.

Gurudas Das limits his paper to five limits to Economic Development of North-East Region. Within these five limits, he raised a number of questions and issues as contradictions between goals and social choices. Having discussed the limits and the constraints caused by them, he seems a light at the end of the tunnel in the form of Plantation--as the plausible leading sector. He therefore concludes by saying that 'the only commercially viable sector is the plantation for the hills of the region where large scale private investment is possible.'

T. Cajee raises many issues. Why grass-root entrepreneurship is lacking among the local people of the state of Meghalaya especially in the state capital city of Shillong? He cited the attempts made by the earlier local entrepreneurs like Babu Jeebon Roy and Rev. J.J.M. Nichols Roy. But unfortunately the noble attempts made by these two stalwarts seemed to have been buried six feet down along with their passing away.

Anjan Thakur dwelt into the historical past of the North-East Region as well as its present multifarious problems. He contended that the region is marked by its plurality of ethnic, religious and linguistic groups who are against different levels of development. Therefore, he suggests that a model must devise policies to avoid creating more division among the people so that industrial development can take its firm root.

P.J. Goswami feels that North-East India needs to have entrepreneurial development programme. He expects to North-Eastern Council and other agencies to undertake this programme.

Mrimoyee Banerjee stresses on two broad social issues:(i) norms of the traditional society impeding the process of industrailisation, and (ii) whether rapid industrialisation will bring about undesirable cultural disorganisation. Though Meghalaya offers considerable scope of industrialisation, the state is likely to continue to be industrially backward for a long time. She, therefore, suggests that there should be sufficient motivation, personal efficiency and self-confidence.

Samir K. Das, bases his paper on three premises:

(1) The issue of globalization and Indian economy,
(2) Ethnizisation of market economy,
(3) Operation of globalization and ethnic assertiveness.

Ethnic assertion acquired a new legitimacy but this itself bring negative efficiency, opined the author.

Sanjib Kr. Barkakoti and joint-paper by P.C. Dutta and B.C. Pradhan dealt with the issues like inter-disciplinary approach and inter-change of ideas between the social scientists and entrepreneurs as well as sufficient attention to be made for development of agriculture. V.S. Mahajan stresses on developing a common market in North-East India notwithstanding the political barriers. P.C. Dey observes that the percentage of people under poverty line is less in North-East India than outside the region, but this situation might not be permanent.

N.C. Roy and P.K. Kuri hold that the local entrepreneurs of Arunachal Pradesh shy away from business activities as the institutions of market insurance are not developed properly.

M.C. Behera and Helena Mantaw point out that growth of private sector is less than the public sector in Arunachal Pradesh. A case study among the Khamtis showed that there was no attempt at primary accumulation of capital and the production was mainly consumption-oriented. The entrepreneurs came mainly from the rich elite families.

S.S. Devbarman's paper on Tripura refers to the demographic changes and the impacts of this change in the state. The tribal society of Tripura has reservations regarding industrialisation. The issue of rehabilitation of the displaced persons in the process of industrialisation was raised.

A. Rajmani Singh and Bibhuti B. Pradhan, dealt with sociological constraints of development in Manipur. They hold that the prevailing family system, lack of business culture and dearth of social movement are responsible for slow industrialisation in the state of Manipur.

The future of North-East India depends on planned economic development. The rapid development of infrastructure is a vital requirement. Roads, public transport communication, adequate energy development, irrigation, flood protection measures and human resource development including public health education should be undertaken on a priority basis. Sociological constraints to economic development are not insurmountable. Development cannot be imposed from above. Planning should not only be people oriented but should be decentralised within a broad frame. North-East India should learn from the success and failures of industrial development especially from the developing countries.

Shillong

B. DATTA RAY
P. BAISHYA

2

STATUS OF AND SOCIOLOGICAL CONSTRAINT ON INDUSTRIAL DEVELOPMENT IN NORTH-EAST INDIA

— J.B. Ganguly

Why Industrialization in North-East India?

The economy of the north-eastern region is still predominantly agrarian. Since the beginning of the planning era, considerable amounts of investments have been made for the development of the social sector (health, education and culture) and the physical infrastructure. Constitutional reorganization effected in the region has led to the dismemberment of Assam and creation of new states, such as, Meghalaya, Mizoram, Nagaland and Arunachal Pradesh. Tripura and Manipur have also been upgraded into the status of full-fledged states. Structural decentralization in the administration of States by creating Autonomous District Councils has also been carried out.

An important consequence of such changes has been marked expansion of the tertiary sector comprising mainly the government services providing employment opportunities for the growing number of job-seekers. Joining politics as a profession has also become an avenue for many youths in the region. But such developments have not been matched by the expansion of the primary sector (agriculture and allied activities) or that of the secondary sector (industries) of the economy. Thus, structurally, the development process in North-East India has been unbalanced one, for which reason it cannot be a sustainable one. No wonder, the problem of educated unemployment in these States has already assumed serious proportions (see Table 2.1) threatening the social, political and economic stability, peace and order in the region.

TABLE 2.1 : Number of Applications on the Registers of Employment Exchanges in the Seven States (at the end of December 1986)

(in '000)

State	No. of registrations effected during Jan. to Dec. 1986	No of placements effected during Jan to Dec. 1986	No of applicants on the registers at the end of Dec. 1986
Arunachal Pradesh	3.5	0.4	15.2
Assam	209.1	5.2	812.3
Manipur	41.7	0.9	258.8
Meghalaya	5.6	0.2	22.7
Nagaland	4.3	0.4	20.4
Mizoram	7 7	0.6	30.6
Tripura	14.4	2.0	107.4

Source : Director General of Employment & Training, New Delhi, quoted in NEC, Basic Statistics of North-Eastern Region 1995, p. 142.

Numbers of applicants on the live registers do not exactly measure the numbers of unemployed; yet these figures are indicative of the fact that the North-Eastern States are saddled with the serious problems of growing number of job seekers. We may also get a broader perspective of the unemployment problem from the data about workforce participation, employment and unemployment scenario in the region. This is given in Table 2.2.

TABLE 2.2 : Workforce Participation Employment and Unemployment in NER

State	Workforce participation rates 1991	Employment in organized sector (lakh)	Unemployment as a % of labour force (1987-88)
Arunachal Pradesh	46.24	—	0.2
Assam	36.09	10.47	5.6
Manipur	42.18	0.56	2.2
Meghalaya	42.67	0.69	0.3
Mizoram	48.91	0.34	0.1
Nagaland	42.68	0.66	4.5
Tripura	31.14	0.98	4.4
India	37.46	268.19	3.8

Source : Economic and Political Weekly, May 21 1994, p. 1306.

The table shows that unemployment rates in Assam, Nagaland and Tripura are higher than the all-India rate of 3.8 per cent. Unemployment in the other four states are lower than the all-India rate, but it is so because their economies are predominantly subsistence agriculture based; therefore visible unemployment is not that prominent. Yet the extent of educated unemployment in all these states is quite alarming as the picture in Table 2.1 indicates.

The distortions in the structural process of development may be noted from the facts about the sectoral distribution of State Domestic Products of these States as given in Table 2.3. These data have been compiled by the Tata Consultancy Services.

TABLE 2.3 : SDP and its Sectoral Distribution in 1984-85 (at 1970-71 prices)

(Rs. crores)

State	Sector						Total	
	Primary		Secondary		Tertiary			
Arunachal Pradesh	29.20	(53.3)	3.38	(6.3)	22.16	(40.4)	54.74	(100)
Assam	664.30	(50.8)	173.00	(13.3)	469.40	(35.9)	1306.70	(100)
Manipur	40.70	(45.4)	6.33	(7.2)	42.51	(47.4)	89.54	(100)
Meghalaya	32.59	(39.9)	5.38	(6.6)	43.67	(53.49)	81.64	(100)
Mizoram	7.71	(28.9)	0.67	(2.5)	18.33	(68.6)	26.71	(100)
Nagaland	22.60	(28.9)	1.96	(2.5)	53.73	(68.6)	78.29	(100)
Tripura	88.77	(61.00)	5.33	(3.7)	51.43	(35.3)	145.53	(100)

Source : Tata Consultancy Services, A Perspective plan for NER Phase I, p. 86.

Note: Figures within brackets indicate percentages.

It may be noted from the table that the secondary sector consisting of mining and manufacturing activities accounts for very low proportion of SDP—much below one-tenth of that excepting for Assam—of each state. The tertiary sector includes construction, transport, power, services and others. For these states, however, the government services are the most significant item. The primary sector's contribution to SDP in Meghalaya, Mizoram and Nagaland is much below the level obtaining in other states. Even a cursory glance over the sectoral distribution of SDPs of the North-Eastern states will indicate the necessity of expansion of the secondary sector, in other words, development of industries, for accelerating the rate of growth of the SDP in a balanced manner and providing employment opportunities for the working population.

The need for expansion of the secondary sector will be also clear from the facts about occupational distribution of main workers as revealed by the 1991 Census. The position is shown in Table 2.4.

TABLE 4 : Proportion of Main Workers to Total Population and Distribution of Main Workers by Type of Occupation as in 1991.

(in terms of percentage)

State	Main workers	Cultivators	Agri. labourers	Household ind. processing, servicing & repairing	Other workers
Arunachal Pradesh	45.22	60.36	5.12	0.19	19.47
Assam	31.19	50.90	12.08	0.88	11.11
Manipur	38.55	61.77	6.69	5.80	15.30
Meghalaya	40.32	55.31	12.51	0.40	14.75
Mizoram	42.09	61.35	3.28	1.02	22.61
Nagaland	42.29	72.65	1.41	0.38	17.19
Tripura	29.09	38.09	23.38	1.42	19.06

Source : Census of India, Paper 2 of 1992, as quoted in NEC, Basic Statistics of North-Eastern Region 1995, p. 14.

For the 1991 Census 'those who had worked for the major part of the year' that is, for at least 183 days, have been termed as 'main workers'. Even as proportions of population occupied as main workers are quite low, more than two-thirds of such workers are dependent on agriculture and allied activities for their livelihood. The North-Eastern States have a tradition of several cottage industries and a number of artistic and useful handicrafts. Yet this sector provides occupation for less than one per cent of main workers in Arunachal Pradesh, Assam, Meghalaya and Nagaland. Only in Manipur this proportion is 5.8 per cent while in Tripura and Mizoram these are 1.42 and 1.02 per cent respectively.

The Census category of 'other workers' include 'factory workers, plantation workers, those in trade, commerce, business, transport, mining, construction, political or social work, all government servants, municipal employees, teachers, priests, entertainment artists, etc.' Given the low level of employment in the organized sector (see Table 2.2) excepting for Assam, it may be safely concluded that most of the other workers in the North-Eastern States are outside the category of factory workers.

The problems of low level of workforce participation and growing unemployment viewed in the context of the predominance of the primary sector in the sectoral distribution of SDP and in providing livelihood for more than two-thirds of the main workers reflect the sectorally unbalanced pattern of growth being experienced by these states. Such a process cannot be a self-sustaining and robust process of growth. The problems of unemployment and poverty also cannot be tackled by such a pattern of growth. The process of industrialisation will help bring about occupational diversification and achieve higher rate of growth of SDP as development of industries will entail adoption of higher technology, rises in labour productivity and rates of accumulation and investment. This will also give a spurt to the growth of the primary sector by making it possible to modernize that sector by supplying inputs and creating increased demand for primary products and absorbing surplus labour thrown up by that sector. In fact, there is a kind of symbiotic relation between the growth of agriculture and that of industry.

Development of industries is not only required for bringing about structural balance in the economy and diversification of productive activities for expansion of employment opportunities but also to make the process of development a sustainable one through maintaining ecological balance. Too much of dependence on farming of land for sustenance of the population will lead to depletion of renewable resources and destruction of bio-diversity. But the technology of production, operational scale and input-output structure of developing industries in the region should be in conformity with resource endowments and physiographical features of the North-Eastern states.

The Existing Industrial Scenario

Structurally, the industries sector is composed of the traditional household industries run by the innumerable households using traditional technology and using locally available forest resources and agricultural, plantation and horticultural products, and the industrial units developed in the modern organized sector which use the region's mineral resources as main inputs applying higher technology.

The third component of the industry sector relates to the tea plantation industry. Though plantation of tea crop is an agrarian operation, the final product comes out through manufacturing process.

In Table 2.5,the position about large and medium scale and small scale industries in these states is indicated.

TABLE 5 : Number of Large and Medium and Small Scale Industries in N.E. States

State	Large and medium scale industries No. of units on 31 March 1994	Number of small scale units developed as in 1988 (provisional)
Arunachal Pradesh	17	374
Assam	118	10,210
Manipur	6	2,892
Meghalaya	7	1,000
Mizoram	1	1,866 (estimated)
Nagaland	16	509
Tripura	1	3,523

Source : NISIET, Guwahati, quoted by NEC, Basic Statistics of North Eastern Region, 1995, p. 149.

The actual number of working small scale units are much less. Principal characteristics of SSI units may be noted from Table 2.6.

TABLE 2.6 : Principal Characteristics of SSI Units (As in March 1988)

State	Number of units	Employment (number)	Production (value in Rs. lakh)	Capacity utilization (percentage)
Arunachal Pradesh	326	2,771	2,624	51.23
Assam	4,430	34,475	30,235	19.31
Manipur	2,078	10,216	2,988	65.37
Meghalaya	587	3,780	2,700	55.25
Mizoram	917	4,223	1,470	71.88
Nagaland	183	3,059	11,247	46.29
Tripura	809	10,069	2,957	40.76
Total	9,330	68,593	54,221	

Source : NISIET, Guwahati, quoted by NEC, *ibid.*, p. 150.

In the entire North-Eastern region only 9,330 small scale units were in working condition in 1988 providing employment for 68,593 persons. In terms of capacity utilization, the picture is quite gloomy. No wonder, as many as 3,065 units of SSI out of a total of 12,395 closed down.

The position about the household sector will be known from the fact that in 1992 there were 95,129 craftsmen in the seven North-Eastern states taken together, who produced handicrafts of the value of Rs. 6613.1 lakhs. (NEC, *ibid.*, p. 155). In the powerloom industry, out of 1,638 authorized powerlooms only 629 were installed as in 1988. But only 153 of installed powerlooms were active in that year. There were 6 mills with authorized spindles of 1,45,340 in 1988. But number of installed spindles were 1,00,042 (*ibid.*, p. 152). In 1988 there were 13,726 handlooms out of which active commercial ones number only 1,343.

From the above facts it is evident that the household sector is still far from becoming an important area of industrial activity to expand employment opportunities and income. The process of industrialisation in the modern organized sector also, because of certain structural characteristics, has not been an overall growth boosting one. Tea industry was developed by foreign enterprise and capital mainly as an export-oriented activity, manifesting an enclave type of highly organized capitalist sector surrounded by subsistence form of low technology and non-surplus generating farm economy. It had almost no spin off effect on expanding productive activities in the non-farm sector. After the foreigners left, tea gardens have come to be run by Indian entrepreneurs, most of whom hail from outside the region.

The same trend continues even in the post-Independence period. A majority of the industries set up in the modern organized sector, which are not state enterprises, have been developed by outside enterprise. Role of local capital and enterprise in the starting and running of these units has been minimal. The majority of the industrial workers have come from outside the region. These industries have been using up local resources without generating perceptible multiplier effect on the growth of regional employment and income. Leakage of resources and income from the region is dampening the process of accumulation and industiral growth on a sustainable basis.

The Structure of Industrial Economy to be Built Up

Nearly 70 per cent of the territorial spread of the North-Eastern States (2.55 lakh sq. kms.) covers hill terrain interspersed with innumerable hill streams and a number of rivers. No wonder, hill hamlets are widely scattered. The level of urbanization is also quite low: only 13.89 per cent of the population lives in towns. The region's surface transport link with the rest of India is only through a narrow corridor in North Bengal. Water transport facility between NER and other parts of the country is also restricted since this involves passing through the waterways in Bangladesh. Moreover, there is a growing opposition from different ethnic groups to the extension of railway lines into the territories of their respective states out of an apprehension that easy flow of traffic will result in rising rate of migration of population from outside. For the same reason these groups are strongly against the abolition of the Inner Line pass system restricting entry of people from other states.

For all these reasons prospects of development of transport and communication network are seriously handicapped. In such a scenario, the industrialization programme in these states need to be structurally decentralized by setting up of small scale and household industries based on the locally available agricultural, forest and other resources using labour intensive technology and producing goods and services for meeting both local demands and exports to other regions. For the latter purpose stress needs to be given on high value low-volume products.

There are, however, certain lines of production, such as, oil refining, natural gas based industries, mineral extractions, etc where production will have to be organized on a scale that will enable enjoyment of economies of scale. These should preferably be in the public sector. Of course, in the current milieu of the country's economic system and ideology the government has been encouraging and providing incentives for the private sector to start industrial units in the region. But taking up of mega projects and location of very big industries in the region using high-tech operations creating opportunities mainly for skilled labour from outside the region will not help the process of development of the people and surrounding area of their locations. On the contrary, it will cause large scale displacement of people from their habitats and means of livelihood. Payment of compensation and alternative locations for settlement can hardly be adequate and effective as the past dismal experiences in this regard in different parts of the country would suggest. Such a programme of industrialisation will only help create enclaves of high-tech industrial activities in the midst of primitive method of ekeing out of an existence depending on traditional non-surplus generating economic operations.

In our view, it is the small scale and household sector which should occupy the core position in the successful industrialization programme in the NE states as a means for diversifying productive activities, generating surplus for enhancing the overall process of accumulation and investment without which economic development on a sustained basis will not be feasible. Economic development must not mean jobless growth. It must expand employment opportunities on a wider scale and growth of income.

Sociological and Cultural Dimensions of Industrialisation

The process of industrialisation through the development of small scale and household industries on a wide scale will entail application of necessary entrepreneurial skill in mobilizing capital, adopting higher technology for turning out cost-effective output of goods and services, marketing of output etc. The traditionally run household and cottage industries will have to compete with the high-tech large scale industries. The former cannot survive such competition without adopting appropriate technology, improved management system and, of course, government support at least up to a certain period of time. Such a pattern of development need to be preceded by social development, that is, spread of literacy, education and training in the required skills, etc., and the promotion of the culture of entrepreneurship. The whole process involves changes in the social framework through the propagation and absorption of new ideology and values.

The literacy ratio and educational attainments of the younger generation in the North-East States have been steadily rising. Considerable progress has also been achieved in the field of higher education—both general and technical. Access of the people to medical and health care facilities has been widening. Development of infrastructure, such as, roads and transport facilities, communication lines, power-supply, administrative bodies covering even the remote areas, etc. combined with political development involving creation of more states and the Autonomous District Councils, etc. have been opening up the possibilities of achieving further social development. Yet certain constraints have been impeding the process of modernization and change. Traits of localism, primitivism, self-sufficiencism, etc. are still quite in evidence.

The process of industrialisation is one of the facets of the process of modernization, and the North-Eastern States have been making efforts to achieve social, economic, political and administrative developments on an unprecedented scale. Necessarily, the cultural matrix has been also changing. Such a process cannot be frictionless, and it is quite evident in the form of ethnic disturbances and growing differentiation in the social framework.

The process of development in these states has been predominantly government-induced and government-financed. But progressively the individual initiative within the framework of community support has to carry forward the process of development an important component of which must be the process of industrialisation. This calls for the cultivation of the spirit of enterprise and initiative. In this respect these states are at a disadvantage in the sense that the value of the legitimacy of entrepreneurship is still not very strong here. Because of several restrictions on free movement of, and transactions in, inputs including manpower between the rest of India and this region and reservation of jobs, trading rights, etc., the market system is not opening up and various vested interests are emerging in the society. This trend has been leading to the rise of the rentier class, and the share of rent in the total income has been rising. This acts as a brake on the growth of accumulation of capital for investment in productive activities and cultivation of the spirit of enterprise and risk-taking.

According to the psychological approach to the process of economic development, "a society with a high level of achievement will produce more energetic entrepreneurs who, in turn, produce more rapid economic development . . . it must satisfy us to have learned that high need for achievment leads people to behave in most of the ways they should behave if they are to fulfil the entrepreneurial role successfully as it has been defined by economists, historians, sociologists . . . ." (McClelland 1971: xii-xiii). There is truth in this assertion which explains the slow pace of development of entrepreneurial skill in this region.

J.A. Schumpeter has outlined the role of the entrepreneur in bringing about economic development. The entrepreneur carries out new combinations which may mean the introduction of a new good and that of a new method of production, opening of a new market, finding out of a new source of supply of raw materials or half-manufactured goods and carrying out of new organization of any industry (Schumpeter 1961). Schumpeter has not, however, discussed the social and cultural environment that favours the growth of enterprise. In fact, the mainstream economists starting with the premise that an individual has the basic motivation to maximize his gain, assume that "entrepreneurial activities will emerge more or less spontaneously when economic conditions are favourable." The favourable conditions are: availability of capital, access to markets, labour supply, raw materials and technology. But it is being growingly realized by the sociologists, anthropologists, historians and psychologists that "noneconomic factors such as social norms and beliefs, psychological motivations for achievement, the legitimacy of entrepreneurship", etc. help create conditions favourable for development of entrepreneurship in the society (Berger 1992 : 3-4).

In the light of such an approach Berger has defined entrepreneurship as "innovative and value-adding economic activity. The individual, for example, who takes a few battered vehicles and turns them into a taxi service, thus providing new services, new employment oppertunities, and a new source of tax revenues may be considered an entrepreneur" (*op. cit.*, 8). In this sense the culture of entrepreneurship is in evidence in different parts of North-East India, but it has yet to assume the character of a widespread phenomenon.

There are several government schemes in operation, such as, the establishment of District Industries Centres, provision of financial assistance and loan for employment generation among unemployed youths, TRYSEM, etc. and several official bodies for providing technical and marketing assistance for starting and running of small industrial units by the local entrepreneurs. One of the latest in the series is the establishment of North-Eastern Development Finance Corporation. Annual flow of resource from the centre for the planned development of this region is also quite substantial. Undoubtedly this has been bringing about some growth and diversification of economic activities under the initiative of local entrepreneurs. But the initiative and enterprise of individuals for surplus-generating productive activities, particularly manufacturing activities, are still not a widespread phenomenon. The reason for this has to be searched for in the cultural milieu. The culture of entrepreneurship has still not been a vibrant force of social change in the region.

One vital impediment for entrepreneurial urges in the region is too much of bureaucratization and centralization of the decision-making process. All plans of development of this region are ultimately formulated and determined by the Centre. Even the North Eastern Council has very little freedom to formulate plans for implementation for the integrated development of the region. Of course this regional planning body itself has also failed in associating local talent and leadership in carrying out its objective of fulfilling regional aspirations. Easy flow of money for implementing exogenously formulated development schemes and other projects has been leading to growing corruption in social and political life. Such an environment is not congenial for the flourishing of the culture of entrepreneurship.

REFERENCES

Berger, B. (ed.) (1992): *The Culture of Entrepreneurship*, Tata McGraw Hill, New Delhi.

E.P.W. Research Foundation (1994): Social Indicators of Development for India-II: Inter-State Disparities, *EPW*, May 21.

McClelland David (1971): Psychological Approach to Modernization as quoted in A.R. Desai (ed.). *Essays on Modernization of Underdeveloped Societies*. Vol I, Introduction.

North Eastern Council (1995): Basic Statistics of North Eastern Region.

Schumpeter, J.A. (1961): *The Theory of Economic Development*, OUP.

Tata Consultancy Services, (N.A.): A Perspective Plan for North Eastern Region, Vol I.

3

SOCIAL RESISTANCE TO DEVELOPMENT: AN ANALYSIS OF SITUATION OF NORTH-EAST INDIA

— M.N. Karna

If social change is an objective reality, development is embedded in ideology. This ideology in a modern state is the product of historical experience and political change. The transition from feudalism to capitalism to socialist transformation in the West is nothing but an ideological transformation. The developing countries of Asia, Africa and Latin America is experiencing a similar alteration in their ideology of development which is essentially anti-colonial in content and liberal in form. In this sense, development is not merely an empirical process devoid of any well conceived direction reflecting historical forces and qualitative character of its society. It is a coherent ideology to bring about well defined transformation in the life of the people. When development is only taken as a programme, the very essence of its qualitative importance is lost. The path of development instead of taking a desirable direction may lead to unfavourable changes in the economic structure and social relations of the people. Directionless development is no development at all.

For the most countries of the Third World, this is a crucial question. The legacy of colonialism and colonial exploitation has brought them to a stage when they are facing a serious crisis of ambivalence. While outlining their ideology of development they face a dilemma created by persisting influence of Western ideology and growing awareness of their own national identity. Consequently, no consistent ideology has developed in most of these countries resulting into a slow pace of development.

Any discussion of development in India must begin in this perspective. But the situation here is hazy and nebulous. Not only the policy and programmes of development launched for different communities and regions are directionless but even the framework in which this is explained fails to comprehend the various issues adequately. The conceptual scheme adopted for the present discussion on constraints of development itself reflects such a limitation of analysis and rigorous examination. To identify social and educational constraints and tribal practices and customs as independent sets of factors responsible for tardy pace of development in North-East is naive and simplistic. Unfortunately such a facile scheme suffers not only from methodological drawbacks but involves far reaching policy consequences for the intended path of development.

The idea that India's socio-economic backwardness in general and North-East's in particular is rooted in its traditional institutional structure does not provide us with a proper and adequate perspective to understand the reality of the situation. Whatever role the traditional institutions might have played in bringing and perpetuating poverty and economic backwardness, the slow rate of economic growth has definitely been more due to a long spell of colonial exploitation. Several new arrangements were made even in secluded and 'excluded' areas to suit colonial interests. Even some baneful social practices were utilised to facilitate colonial goal. Thus perceived we must not exclude the role of impediments and constraints from our purview that were created by prolonged foreign rule. There is no denying the fact that the structure of traditional Hindu society in Central India and isolated social organisation with associated psychological insulation in tribal regions has partly contributed to the creation and maintenance of a very backward economy and social system. But to assign primacy to this factor as compared to the barriers imposed by the colonial administration will be distortion of facts and exaggeration of the reality.

Another unsatisfactory dimension inherent in this logic as applied to North-East is whether social and educational constraints are responsible for arrested growth or such a backwardness itself is the result of slow pace of development. The issues involved here are not merely academic but substantive. Every social system possesses both the elements, one that stimulates change and the other which resists it. It is the ideology of development which articulates these elements in a desired direction to fulfil its goal. What we, therefore, require in the present context is not only an identification of social constraints found in numerous communities of North-East but also a proper understanding of those elements in social organisation which facilitate change and transformation. Accordingly, we should develop a scheme of inquiry which takes care of both sets of factors: barriers and stimulants of change. The framework being suggested does not contradict altogether the popular notion of constraints of development but attempts to give them rigour and precision.

In speaking of constraints there has been another tendency to see them in "tradition-modernity" framework. Under the influence of western sociology especially American conceptual formulations societies or nations of the Third World have been characterised as 'traditional' as against the First World which are regarded as 'modern'. Besides several other differences, the traditional societies are supposed to possess some peculiar features not generally found in modern western societies. Behaviour in traditional society is governed by custom not by law. The social structure is hierarchical. The position of individuals in society is ascribed not achieved. Economic productivity is at the level of subsistence. Since such societies are closed and immobile, they experience to tension as in most cases tension is mainly concerned with the conflict between tradition and modernity. The oft-quoted theoretical model of Talcott Parsons has also been used to explain the tradition-modernity dichotomy. The scheme attempts to structure the relevant relationships in terms of the "pattern variables" in the attempt to state the basic factors comprising a framework in which entire social system can be studied and compared. The five dichotomies which express these choice alternatives called pattern variables have been listed by Parsons[1] as follows:

(a) affectivity *vs* affective neutrality,
(b) self-orientation *vs* collective orientation
(c) particularism *vs* universalism
(d) ascription *vs* achievement
(e) diffuseness *vs* specificity.

Applying this to the question of development it has been suggested that the first set of variables—affectivity, self-orientation, particularism, ascription and diffuseness are broadly associated with backward economies as against the other five found in an advanced society. But in a somewhat different way the traditional societies are facing these constraints because these alternatives determine the pattern of economically relevant behaviour. The contrast between traditional and modern societies in terms of the contradiction between the two sets of pattern variables is based on the assumption perhaps that they represent two extremes on an evolutionary scale. Such a theoretical assumption is not tenable because possibility of constant dialectical evolution of tradition cannot be denied. Moreover, the traditional society is by no means extremely traditional and modern society devoid of tradition. Such a functional scheme of inquiry attaches secondary importance to historical forces of change which may be introduced from outside the system. Even these reasons are sufficient to discard this framework in the present discussion.

What I have attempted to highlight in the foregoing paragraphs is the limitations of the framework which endeavours to explain the constraints of development in a structural-functional manner. It is my contention that the social constraints of development in North-Eastern region of India must be viewed in the historical context. Except geographical contiguity the region does not form a homogeneous whole. Each unit has its own peculiarity from the points of view of social organisation and cultural pattern. The enormity of the problem is further reflected in a large number of tribal groups which inhabit the area. Despite the socio-cultural heterogeneity it is possible to formulate a systematic approach to develop if we go by historical analysis that does not consider the region as static, timeless and spaceless in character. We cannot elucidate the role of social institutional constraints in their complexities purely in terms of the existing situation. We have to refer to the historical experiences under which the entire region has had uniform impact. What I propose to do now is to dwell on some important aspects of indigenous social life which are directly associated with the development question in North-East. This will be taken up at two lavels, first at the level of individual personality and secondly at the level of social institutions.

Since change is initiated in the minds of the people, their attitude towards life and work are directly intertwined with the question at issue. Unfortunately, we do not have any systematic study of what one may call 'tribal psychology'. However, keeping the overall civilization growth in view it is not difficult to point out some of the common features of such societies at the attitudinal level. Superstitious beliefs and irrational outlook, lack of competitiveness and ambition, reverence for the past and fear of the new, submissiveness to authority and exploitation are some of the major constraints at the psychological level which are normally highlighted in relation to tribal societies of North- East.[2] Such attitudes towards life and work are the products of social environment not of biological instincts. 'The individual no more act upon the world than the world upon the individual'. Those who assign importance to these factors and hold tribal responsible for these drawbacks tend to look for certain 'modern values' in societies which had been based entirely on different value structure. An important instance is the notion of competitiveness which is definitely the outcome of the capitalist mode of production. To look for such values in indigenous societies that have been traditionally based on mutual interaction and exchange is to seek effects without a cause.

How far have these attributes taken firm roots in the minds of the people? What I mean to suggest is that whether these elements of people's experience has been brought into systems of thought and values to defy possible change and transformation. For instance, the traditional and dominant Hindu world views have been based on doctrines of *maya, karma and dharma.* Such philosophical doctrines have influenced minds of the people of ages insisting on extreme conformism in practice. The attitude of fatalism, compulsiveness of caste obligations, secondary place for secular values are some of these elements that are incompatible with the moral sense of modern man. I am of the view that in the tribal societies of the North-East we do not find any such system of thought and value providing normative-philosophical support to the negative ideas of the people. Hence these value components are not difficult to be replaced by rational, scientific and secular outlook. Modern education can play a liberating role if properly planned and executed.

Coming to the social institutional dimension of the problem we can begin from the village community. Like other regions of the country the village in North-East India has been more than a collection of individuals. The nature of ecological setting and demographic features had led to close knit and well integrated structure functioning on the basis of self-regulation and self-government. The village leadership has been based on status which has carried with it a well defined code of obligations and duty. Continuity and stability of the tribal social structure could be maintained through such a village community. In most of the cases these villages have been the extension of lineages and clans. In this sense a tribe and its villages have been a world within itself having a few external ties.

It will be interesting to point out here that some of the components of this village community are taken today as constraints in socio-economic development. But the local level institutions such as chieftainship and village government which are considered to be stumbling blocks now are not the creation of tribal social process itself. It is clearly the consequences of colonial legacy. The system of chieftainship, for example was developed by the people to maintain a self-zamindar. But the colonial administration found in these chiefs a very convenient and powerful ally who could be utilised to accomplish colonial interests. It is through this process that in most of the tribal communities democratic chiefs became hereditary ones. In this sense, the colonial rule had in fact a vested interest in the continuation of India's social stability.

Similarly communal control over land is another important feature that attracts our attention in this context. The social organisation of *jhum* cultivation does not allow the individual ownership of land as does the settled agriculture. *Jhuming* is labour intensive, particularly in its initial phase when land is cleared for cultivation. Under such a system the control over land is exercised either by the clan or the village but rarely by the individual household. Such a communal ownership is found in majority of the tribal groups. However, several distortions have taken place in the system and we find growing privatization of land. But the fact of the matter is that community ethos and values associated with agricultural land and forests continue to be maintained.

The development administrators today consider this system of land tenure and modalities of land distribution as serious constraints in replacing *jhuming* by settled cultivation. Hence the established principles of individual ownership is advocated for this region as well. It is also being contemplated for providing institutional credit as in the absence of individual ownership it will not be possible to do so.

I would like to make it clear that the transition from communal ownership to individual ownership of land started during the British period and has been going on even now. Nevertheless the dominant practice continues to be communitarian. Unfortunately, a somewhat egalitarian system is being treated as a constraint in development because it goes against the established thinking of the government agencies which is in tune with the system prevalent elsewhere. The policy makers perhaps do not realize that the strategy adopted in other areas may lead to a serious social implication in this part of the country. This can be illustrated with the help of concrete example.

The communal land tenure system, distortions notwithstanding, had not permitted much internal differentiation within the community in terms of income and wealth. It has resulted in the absence of sharp class distinction in most of the tribal communities. Iniquitous norms and inegalitarian values are yet to be internalized by the individuals and institutionalised by the group. Self-help, self-reliance and community sentiment which helped them to sustain through the difficult days of hills and forests continue to guide them even in the age of government subsidy and help. Naturally, if we ignore these facilitating factors and go on viewing them as constraints, it is going to create a serious problem for the region. A directionless investment and subsidy will lead to parasitic development giving rise to what one of our Naga research scholars has said a 'sponsored society'.

As a matter of fact numerous new objects of resistance have emerged in these societies in the wake of changes taking place during the last few decades. A potent obstacle to development today is individuals and groups that fear a loss of power, wealth or prestige. Should development gain prominence? Emerging internal differentiation and growing inequality in these indigenous societies have given rise to a class of people which has vested interest in the backwardness of these societies. It consists mainly of rich and middle landowners, traditional social leaders and new professionals having landed interests. A notable feature of this class is that while confronted with the disgruntled groups the different segments of this class come closer to protect their interests but whip up passion to mobilise their own people for other immediate gains. As such, this group takes the form of a class on one occasion but goes back to the traditional tribal appeal on the other. Thus the underdevelopment of these societies is in the interest of this class.

Then there is a question of resistance to change on the grounds of "ideological traditionalism". The basic intellectual and religious assumptions with regard to existing power relations, morality, welfare and security tend to be adversely disposed to change and development.

REFERENCES

Talcott Parsons and Edward A. Shils, *Toward a General Theory of Action*, Cambridge, Mas., 1951, pp. 49, 76-7.

See for details, *Report on Development of North Eastern Region*, National Committee on the Development of Backward Areas, Planning Commission, Government of India, November, 1981.

4

SOCIO-CULTURAL FACTORS OF ECONOMIC DEVELOPMENT WITH SPECIAL REFERENCE TO NORTH-EAST INDIA

— Prabin Baishya

Introduction

The very title of this chapter may cause some shuddering to the pseudo-Marxists who lay over-emphasis on economic factors determining the course of human history and to the bitter critics of Marxism who with a view to throw over board this humanitarian science try to portray it as an *'ism'* of economic determinism. No doubt Prof. Marshall had also stressed, after Marx and Engels, that 'Man's character has been moulded by his every day work and the material resources which he thereby procures more than by any other influence unless it be that of his religious ideals . . ."[1] To allay the misconception about Marxian economic determinism and to stress the role of socio-cultural factors in the development of human society "two points must not be overlooked" said Engels: (1) "Political, juridical, philosophical, religious, literary, artistic etc. react upon one another and also *upon the economic basis"* (emphasis added), and (2) "men make their history themselves, but not as yet with a collective will according to a collective plan or even in a definite delimited given society. Their aspirations clash, and for that very reason, all societies are governed by necessity, the compliment and form of appearance of which is *accident*" (emphasis original).[2] Prof. Rostow while propounding "an alternative to Karl Marx's theory of modern history" also holds that "economic change is itself viewed here as consequence of political, social as well as narrowly economic forces . . .

and many of the most profound economic changes are viewed as the consequence of non-economic human motives and aspirations".[3]

As it is well known, all the seven states of North-East India are clamouring for economic development. Per capita income in six of the seven states remained far below the all-India average. However, it needs no emphasis that the arithmetical mean of state or national per capita income in a society with skewed income distribution[4] bears little truth without showing the upward and downward deviations. Prevalence of 51.96 per cent poverty in 1973-74, 58.55 per cent in 1977-78, 41.40 per cent in 1983 and 37.47 per cent in 1987-88 and 1993-94 in Arunachal Pradesh with her per capita income of Rs. 3679 standing above the national average of Rs. 3285 in 1987-88 is a pointer to the weakness of the concept of per capita average. The incidence of poverty in the other six states is also not less,[5] it was above 50 per cent in 1973-74, 55 per cent in 1977-78, near about or above 40 per cent in 1983 and around 35 per cent in 1987-88 and 36.46 per cent in 1993-94. This poverty exists in the midst of "super abundance" of a few; the number of wealthy Nagas rolling in riches with their drawing rooms furnished with "wall to wall carpets," electric gadgets from toaster and kettles to shaving sets and vacuum cleaners, refrigerators, radio and hi-fi sets, tape recorders, expensive cameras, costly colour television sets and 'boasting of them' are example of the affluence a few Naga families in the midst of poverty of nearly 51 per cent of the Naga people in 1973-74 when Prof. Horam, himself a Naga scholar, had observed the socio-economic scenario of Nagaland.[6]

Transitional Asiatic Society

It needs no stress that the population of the entire North Eastern region excluding an Aryanised segment in the Brahmaputra and Barak Valleys of Assam belongs to the autochthonous groups of the Indo-Mongoloid and/or Mon-Khemar races. Till the nineteenth century when the region was annexed to the British empire (first Assam in 1826 and last Mizoram in 1892), the related gentes and phraties united themselves into tribes with a common dialect under a chief occupying a particular territory and their evolutionary stage, according to the schemata of Morgan[7] was probably the uper status of Barbarism or of civilisation. For instance, "among all Naga tribes in the days before Christianity came to the Naga Hills, every village was not only a religious unit, but also politically and economically a distinct unit"[8] with a council of village elders and a chief.

In the Arunachal Pradesh "at the least, the People had not enough food . . . their life was distracted by war, kidnapping, slavery and cruel punishment. They were not free; weaker tribes had to pay tribute to the strong, rich and powerful chiefs grew richer on the labour of hundreds of serfs; freedom of movement was severely restricted by inner-village conflict." On other economic front, three types of land tenure prevailed among the tribes, (1) individual ownership for residence and cultivation after common land was parcelled out, (2) Clan land of pasture, burial ground and tracts of forests belonging to the first clearers and (3) common village land of pasture and forests along the peripheries. Cultivation was under *Jhuming* which was taken up by the whole village in the form of "a co-operative enterprise". Hunting, fishing and food gathering was a common feature of the tribes and distribution of the game was done "according to certain traditional rules".[9]

The Jaintiyas and Khasis of Meghalaya had their own social ana economic units. In the matrilineal society based on chieftainship of Dalois and Syiems chosen by a council of village elders known as Kur or Darbar, the Kur or clan is reckoned through the mother line and all properties are supposed to belong to the mother, i.e. the clan. Land rights were also similar to other tribes; Ri Kur land was held jointly by a clan or group of clans after the main clan was broken due to its large size. Rai Raid land did not belong to any particular clan, but to the whole community or a number of clans occupying a particular area or some villages. But in the midst of communal land ownership private ownership of land had also emerged; the ruling families of Syiems, Lyndows, Myntries, Basans, Dalois and Patars had their Ri Kynti or private service land. However, usufruct of individual families over Ri Raid land converted to Ri Kynti had also emerged in the 19th century although the occupants could not dispose of their land without the consent of the clan.[10]

Examples may be multiplied about different evolutionary status of the tribes of the North-East and their cultural upliftment through a gradual process of Hinduisation and Christianisation sometimes called detribalisation. Probably suffice it to depict these communities as traditional "Asiatic Societies" as Marx had called the ancient village communities of India whose economy was based on possession of common land, blending of agriculture and handicrafts in a self-sufficient village where products were destined for direct consumption and the surplus, if any, went to the chief who was the judge, police, tax-gatherer and book-keepr or was bartered in the village fair—the occasional meeting ground of people of different clan or communities.[11]

In the terminology of the Netherlands East Indies Civil Servant in Indonesia and later on Professor of Eastern Economics at Leiden University, Dr. J.H. Boeke, the socio-political status of these communities may also be called an "indigenous social system" of its own type in which the economy was basically "precapitalistic". The characteristic feature of a precapitalist economy is a backward sloping supply curve for efforts and risk taking, the predominant characteristics of a capitalist economy. He cites examples of a backward sloping supply curve from Indonesia, "if three acres are enough to supply the needs of the household a cultivator will not till six; when rubber prices fall, the owner of a grove may decide to tape more intensively, whereas, high prices may mean that he leaves a larger or small portion of his tapable trees untapped."[12] This happens because the needs of the indigenous societies were limited. The other feature of these societies is the absence of "profit seeking" which is the *sin qua non* of capitalist production. Similarly, there is no mercantile class in these societies to convert their trade capital to industrial ventures which was the most important characteristic of the development process of European capitalist societies in the 16th and 17th centuries.

On these precapitalistic tribal economies of the North-East based on the foundations of an indigenous social system was imposed by the colonialists through their administrative officers and other agents, what Prof. Boeke calls "an imported social system" and "most frequently the imported social system is high capitalism. But it may be socialism or communism just as well or a blending of them." Certainly, the indigenous societies with a cultural heritage of co-operative enterprise particularly in agriculture with communal land ownership, might have by-passed the capitalist phase of development and proceeded towards building up an egalitarian modern society based on modern co-operative lines of production. But the rising bourgeoisie of England had introduced capitalism which created a "dual society" with "the disintegration" of earlier forms of social and economic organisations resulting in the "clashing of an imported-social system with an indigenous social system of another style."

The general feature of the clash between the indigenous social system and the imported social system of high capitalism was observed in the Naga society by Prof. Horam: "beneath a crude exterior of nakedness and headhunting, they possessed an indigenous culture, an effective system of self-government . . . They had some admirable institutions such as houses for young men. Besides, they had always been self-sufficient in food and were adept weavers. True, the needs were limited, but they had lived thus for centuries and had managed to remain a people full of zest and vigour. Though the government officials and the bringers of Christianity did not mean intentional harm, they very often in their misguided zeal sought to pack into a couple of decades changes which should normally have taken centuries even in an alert continent like Europe. This was introducing abrupt change and forced growth at an abnormal pace and the results have been more revolutionary than evolutionary."[13]

Certainly, the whirlwind of changes had overtaken the "simple and uncultured life-style" of the tribes throughout the entire region. The spread of Christianity by the "White Missionaries" had removed superstitions, introduced cleanliness, schools and hospitals. Then other changes came about; people started acquiring modern material equipments like lamps, lanterns, matches, battery torches, boots, shoes, umbrellas, modern kitchen utensils and even guns. Changes came over even in food habits; new items of vegetables, fruits, pulses and the like were added to their delicacies. The youth become conscious of their beauties; they were after tailored clothes; "a number of tribal people have taken to full European dress, it is very rare to see any one of them in Dhoti." A "youth in smart English clothes and a Sola Topi will not obey his tribal chief who looks so 'jungly' in his classic attire; girls in meretricious blouses and even trousers with lipstick on their lips and phoney trinkets in their hair, are already showing signs of rebellion against the discipline of the community" observed Verrier Elwin in the last fifties about the changes that took place among the tribes in Arunachal Pradesh.[14]

Irreversible Trend

Whether the maelstrom of changes are for the better or worse is a matter of speculation and of philosophy of life. Today, people everywhere in the world are after material progress. "What is called economic development," says Prof. Galbraith, "consists in no small part in devising strategies to *overcome* the tendency of men to place limits on their objectives as regards income and thus on their efforts"; "goods which by their novelty appeal to vanity or to emulative or competitive adornment or display are now considered more legitimate." In the underdeveloped countries and regions within them "the effort inspired by the introduction of modern consumer goods—cosmatics, motor, scooters, transistors, radios, canned food, bicycles phonogram records, movies, American cigarettes—is recognised to be of the highest importance in the strategy of development."[15] And this is the stage to which the exposure of the tribes of the North East has brought about the blessings, if not the blemishes of high capitalism! And Pandit Nehru rightly expressed his doubts; "how far the normal idea of progress was beneficial for these people and indeed, whether this was progress at all in the real sense of the word?"[16] And what is "the quality of human character" that is being evolved in the process?

The old values of the tribal societies have crumbled down; religions of the primitive societies often condemned as paganism or animism which upheld the mechanical solderity and were strong sources of promoting ultruism and restraining egoism[17] have been replaced by new ones under the garb of Weberian Protestant Ethic and Capitalism which have glorified the spirit of economic individualism and egoism. This spirit, while breaking down the traditional economic system of co-operative enterprise and egalitarian principles of distribution, has encouraged individual initiative and "a moral familism" in the struggle for enriching oneself and has created an atmosphere where "individual freedom . . . meant in the main freedom to make money." And "the society approves and applauds money making as the highest social purpose". Even public officials of the state are responsive to the opportunity for pecuniary gains and "sell themselves or their decisions for what they are worth to buyers."[18]

This money making spirit has created, besides new economic classes, a state of anomie; the society has split horizontally; while the ignorant and illiterate mass of the older generations still remain traditional with taboos, mores and folkways, the youth is torn between the impulses of tradition and modernity.[19] Small wonder, Lord Jesus came with a sword "to set sons against their fathers, daughters against their mothers, daughters-in-law against their mothers-in-law."[20] And it is certainly so, the youth has risen in revolution against the old social order.

Revolution of Rising Expectations

They youth through their socialisation process of education outside their homes and exposure to the outside world in the towns and cities have become acquainted, through demonstration effect, with the benefits of a higher civilisation of high mass-consumption and have come to desire and demand the goods of higher level. This psychological attitude is not, however, a peculiar social phenomenon of the youth of a particular tribe, ethnic or linguistic group. "All over the world there has been a rising tide of expectations. Burmese will not starve quietly while they see Europe and Japan prospering. The black community within America is no exception. They are not content to sing spirituals and hope for better future," says Prof. Samuelson.[21]

But there is a gulf, a very wide gulf between their aspirations for consumption exenditures and income accruels necessary to fulfil the expectations. An alert and active awareness about their aspirations and social goals would have made them work hard like the American multi-millionaires, working right up to the last days of their consciousness[22] for efficient production of goods and expansion of output through replacement of pre-Newtonian technology by modern techniques of production. And this is a question of "human motivation," "a temptation to take a chance and a feeling of satisfaction," as Lord Keynes,[23] had termed it, in undertaking new ventures like that of a modern farm or a modern factory that would have enabled the youth to earn more and live a conspicuous life. In the above context there should emerge a new elite group of non-conformists or what Prof. Hoselitz calls 'social deviants' with a creative imagination and vision to undertake new economic activities in the form of capitalist enterprise within the parameters of the given socio-economic system. He cites the example of the Maori tribes of New Zealand where a new leadership had changed the goals of the Maori society. In Japan also, he says, the first stage of economic development was triggered off by a wiser section of the elite.[24] But in the North-East such an elite group with creative imagination and constructive impulse is yet to emerge, rather the educated youth seem to have taken a negative attitude to a work culture of' "soiling their hands" which is considered a disgrace. With the spread of education "the proverbial dignity of labour among these hill folks," says Prof. Horam, "is fast on the decline, for not even the mediocre educated persons work on the land, preferring to work at a desk for a mere pittance."[25] Even engineering graduates "expect desk jobs and recoil from the prospect of physical contact with machines," was the general observation of the Nobel Laureate Prof. Myrdal.[26] In the situation a sense of frustration and alienation has engulfed the youth for their failure to adapt themselves to the industrial culture of high capitalism.

Therefore, the grievances of the youth, besides the contradictions between traditional elites weilding power and position in the traditional society on the one side and the so-called western educated elite desiring to capture social and political power from the former on the other, have been directed mostly against the newly ascending immigrant groups in trade, commerce and industry who are allegedly exploiting the indigenous people. The youth have also their long standing grievances of historical neglect of development of the region and great disparties in the levels of development between different regions of the country have also strengthen this feeling. Hence some insurgent groups have directed their anger and energy against the amalgamation and unification of the region with the Indian Union. These young elites, while using Gramscian terms like 'hegemony of the Indian State' without clarifying 'who holds state power' at the moment and without a clear alternative socio-economic programme for economic development of the region or a particular area which they call 'land' (sovereign state) have turned secessionists. Apart from the question of confusing the rights of nationalities to cultural self-determination (use of one's own language, literature, development of spiritual as well as material culture) through political autonomy within the Indian Union with the rights to political self-determination through secession (according to Lenin oppressed nations and nationalities have rights to secede)[27], the secessionists may pose to themselves the question if they would be able to develop infrastructures, build up modern industries etc. without capital inflow from outside the region and up-dated technology from foreign countries. And on the question of exploitation, the secessionists are expected to know that the emergence of an indigenous bourgeois class like the ack bourgeoisie in the American ghettos[28] shall not salvage the working class to the pilgrimage of paradise in the given socio-economic system; anarchy in production and distribution will remain there as it exists today; as the luxury of the rich gives employment to the poor a large segment of the indigenous population will be reduced to the status of white or blue collar wage earner while another section shall suffer from underemployment and unemployment and languish in poverty and squalor as "there are many poor people left in the industrial countries and notably in the United States" and "they are those who have not been drawn into its (industrial system's—added) service or who cannot qualify."[29] And therefore, in the not too far distant future the indigenous bourgeoisie like his black counterpart in America shall join hands with the immigrant exploiters and it will make little difference who is exploited by whom.

The insurgency in the North-East needs further indepth analysis in the context of ethnic violence between the Nagas, Kukis, Meiteis, Bodos, Santhals etc. and fatricidal combats among the Nagas, Bodos etc. themselves killing the members of the political rival groups. Space does not allow us detail elaboration; suffice it to say that the insurgents using Marxian terms like socialism, Gramscian terms like "subaltern classes" have, instead of leading the masses, divided the subaltern classes on ethnic lines which in the context of the need for uniting the working class is an anathema to Marxian-Gramscian principles. Their commando tactics by dividing the subaltern groups on ethnic lines and without mass following (masses cannot be led by totting the guns while extortion alienates, rather antagonises the middle class) seems nothing but "the mark of a fool"—to use a Gramscian term. On the question of secessionism too, the insurgents may take a lesson from Gramsci himself—a Sardinian nationalist first turning into an Italian nationalist and subsequently to an internationalist,[30] of course remaining always aware of and fighting for regional problems of Southern Italy and for the national democratic question under the fascism of Mussolini after October 1922. However, if there is a fusion of progressive and reactionary political leadership under the guise of regionalism and medieval particularism of petty states (most probably foreign agents have assimilated to divide the people on ethnic lines for the benefit of the neo-colonialists), the problem stands on a different footing calling for the emergence of an alternative leadership based on the philosophy of praxis.

Conclusion

Economic development aims at leading the human society from a lower to a higher stage of material civilisation through a process of challenge and response. In this race several communities may be said, to use a metaphor of the great historian Toynbee,[31] to be lying torpid upon different ledges on a mountainside, with a precipice below and a precipice above. The race of the communities of the North-East for economic development may also be likened to the companions of the sleepers who have risen to their feet and have started to climb up the face of the cliff of capitalist civilisation. The journey, however, is arduous, the changes of its course are over rapid. But in the myopia of short term individual needs and gains, let us not lose sight of climbing up the cliff beyond the immediate one where social needs and gains should get topmost priority.

The goal above calls for freeing the productive forces from the fetters of the present day industrial system based on money-making motive so that human civilisation may march towards a stage of high mass-consumption, from necessity to freedom, with a *human face*, a stage, Marx had so forcifuly pleaded for. As Rostow[32] admits. ". . . on one point Marx was right—and we share his views: . . . it is the adventure of seeing what man can and will do when the pressure of scarcity is substantially lifted from him". And let us see to the possibility of a civilisation "when all can share the choices open in the stage of high mass-consumption and beyond."

REFERENCES

Marshall, Alfred, *Principles of Economics*, Macmillan, London, 1890/1956, p1.

Letter from Engels to Borguis, London, Jan. 25, 1894 in *Mark-Engels Selected Works*, Progress Publishers, Moscow, 1968, pp. 704-5.

Rostow, W.W., *The Stages of Economic Growth*, Cambridge University Press, New York, 1960/1969, p. 2.

There were about six lakh households with an income of more than one million in India in 1993-94. Ref. Natarajan, Estimates of the Number of Very Rich in India, Working Paper No. 55, National Council for Applied Economic Research, Delhi, 1995, p. 28.

Alagh, Y.K., "Poverty and Food Scarcity", Paper in *EPW*, Dec. 30, 1995, Tables 2, 3, 4, 5 and *Assam Tribune*, Jan. 26/1997.

Horam, M. (A), *Naga Polity*, Low Price Publications, Delhi, 1975/1992, pp. 134-35.

Morgan, Lewis Henry, *Ancient Society*, K.P. Bagchi, Calcutta, 1877/1992, pp. 65,80.

Horam, M. (A), *op. cit.*, p. 61.

Elwin, Verrier, *A Philosophy of NEFA*, Shillong, 1957/1960, pp. 47, 64, 71 & Hoselitz, Bert F., *Sociological Approach of Economic Growth*, Vakils, Feffer and Simons, Bombay, 1960, p. 14 for the principles of distribution among tribes.

Mathew, T., Report of the Land Reforms Commission for Kashi Hills, 1975, paper in *Tribal Economy of the North Eastern Region*. Mathew, T. (ed.), Spectrum Publications, Guwahati, 1980, pp. 107-12 & Mazumdar, D.N. *et. al, Tribal Occupational Mobility*, Research India Publication, Calcutta, 1964, pp. 29-31.

Marx, Karl, *Capital*, vol. I, Progress Publisher, 1954/1977, p. 338. The term "Unchangeable" was used by him in the sense of stability of a community in the midst of rise and fall of dynastic kings and monarchs which was not the concern of the village people.

Boeke, J.H., Economics and Economic Policy of Dual Societies (New York 1953) and other works quoted extensively in Higgins, Banjamin, *Economic Development, Problems, Principles and Policies*, Central Book Depot, Allahabad, 1963, pp. 274-80.

Horam, M. (B), *Social and Cultural Life of Nagas*, Low Price Publications, Delhi, 1972/1977, p. 98.

Elwin, Verrier, *op. cit.*, pp. 119-23.

Galbraith, John Kenneth, *The New Industrial States*, Oxford and IBM Publishing Co., Calcutta, 1967, pp. 270-71.

Nehru, Jawaharlal, Foreword to the 1st. edition of Elwin's work cited, No page number dated 16/2/57.

Giddens, Antony, *Capitalism and Modern Social Theory, Marx, Durkheim and Max Weber*, Cambridge U. Press, 1992/1994, pp 70, 106.

Galbraith, J.K., *op. cit.*, pp. 291, 299.

Baishya, P., "Urbanisation in the North East," unpublished Seminar paper, 1995.

Holy Bible, *Good News Edition*, Bible Society of India, Bangalore, no year of publication, Book 2, Mathew 10(34), p 15.

Samuelson, Paul A., *Economics*, 8th international students edition, McGraw Hills 1970. p. 788.

Gramsci, Antonio, Selection from Prison Notebooks, Ed. Hoare Q & G.N. Smith, Orient Longman, Hydarabad, 1996, p. 284.

Keynes, John Maynard, *The General Theory of Employment, Interest and Money*, Macmillan & Co, Londan 1936/1964, p. 150.

Hoselitz, BF, *op. cit.*, pp. 22-23, 27-28.

Horam, M., *op. cit.*, (B), pp. 99-100.

Myrdal, Gunnar, *Asian Drama*, Vol. II, Penguin Books, 1968, p. 1127.

Lenin, V.I., *Collected Works*. Vol. 20, pp. 412, 417, 425. (Progress Publishers, Moscow, 1964)

Samuelson, P. *op. cit.*, 785-86.

Galbraith, J.K., *op. cit.*, p. 318.

Gramsci, Antonio, *op. cit.*, p. 232 and XIX respectively.

Toynbee, Arnold J., *A Study of History*, Vol. I, Oxford University Press, New York, 1965, p. 69.

Rostow, W.W., *op. cit.*, p. 166.

(This is a revised version of a paper presented in a Seminar on Sociological Constraints to Industrial Development in North East India organised by the North East India Council for Social Science Research on July 26 and 27, 1996 at Shillong).

5

INDUSTRIALISATION IN NORTH-EAST INDIA: 'AN ART OF THE POSSIBLE'

— A.K. Maiti and
S. Chakrabarti

There has been a growing body of economic theories on regional development. Economic development as a result of economic activities is not an inevitable process but an "art of the possible." This may be done by a variety of co-ordinated measures designed to control the free play of social, economic and other forces. But, the questions which immediately arise are: who is to co-ordinate those forces? What are the goals that are being set up by the co-ordinating agencies? what co-ordination and planning measures are deemed necessary to attain the goals? The broad theory of development holds that the planning measures would be the precise application of development policy particularly the degree of priority that a country would allow. Industrialization is one of the important components of planning measures and organic to the economy as a whole. It promotes economic changes and also make social and institutional changes. As essential force of development it gives rise to new sets of values and new concepts of societal structure. Industrialization depends on many factors which are linked with environmental and human problems.

This chapter is based on the premise that economic growth without commensurate improvement and progress for the mass of population cannot be termed development. Again, industrialization has many problems of its own, namely, problems of capital formation, capital attraction, marketing, labour problem, problems of imbalances as well as those of natural and physical environment. The intensities of these problems differ not only between countries but also among the regions within the same country. So the industrial problems and pattern in one country is likely to differ from that in the other. For example, Switzerland with two-third of its geographicl area mountainous and having no mineral resources is very handicapped for industrial development compared to India which is much advanced in all these respects. But Switzerland has sources of hydrolic energy, scenic beauty and an advantageous position astride international route ways. But her concentration on high quality goods for export markets by the application of high skilled labour and capital, she had overcome the disadvantages of being handicapped in heavy industries. She concentrated in manufacture where precision and quality predominated and put emphasis upon selective rather than mass market. Likewise, what is possible in one region or state within India may not be possible in other due to diverse geo-ecological and natural resource endowment situation.

In the North-Eastern region it has been observed that agricultural income is not increasing due mainly to physical constraints although there has been attempts for agricultural development. So industrialization would be necessary to absorb the shocks generated by the dwindling agriculture and occupation allied to agriculture, namely, animal husbandry, bee-keeping etc. But what kind of industrialization would be appropriate to the North-Eastern states? We would generally argue for an eco-friendly and sustainable industrialization. Because, industrialization would not mean just setting up a few factories or closing the old units and go for so-called modern high-tech units. Neither blind submission to the dictates of International Bank for Reconstruction and Development (IBRD), International Monetary Fund (IMF), the Multinational Companies (MNCs) etc. and allowing extra powers to the industrial magnets nor consideration of profitability as the only criterion should be the way towards industrialization. For industrialization of a particular region or country, one should not blindly follow the international made-easy remaining indifferent to their own natural and human resource endowments. Not only in case of North-Eastern India but also in case of India as a whole there is lack of appropriate attitude towards comprehensive development while formulating industrial policies. With these in view, there should be industrialization as a part of development of the North-Eastern region of India rather than setting up a few profit-yielding and eco-degrading factories here and there in this region.

Factors Influencing Industrialisation

The nature and scope of various industries and the possibilities of their adoption are influenced by certain limitations, namely, lack of skilled labour, lack of capital, lack of market and lack of infrastructural facilities. These impose restraints upon the kind, size and scale of industrial development. Lack of skilled labour remained a product of our system of education and indifference towards people's well-being. Again, underutilization of skilled labour remained in-built into our age-old reluctance towards investment, especially in sectors which do not yield quick profit. Scarcity of capital is again entwined with lack of infrastructural facilities. These form a vicious circle which discourage industrialization. Profit maximization being the main driving force of capitalism, there cannot, in general, be any employment beyond the point where marginal productivity is less than wage.

Now, how do one calculate the marginal productivity of a labour with wild diversities in the factor market which again is influenced by undeveloped product market? Both socially productive labour force as well as the various aspects of social production relations differ in different types of industrial activities in different areas. These problems therefore need be tackled not only from the economic but also from socio-cultural perspectives. Theoretically, in examining the character of industrial development in the states in our country, the classical doctrine of comparative advantage may have some application. But in practice, it may not be so in the initial phase. The theory underlines the optimum use of resources and invokes international levels of cost comparison. But a substantial body of industries cannot be assessed this way for their products really do not enter into the world trade. Again, comparative costs are not static. From these considerations the government's intervention becomes a necessary instrument of industrialization in developing nations as ours.

Added to these are socio-political factors. Mainly due to lack of organisation and consciousness of labour the relevant data on industrial labour and enterprises with which they are associated are not available. In our country, numerically small sector employing 10 or more workers with power or 20 workers without power are to be legally registered as factories for which survey data are available. Among the non-registered factories, named as unorganised or informal sector industries which are family based, cottage or household units and which do not use wage-labour, gets no industrial loan/supp. rt from financial institutions or the organised market. They often carry on with great disadvantages. The head-count of such non-wage industrial or manufacturing workers, designated as artisans, far outnumber the labour in the registered industrial sector. The so-called distinction between organised and unorganised industrial sector, however, does not reflect the concrete economic problems not to speak of other problems in the industrialization process. If we are to look into all these problems, the approach towards industrialization should be the best possible utilization of indigenous materials and the skills of labour force available in the area. The major obstacle for developing countries remain their dependent relationship with highly developed countries. The concept of development remained ambiguous and controversial having economic as well as non-economic dimensions. In situation where capital is scarce, one cannot expect a capital intensive heavy industry to be set up in an area where neither indigenous material nor labour would be of any use. That is why, it is necessary that industrial policy to be pursued in such an area should be from the point of view of an in-ward oriented economy. Such policies created high growth in some countries, most notably in North Korea and China. There is however limitation of such industrialization from the point of view of marketability of their products in the international fields. Even then a few economies in the Central America and Africa successfully earned foreign exchange in this process (Nicaragua, Mozambic, Ethiopia and most notably, Cuba).

With the small size of the domestic market and the general poverty of the North-Eastern states in India, large scale industrialization programme would be largely inapplicable. Moreover, the disadvantageous geo-ecological location of these states (in a seismic zone) also come on the way of establishment of heavy industries. More importantly, there are some social and political factors which inhibit the import of capital from outside.

In the last four decades there has been little or no investment in North-Eastern region by the private entrepreneurs. Because private entrepreneurs want direct investment and are not in favour of portfolio investment. If such port-folio investments could be encouraged by the state governments there would have been better utilization of indigenous raw materials, the product mix or change in product design suitable to local markets. Use of local skills and capacity might have stretched the existing potential to a considerable extent. Even certain kinds of highly specialised products of this region on their own merit would find their way to international market. For example, specialised textile and silk materials, cane wares, wooden products, processed fruit, resin etc. are some products which could easily and efficiently be produced in the states and would earn substantial amount of foreign exchange for the economy. Instead of this, the policy pursued in these states remained orthodox and did not try to appropriately combine both inward looking and outward looking industrialization which was the need of the area.

Though late, it would be worthwhile to give a fresh look into the potential of industrialization of North-Eastern states in view of the present status of industrial situation both in registered as well as non-registered industrial sectors.

In the following sections we present a few salient points regarding present industrial scenario in the North-Eastern states.

Work Force

Work force consists of members of the population in 16 to 65 age group who are employed (main worker), marginally employed and involuntarily unemployed. The figure of involuntarily unemployed persons are neither available from census data nor from unemployment register due to inefficient system of functioning of the Employment Exchanges. The unrecorded unemployment is much higher than the recorded unemployment. It is possible that around 5 to 7 per cent of the total population comes under unrecorded unemployed category. However, due to non-availability of data regarding this we would be depending on the census data (vide Table 5.1) to describe the work force. Table 5.2 describes the percentage share of workers to total population in 1981 and 1991, showing a general trend of decreasing number of main workers to total population. In other words, unemployment is on the increase. Except in the case of Mizoram, the share of work force to total pupulation has decreased. If we add the number of involuntarily and wholly unemployed persons it may still be higher. In a region with a population of above 31 millions (vide Table 5.1), the total work force would be about 19 millions. But according to census data we get 11.77 millions as the total workers in 1991 of which 6.78 millions are attached to agriculture.

TABLE 5.1 : Population, Workforce and their Distribution in North-Eastern States, 1991

States	Population	Total worker	Main worker	Marginal worker	Cultivator	Distribution of Main Workers: Agriculture labour	Household industry worker	Other worker
Arunachal Pradesh	858392	407362	389621	17741	237918	19074	2480	130149
Assam	22294562	8108785	7068363	1040422	3622017	911386	177149	2357811
Manipur	1826714	758204	682448	75756	389690	63350	48352	181056
Meghalaya	1760626	758118	719205	38913	404561	95895	7151	211598
Mizoram	686217	338724	290215	48509	176713	10835	3609	99058
Nagaland	1215573	537314	505179	32135	344666	23889	7649	128975
Tripura	2744827	860752	793457	67295	301856	186671	15487	289443
N.E. States	31386911	11769259	10448488	1320771	5477421	1311100	261877	3398090
* All India	836605522	314903642	285422913	29480729	110588822	74649217	10373091	89811775

* Excludes Jammu and Kashmir.

Source : Census-1991, Govt. of India.

TABLE 5.2: Percentage Share of Worker to Total Population

	Total Worker		Main Worker		Marginal Worker	
States	1981	1991	1981	1991	1981	1991
Arunachal Pradesh	52.63	47.46	49.61	45.39	3.02	2.07
Assam	N.A.	36.37	N.A.	31.70	N.A.	4.67
Manipur	43.20	41.51	40.35	37.36	2.85	4.15
Meghalaya	45.92	43.06	43.43	40.85	2.49	2.21
Mizoram	45.44	49.36	41.73	42.29	3.71	7.07
Nagaland	48.23	44.20	47.53	41.56	0.70	2.64
Tripura	32.27	31.36	29.64	28.91	2.63	2.45
All India	36.77	37.64	33.45	34.12	3.32	3.52

Source : Census-1981 and 1991, Govt. of India.

Industrial Performance in North-Eastern States

Let us look at the performance pattern of different industries in different states of North-Eastern India between 1984-85 and 1992-93 for which data are available from Annual Survey of Industries, conducted by Central Statistical Organisation (CSO), Government of India. It is a common knowledge that these data have been supplied by the owners and/or the management of the industries and not by the workers. Since we have no other sources to depend upon, we would base our discussion on the data supplied by CSO.

The indicators by which the prospect of an industry is generally measured are gross output per employee and ratios of fixed capital to output, net value added to output, fixed capital to net value added and net fixed capital formation to net value added. Such measures are done from the view point of the entrepreneurs. Table 5.3 gives the selected ratios relating to industrial sectors in North-Eastern states in different years. Gross output per employee generally showed an upward trend over the years although remained a little lower than all-India figures. Net value added to output, a key measure for entrepreneurs, also remained either higher or equal to that of all-India figures in all states of North-East except in Manipur in one particular year, 1992-93. Net fixed capital formation to net value added in 1992-93 was 0.03 in India as a whole whereas it was 0.53 in Meghalaya, Nagaland, Tripura and Manipur showed negative values which needs an explanation. Is this might of

TABLE 5.3: Selected Ratios Relating to Industrial Sector in North-Eastern States and India

	Year	India	Assam	Mani-pur	Megha-laya	Naga-land	Tripura
Gross Output per Employee	1984-85	1.34	1.16	0.35	0.41	N.A.	0.24
	1985-86	1.61	1.52	0.18	0.74	N.A.	0.25
	1990-91	2.83	2.44	0.28	0.53	1.47	0.31
	1992-93	4.23	2.83	0.15	1.02	1.16	0.69
Fixed Capital to Output	1984-85	0.52	0.37	0.27	3.25	N.A.	0.37
	1985-86	0.50	0.27	0.50	0.93	N.A.	0.37
	1990-91	0.46	0.33	1.00	6.10	0.32	1.48
	1992-93	0.52	0.43	0.75	4.82	1.70	0.57
Fixed Capital to Net Value Added	1984-85	2.63	1.41	0.94	8.62	N.A.	0.99
	1985-86	2.58	1.06	1.00	13.00	N.A.	1.57
	1990-91	2.47	1.30	1.00	20.00	1.80	8.88
	1992-93	2.71	1.93	-6.33	10.26	11.60	1.77
Net Value Added to Output	1984-85	0.20	0.26	0.30	0.38	N.A.	0.37
	1985-86	0.19	0.26	0.50	0.07	N.A.	0.23
	1990-91	0.19	0.25	1.00	0.34	0.18	0.17
	1992-93	0.19	0.22	-0.12	0.47	0.15	0.32
Wages to Value of Output	1984-85	0.06	0.04	0.31	0.16	N.A.	0.17
	1992-93	0.05	0.04	0.06	0.20	0.12	0.16
Net Fixed Capital Formation to Net Value Added	1984-85	0.30	0.15	0.08	-0.03	N.A.	0.003
	1992-93	0.30	0.06	-0.85	0.53	-0.03	-0.01

Source: i) Annual Survey of Industries: 1984-1985 and 1992-1993, C.S.O. Govt. of India.

(ii) Report on Currency and Finance 1993-94; Vol. I: *Economic Review*.

capital? It is possible when capital might have been exported out of these industries by the outside entrepreneurs settled in these states. Fixed capital to output in case of India as a whole in 1992-93 was only 0.52 whereas the corresponding figures for Meghalaya, Nagaland, Manipur, Tripura and Assam were 4.82, 1.70, 0.75, 0.57 and 0.43 respectively. So all the states except Assam evidenced more capital intensity in the production process compared to that in India as a whole. This is about capital. Now, we should see the gains of industrialization which was accrued to labour. The wages' share to output remained as low as 0.04 to 0.06 not only in these states but also for India as a whole.

In case of Tripura, Manipur and Nagaland the ratios were a little favourable for workers in some of the years. But there is no indication of rising share of wages to the value of output.

From the workers' view point or from the view point of the society as a whole rising share of wages to value of output should be treated as favourable industrial climate. Unfortunately, from this consideration, there has been steady decline in most of the industries in all the states in North-East India. In food processing industries, wages' share was 0.01 and 0.04 between 1984-85 and 1992-93 in Meghalaya. The corresponding figures for Assam, Manipur, Tripura were 0.03 and 0.03; 0.02 and 0.01; 0.03 and 0.03 respectively. In case of Nagaland it was 0.09 in 1992-93 (vide Appendix I to VI). How much more sacrifice one can expect from the workers for industrialization? In case of India as a whole the wages' share to output remained 0.06 in 1984-85 and 0.05 in 1992-93.

It was apparent from the data that food processing (20-21), rubber-plastic (31), gas steam generation (41), wool-silk and fibre (24), wood and wood products (27) and repair of capital goods (39) are some of the industries in Assam which experienced positive net capital formation. In Assam the overall industrial performance remained favourable over the period between 1984-85 and 1992-93 although there was a slight decline in the rate of capital formation. The industries which might have been responsible for the decline in the rate of capital formation were food products,wood and wood crafts, basic chemicals (36), non-metallic mineral products (32) and transport equipments (37) where output capital ratios dwindled. But output per employee increased in each of the industries barring basic chemicals. So industrial climate in Assam is favourable in the existing industrial situation for the entrepreneurs. By rule, productivity per unit of labour has increased over the said period and the share of wages to the value of output remained static considering the overall situation and this remained as low as 0.04. Assam is not unique in North-Eastern India.

Industrial survey data reveal that productivity of labour as well as output per employee showed a tendency to increase in Manipur, Meghalaya as well as in Tripura. The data on Nagaland, Mizoram and Arunachal Pradesh are not available from the source we are quoting. Industrial Survey data leave no scope to think of bad performance on the part of the workers. Output capital ratio showed some decline in food processing, wood craft, paper products (28), repair services (97) in Manipur. Meghalaya and Tripura. In the electricity (40) sector of Tripura there was also decline. But it is a common knowledge that capacity in these sectors was not fully utilized. Work was not undertaken for full-capacity utilization due mainly to the problems of management as well as loss of working hours for political disturbances in Meghalaya, Manipur and a part of Assam. The government blamed the extremists and vice-versa.

The next question is whether capital formation is encouraged or allowed by the entrepreneurs themselves? In case of industries which deal with mass consumption articles, profit accrued to are not generally ploughed back in full. It finds its way to conspicuous consumption, speculative investment or investment in real estate and/or other fields outside North-East by the entrepreneurs.

One more thing need be highlighted regarding workers' sacrifice to the cause of industrialisation.

While calculating net value added, the prevalent practice is to assess the value of output (revenue) net of costs. So the figures on net value added presented in industrial survey data give total revenue net of all costs of inanimate inputs. In order to claculate labours' share to net value added, wages should not be included into the costs. Wages' share to this surplus would indicate the rate of exploitation of the workers. So one can easily construct the rate of exploitation from the industrial survey data of different states as well as in India as a whole. Table 5.4 shows the rate of exploitation of labour over time (1980-81 to 1992-93) in different states as well as in India as a whole. From the table it is clear that the workers' share to surplus show monotonically declining trend in Assam between 1980-81 and 1990-91 except in 1983-84 and 1988-89. However in 1991-92 and 1992-93 there was slight improvement. The same trend has been observed in Manipur. But in case of Meghalaya there seem to be some improvement over 1980-81 (0.14) in 1992-93 (0.43). The industrial survey data show negative values of net value added in some of the years in some states (e.g. Manipur in 1992-93, Meghalaya in 1985-86).

Again in some years the wages exceeded net value added, e.g. in Meghalaya in 1990-91 and in Tripura in the years 1988-89 to 1990-91, which implies that the industries may have to shut down.[1] In case of Tripura the share dwindled from 0.72 to 0.50 between 1980-81 and 1992-93. In case of India as a whole wages share to net value added was one-third between 1980-81 and 1981-82. In later years there was decline in the share of wages (though not monotonic) and became as low as 0.23 in 1992-93. So in case of India as a whole the rate of exploitation of

TABLE 5.4: Ratio of Wages to Surplus (Net Value Added) in Different States in N.E. India Over Time

Year	All India	Assam	Mani-pur	Megha-laya	Tri-pura	Mizo-ram
1980-81	0.33	0.25	0.71	0.14	0.72	N.A.
1981-82	0.33	0.22	0.91	0.34	0.78	N.A.
1982-83	0.28	0.20	0.75	0.33	0.67	N.A.
1983-84	0.26	0.18	0.63	0.33	0.65	N.A.
1984-85	0.32	0.14	0.41	0.43	0.44	N.A.
1985-86	0.30	0.13	0.62	−1.77	0.83	N.A.
1986-87	0.31	0.11	0.60	0.56	0.62	N.A.
1987-88	0.32	0.12	0.53	0.51	0.85	N.A.
1988-89	0.30	0.18	0.36	0.25	1.08	N.A.
1989-90	0.27	0.12	0.36	0.74	1.28	0.27
1990-91	0.26	0.11	0.53	1.02	1.24	2.77
1991-92	0.25	0.14	0.68	0.58	1.46	0.53
1992-93	0.23	0.18	--0.47	0.43	0.50	0.82

Source : Estimated from Annual Survey of Industries, various issues, C.S.O., Govt. of India.

worker is on the increase. Compared to developed countries the share of Indian workers is very dismal. In case of the so called advanced countries the wages share is at least sixty per cent of net value added.

From the above results one can sum up that the rate of exploitation of workers is quite high irrespective of the states. Even if we base our analysis on industrial survey data, it is not only the wages' share to the value of output which is unfavourable to workers but the wages' share in the surplus is also discouraging. In spite of all these, the workers are trying to perform while some of the entrepreneurs are trying exit policy and engaging themselves in speculation thereby debarring capital formation in the industrial sector.

The Constraints of Industrialization

India's industrialization had been characterised by lack of quality products and specialization due to inefficiency of R & D. Besides, lack of entrepreneurial initiative and failure to achieve access to international markets have also contributed to this impasse.

Without examining the pitfalls within this process of industrialization and remedying them, the new economic policy from the beginning of the 90s took a very different attitude towards this issue. The exit policy, i.e., disinvestment, devaluation and denationalization have become the corner-stones of the new economic policy. This however is not unique in case of India. This is the part of the policy of imperialism which for its own interests are trying to reduce the developing economies to their hinterlands from which they would mercilessly exploit the natural resources at a low or no cost. It is in their interests again that they would not allow any developing economy to be industrially prosperous lest they could have to compete with them. By queer logic they plead for competitive price and quality products. By now it is clear that their talk of competition is really meant for abolishing competitions. Their talk of liberalization is actually an exercise to destroy international trade on equal footing. Some instances in India are Kentuchky, Coca-Cola, Walls, Kellogg's etc. which showed how they wanted to capture the markets of devloping economies in the name of liberalization. The infrastructure built-up in the last forty years at the cost of the people of India have provided them opportunities to make deep in-road into Indian markets and they now want that the government should not come into their way of intrusion. At the same time, they want that coercive machinery of the states should be deployed for protection of foreign interests. So, the new industrial policy is really a policy of deindustrialization of Indian economy in favour of the Multinational Companies (MNCs) and Trans National Corporations (TNCs).

GATT could be forced on India due to heavy indebtedness of India and crucial dependence on Funds (IMF) and Bank (IBRD) Loans. The inclusion of India in the World Trade Oraganisation (WTO) has practically sealed the path of independent industrialization and there has been a serious infringement on the political and economic sovereignty of India. All initiatives for industrialization by Indian capital has been put into serious difficulties. Small and medium scale industries would be forced to down their shutters and big industrial houses would be reduced to franchises of the MNCs.

This being the industrial climate in India in the present years, North-Eastern states cannot possibly escape the assaults on industrialization if these states remain under illusion of being integrated to Indian 'main stream'. These states could possibly prosper in their own kind of industries without going for products dealt with by the multinationals.

In the previous section, we have shown that the industrial climate in North-Eastern states is not favourable if we consider industrialization from social point of view. The entrepreneurs also have no argument against workers regarding their contribution to industrialization. We have pointed out earlier that industrialization in North-Eastern states cannot and should not mean setting up of heavy industries. Rather it should be based on indigenous resource potential and skill of local human resources. We also argue in favour of specialization in the fields where the workers of this area have developed expertise. There should therefore be proper emphasis on specialised products for which there would be national and international markets and not product diversification which may be suggested by multinationals.

What course therefore the North-Eastern states should adopt regarding industrialization? Industrial progress in these states cannot ignore the fact that the economies of these states are predominantly agricultural. Moreover, there are various local economies even within each particular state. The situation therefore may not be comparable to other states in India where there are less diverse ethnic groups as well as socio-cultural differences.

So economies in North-Eastern India should march on both feet, namely, agriculture and industry. Agriculture and industry should be complementary to each other and not a substitute. In fact, without development of agriculture and allied activities like animal husbandry, sericulture, horticulture. etc. industrial development would be inhibited. The infrastructure necessary for industrialization suitable to North-Eastern India still reamin grossly inadequate due mainly to transport and communication difficulties, lack of facilities for processing of products and gross neglect of these physically handicapped states by the national government. For formulation of appropriate policies of industrialization one need a reliable and comprehensive data base (which we lack) and awareness of the constraints and potentialities contained in these economies.

Socio-cultural Perspectives of Industrial Development

With the ever increasing number and demand of population economic activity need further widening and deepening. Industrialization becomes the logical outcome of not only supplementing but also developing the economic activities of the primary sector. But industrialization per se is generally conceived as setting up of a few factories with high technology and large imported capital. Such setting up of industries generally alienate the local inhabitants from their own land and very often they are put in different social and natural environment following their eviction. On the other hand the few skilled people who get employment in newly built factories do not find any social roots. As a result of such imposed industrialization the question of indigenous people vis-a-vis development are being raised not only in North-Eastern states but also in other states as well. The Uttarakhand movement, the Jharkahnd, the Kamtapuri movement and many different statehood movements in North-Eastern India emanated from such unwise economic policies completely divorced from the social and cultural ethos of the population.

Economic development in the form of industrialization and socio-cultural changes are generally both causes and effects of each other. The institutions as well as socio-cultural attitudes of the people should be closely interacting with each other and try to evolve a harmonious and secular movement towards the future. Under the present circumstances, neither mercantilism nor individual capitalism or for that matter corporate type of business can be the path of progress in economies where traditional societies are predominant. Therefore, industrialization would necessitate specific development culture suitable for the area. Unless the people of the area are not treated as subject of development there would be serious sociological constraints of industrial progress. Institutions should be oriented towards mobilizing people's participation as well as creativity so that a proper industrial climate can be built up. By industrial climate, the capital means subjugation of labour and maximum profit possibility whereas the labour would mean more employment and an egalitaian distribution of the gains of development. This is the point where the government should intervene and should increasingly depend on the will of the people. The people should be taken into full confidence. Otherwise no backward area can be developed and the people as a whole cannot be benefited and the interests of the nation cannot be served. Our academics should, therefore, examine whether industrial policies pursued in any area are oriented towards well-being of the people of the area. If ethics of industrialization of the above kind is followed only then there can be positive contribution towards work atittude. Broadly speaking, the success of any economic plan to a great extent depends on successful development of institution and socio-cultural ethics towards life and work, both for the prupose of formulation as well as execution of a plan.

Concluding Remarks

From the survey of the industires in the North-Eatern India presented above one can make a few broad observations.

All discussion and planning for industrial development necessarily revolve round the potential markets both domestic and international. To succeed, industries must sell their products. A feature which is common to all the underdeveloped areas is the smallness of the home market and unequal competition in the international market. It is therefore necessary to find out a suitable approach where both inward looking and outward looking processes of industrialization can be combined. Again as discussed above we cannot ignore the present economic liberalisation policies helping the MNC's and TNC's for making deep in-road into our home markets. In the face of competition with these international giants the small and indigenous industrial entreprises are likely to lose. In view of these offensives the indigenous industries, especially those in the areas of North-Eastern states, cannot but insist on specialised products for international markets and mass consumption products for the home markets in order that the dominance dependency relationship can be broken and suitable terms of trade can be set up.

The existing situation of industries in these states show the following trends.

(a) The value of output to capital has been increasing in most of the industries. (b) The net value added to capital is also increasing although at a slower rate (compared to India as a whole). (c) The net capital formation is not increasing as expected due possibly to flight of capital from the states. (d) Wages' share to value of output has remained at a very low level (between 1 and 6%).

All the above show a favourable climate for the capital and unfavourable to labour. Even then net capital formation is either static or negative. Increased casualisation of labour in industries with static and/or declining share of wages cannot enthuse the workers who are being alienated from the industries.

It can further be observed that there are great diversities, geo-physical as well as socio-cultural within the North-Eastern region itself. A substantial portion of the region is mountainous although there is a very wide valley in the same region. Industrialization in the region cannot therefore ignore these peculiarities and policies should have adequate flexibility.

The approach we argue for are as follows:

(1) With around 31 million population in North-Eastern states and a great reserve army of unemployed, attempts should be made to undertake industrialization which would generate greater employment. (2) Although earnings of foreign exchange by sale of specialised products of the North-East (as mentioned earlier) is important, emphasis should be given on producing essential consumption goods for the use of the local inhabitants. (3) As the states are located in a seismic zone, setting up of heavy industries and exploration of minerals and oil should be very cautious and discrete. There should not be any insistence on heavy industries in this area so that the eco-balance can be maintained. Since the area has great geo-diversity, the industries should be planned suitably for plane (valley), hilly and plateau regions. (4) Light engineering and electronics industries may be undertaken and arrangement for the development of the skill should be made. (5) Agencies like Indian Council of Agricultural Research, National Dairy Development Board and Central Fishery Institute etc. should devote more attention on maintaining and strengthening bio-diversities so that the environment of this area is improved and reckless denudation of forestry is stopped. (6) The wages' share to output should be improved and workers should be given proper status and 'say' in management. (7) Thousands of small and cottage based industries should be encouraged to come up. (8) Attempts should sincerely be made to check the flight of capital from these states to elsewhere, be it in case of state or individual enterprises. (9) There should be strict vigilance against misuse of state investments.

It should always be remembered that the aim is comprehensive and eco-friendly development of this region of which industrialization with appropriate technology and adequate funding is an important part. By so doing both industry and agriculture and allied to agriculture can proceed in a meaningful way.

REFERENCE

1. It is obvious that the private sector industries are likkely to exit from those industries where the net value added is less than wages. The question then arises why and how the industries can still continue. There are several possibilities: (a) "the loss" is being borne by the public sector units in the industry; (b) the information given by the industies are not correct; (c) the P.F. and other

benefits supposed to be given to the workers are not being deposited by the industries concerned. Moreover, the rental and taxes shown in the balance sheet are paper transaction and not real. We cannot give any observation without having access to all these data. Such data can only be collected by undertaking serious scrutiny of data supplied by the industries.

APPENDIX : I (ASSAM)

Major Industry code	Gross output per employee		Fixed capital to output		Net value added to output		Fixed capital to net value added		Wage to value of output		Net fixed capital formation to net value added	
	1984-85	1992-93	1984-85	1992-93	1984-85	1992-93	1984-85	1992-93	1984-85	1992-93	1984-85	1992-93
20-21	1.18	2.42	0.13	0.26	0.29	0.19	0.45	1.33	0.03	0.03	0.07	0.13
22	0.33	0.99	2.08	N.A.	0.25	N.A.	8.33	N.A.	0.10	N.A.	6.50	N.A.
23	0.47	0.99	0.47	0.37	0.25	0.17	1.92	2.16	0.14	0.16	0.06	-0.28
24	N.A.	1.70	N.A	0.85	N.A	0.19	N.A	4.55	N.A	0.10	N.A	1.22
25	0.20	0.43	0.33	0.24	0.40	0.38	0.84	0.64	0.22	0.25	0.02	-0.05
27	0.80	1.79	0.17	0.18	0.27	0.25	0.61	0.70	0.04	0.05	0.04	0.07
28	0.65	3.12	95.21	1.67	-7.73	0.25	-12.16	6.55	0.06	0.06	-2.49	-0.40
30	10.95	2.22	0.09	1.28	0.20	0.16	0.48	-7.93	0.01	0.14	0.13	1.57
31	1.26	19.41	0.86	0.33	0.24	0.27	3.65	1.21	0.13	0.02	-0.39	0.12
32	0.47	0.76	0.47	0.61	0.28	0.33	1.69	1.85	0.07	0.07	-0.02	-0.01
33	0.68	5.36	0.40	0.21	0.23	0.10	1.78	2.12	0.09	0.02	0.02	-0.64
34	0.77	1.26	0.16	0.09	0.26	0.24	0.59	0.36	0.05	0.08	0.02	0.00
35-36	0.71	1.73	0.28	0.11	0.36	0.32	0.79	0.34	0.09	0.12	0.11	-0.02
37	0.30	0.71	0.07	1.75	0.58	0.41	0.11	4.31	0.35	0.30	0.00	-0.40
39	N.A	0.96	N.A	1.08	N.A	0.53	N.A	2.03	N.A	0.39	N.A	0.03
40	0.20	8.48	6.02	5.77	0.46	0.58	13.01	10.01	0.16	0.03	0.09	-0.04
41	N.A	1.54	N.A	1.99	N.A	0.45	N.A	4.46	N.A	0.15	N.A	1.61
42	N.A	3.04	N.A	0.63	N.A	0.24	N.A	2.65	N.A	0.19	N.A	-0.38
97	0.29	0.57	0.18	0.46	0.42	0.58	0.44	0.79	0.25	0.24	0.07	-0.04
99	0.44	N.A	0.34	N.A	0.39	N.A	0.92	N.A	0.19	N.A	-0.08	N.A
Overall	1.16	2.83	0.37	0.43	0.26	0.22	1.41	1.93	0.04	0.04	0.15	0.06

Source: Annual Survey of Industries: 1984-1985 and 1992-1993, C.S.O. Govt. of India.

APPENDIX : II (MANIPUR)

Major Industry code	Gross output per employee		Fixed capital to output		Net value added to output		Fixed capital to net value added		Wage to value of output		Net fixed capital formation to net value added	
	1984-85	1992-93	1984-85	1992-93	1984-85	1992-93	1984-85	1992-93	1984-85	1992-93	1984-85	1992-93
20-21	1.43	3.51	0.11	0.92	0.24	-0.70	0.44	-1.31	0.02	0.01	0.21	0.03
27	0.30	0.74	0.41	0.50	0.28	0.25	1.46	1.97	0.13	0.08	-0.08	-0.16
28	0.10	N.A.	0.92	N.A.	0.84	N.A.	1.10	N.A.	0.60	N.A.	-0.05	N.A.
32	N.A.	0.39	N.A.	3.66	N.A.	0.20	N.A.	17.94	N.A.	0.17	N.A.	7.94
*38	N.A.	2.18	N.A.	0.34	N.A.	0.15	N.A.	2.22	N.A.	0.05	N.A.	0.23
97	0.15	0.25	0.75	1.00	0.50	0.66	1.50	1.53	0.25	0.59	0.00	-0.10
99	0.16	N.A.	0.29	N.A.	0.19	N.A.	1.57	N.A.	0.21	N.A.	0.29	N.A.
Overall	0.35	1.55	0.27	0.75	0.30	-0.12	0.94	-6.33	0.31	0.06	0.08	-0.85

* Includes indigenous groups 24, 28, 30, 33, 34, 36, and 37.

Source: Annual Survey of Industries: 1984-1985 and 1992-1993, C.S.O. Govt. of India

APPENDIX : III (MEGHALAYA)

Major Industry code	Gross output per employee		Fixed capital to output		Net value added to output		Fixed capital to net value added		Wage to value of output		Net fixed capital formation to net value added	
	1984-85	1992-93	1984-85	1992-93	1984-85	1992-93	1984-85	1992-93	1984-85	1992-93	1984-85	1992-93
20-21	3.54	1.38	0.13	0.27	0.08	0.24	1.55	1.09	0.01	0.04	-0.09	0.09
27	0.40	2.10	0.49	0.24	0.40	0.36	1.24	0.66	0.12	0.04	-0.11	0.07
28	0.20	0.41	0.24	0.26	0.66	0.84	0.36	0.31	0.52	0.68	0.08	0.06
32	N.A.	2.27	N.A.	0.74	N.A.	0.29	N.A.	2.57	N.A.	0.12	N.A.	-0.80
*38	N.A.	1.66	N.A.	0.14	N.A.	0.34	N.A.	0.40	N.A.	0.04	N.A.	-0.02
40	N.A.	0.79	N.A.	8.69	N.A.	0.58	N.A.	14.94	N.A.	0.25	N.A.	1.04
97	0.33	0.27	1.10	0.85	0.47	0.72	2.32	1.18	0.31	0.72	-0.20	-0.09
99	0.42	N.A.	4.15	N.A.	0.37	N.A.	11.11	N.A.	0.15	N.A.	-0.01	N.A.
Overall	0.41	1.02	3.25	4.82	0.38	0.47	8.62	10.26	0.16	0.20	-0.03	0.53

* Includes indigenous groups 22, 23, 33, and 34.

Source : Annual Survey of Industries; 1984-1985 and 1992-1993, C.S.O. Govt. of India.

APPENDIX : IV (NAGALAND)

Major Industry code	Gross output per employee		Fixed capital to output		Net value added to output		Fixed capital to net value added		Wage to value of output		Net fixed capital formation to net value added	
	1984-85	1992-93	1984-85	1992-93	1984-85	1992-93	1984-85	1992-93	1984-85	1992-93	1984-85	1992-93
20-21	N.A.	1.12	N.A.	0.12	N.A.	0.08	N.A.	1.39	N.A.	0.09	N.A.	-0.17
27	N.A.	2.01	N.A.	0.20	N.A.	0.24	N.A.	0.84	N.A.	0.04	N.A.	0.01
28	N.A.	0.11	N.A.	51.70	N.A.	-1.56	N.A.	-33.17	N.A.	0.12	N.A.	0.04
32	N.A.	0.45	N.A.	0.72	N.A.	0.38	N.A.	1.91	N.A.	0.14	N.A.	-0.09
38	N.A.	0.45	N.A.	5.00	N.A.	0.10	N.A.	50.00	N.A.	0.20	N.A.	-5.00
97	N.A.	0.39	N.A.	0.43	N.A.	0.86	N.A.	0.50	N.A.	0.14	N.A.	0.00
Overall	N.A.	1.16	N.A.	1.70	N.A.	0.15	N.A.	11.60	N.A.	0.12	N.A.	-0.03

Source : Annual Survey of Industries: 1984-1985 and 1992-1993, C.S.O. Govt. of India.

APPENDIX : V (TRIPURA)

Major Industry code	Gross output per employee		Fixed capital to output		Net value added to output		Fixed capital to net value added		Wage to value of output		Net fixed capital formation to net value added	
	1984-85	1992-93	1984-85	1992-93	1984-85	1992-93	1984-85	1992-93	1984-85	1992-93	1984-85	1992-93
20-21	0.63	1.43	0.19	0.58	0.22	0.28	0.87	2.09	0.03	0.03	0.03	0.04
22	0.76	N.A.	0.00	N.A.	0.08	N.A.	0.00	N.A.	0.05	N.A.	0.00	N.A.
25	0.31	N.A.	0.75	N.A.	0.21	N.A.	3.62	N.A.	0.24	N.A.	-0.32	N.A.
27	0.05	0.53	1.00	1.53	0.38	0.63	2.67	2.42	0.75	0.26	-0.33	-0.25
28	0.18	0.29	0.38	1.39	0.63	0.41	0.61	3.43	0.47	0.91	0.02	0.09
30	0.90	0.39	0.50	6.85	0.39	0.52	1.29	13.29	0.39	0.27	0.48	1.88
32	0.08	0.22	0.15	0.12	0.46	0.55	0.33	0.20	0.25	0.18	0.01	0.003
33	0.01	1.32	13.50	0.14	-1.50	0.23	-9.00	0.63	N.A.	0.14	-4.00	0.38
34	0.20	0.37	0.16	0.29	0.24	0.31	0.65	0.96	N.A.	0.47	0.06	-0.09
35-36	0.00	1.59	N.A.	0.27	N.A.	0.36	-0.67	0.75	N.A.	0.06	0.00	0.42
*38	N.A.	0.14	N.A.	0.20	N.A.	0.13	N.A.	1.62	N.A.	1.23	N.A.	-0.14
40	0.54	3.50	0.43	0.75	0.77	0.25	0.56	3.06	0.17	0.08	0.01	-0.18
42	0.28	0.39	0.80	0.29	0.43	0.55	1.84	0.52	0.74	0.59	0.32	0.02
97	0.32	0.75	0.25	0.21	0.26	0.46	0.97	0.46	0.56	0.22	0.00	-0.01
99	0.36	N.A.	0.42	N.A.	0.19	N.A.	2.17	N.A.	0.42	N.A.	0.00	N.A.
Overall	0.24	0.69	0.37	0.57	0.37	0.32	0.99	1.77	0.17	0.16	0.003	-0.01

* Includes indigenous groups 22, 25, 26, and 31.

Source: Annual Survey of Industries: 1984-85 and 1992-1993, C.S.O. Govt. of India.

APPENDIX : VI (ALL INDIA)

Major Industry code	Gross output per employee		Fixed capital to output		Net value added to output		Fixed capital to net value added		Wage to value of output		Net fixed capital formation to net value added	
	1984-85	1992-93	1984-85	1992-93	1984-85	1992-93	1984-85	1992-93	1984-85	1992-93	1984-85	1992-93
20-21	1.39	4.19	0.15	0.16	0.12	0.10	1.23	1.66	0.03	0.03	0.06	0.23
22	0.56	1.33	0.11	0.18	0.23	0.25	0.48	0.74	0.06	0.06	0.04	0.18
23	0.74	2.30	0.29	0.27	0.26	0.16	1.09	1.74	0.13	0.09	0.08	0.26
25	0.49	0.89	0.14	0.25	0.25	0.29	0.54	0.85	0.20	0.27	0.02	-0.001
27	0.61	1.54	0.24	0.24	0.22	0.20	0.98	1.23	0.07	0.06	0.06	0.08
28	1.06	3.24	0.65	0.42	0.24	0.21	2.71	1.95	0.08	0.06	0.36	0.19
30	6.03	7.90	0.19	0.44	0.09	0.21	2.04	2.50	0.02	0.03	0.44	0.12
31	2.74	11.52	0.37	0.27	0.18	0.16	2.02	1.61	0.04	0.02	0.13	0.24
32	0.94	2.87	0.46	0.59	0.26	0.20	1.81	2.95	0.07	0.05	0.22	0.27
33	1.92	7.02	0.63	0.71	0.14	0.14	4.37	5.16	0.06	0.03	0.50	0.73
34	1.10	3.08	0.20	0.28	0.23	0.19	0.90	1.50	0.08	0.06	0.08	0.24
35-36	1.42	4.76	0.24	0.26	0.29	0.23	0.84	1.12	0.07	0.05	0.07	0.16
37	1.12	4.06	0.39	0.31	0.26	0.20	1.48	1.50	0.10	0.06	0.19	0.19
40	0.96	4.15	2.72	2.00	0.31	0.33	8.74	6.06	0.09	0.06	1.11	0.59
42	0.96	2.04	0.49	0.29	0.20	0.28	0.43	1.43	0.09	0.11	0.18	-0.07
97	0.39	0.95	0.21	0.18	0.44	0.47	0.49	0.38	0.28	0.22	0.01	0.001
Overall	1.34	4.23	0.52	0.52	0.20	0.19	2.63	2.71	0.06	0.05	0.30	0.30

Source: Annual Survey of Industries: 1984-1985 and 1992-1993, C.S.O. Govt. of India.

6

THE ANOMIE OF A BORROWED ECONOMY

(A preliminary enquiry into the anomic constraints to economic development of North-Eastern India)

— P.C. Dey

The whole economy of N.E. India is a borrowed one in the sense that eighty to ninety per cent of the expenditure of its seven governments is funded by the central government. Per capita central grant and contributions in Assam, Manipur, Meghalaya and Tripura in 1988-89 were Rs. 250, 1010, 850 and 870 respectively whereas the figures under this head for U.P., Orissa, M.P. and Andhra Pradesh were Rs. 80, 150, 90 and 80 respectively. The per capita Seventh Plan outlays (1985-90) of the former afore-mentioned states of N.E. India were Rs. 850, 2529, 2750 and 1760 respectively; for the other states mentioned above they were Rs. 803, 897, 1146 and 841. (The shares of Arunachal Pradesh, Nagaland and Mizoram were much higher on both the counts) As a result of all this we find heavy revenue expenditure (per capita) incurred in the states of N.E. India much heavier than noticed in other states of the country. The end results of this phenomenon are reflected in high physical quality of life index in this region. The author found in one of his exercises ('Economics of Paternalism in the states of N.E. India', The Journal of Jayaprakash Narayan Institute of Social and Economic Studies, Jan-June, 1996, Bhubaneswar) that is was very much higher in N.E. India than most of the other parts of the country. This particular finding was surprisingly in line with figures of population below poverty line published in L.S.U.S.Q.—Statement-No. 469 (1983-84), GOI in the different states. The statement *inter alia* showed that people living below poverty line in N.E. India (percent-wise) are very low than most of their counterparts living elsewhere in the country. But with low level of infrastructural development here this better-off position cannot be sustained. A slight cut in central grant will breakdown this cosmetic economy of N.E. India. in a twinkle of moment.

The borrowed (one may call 'INFLATED' if he likes) economy is creating havoc in this region with all its attendant ills, mostly economic ones—all obstructing its sustainable development. The author laid bare some of these ills in his earlier-mentioned paper. As the central grant was much in excess of utilisation capacity a hugs amount went down the gutter resulting in all pervasing corruption. So the marginal productivity of central grant decreased leading to social tension and divisive tendency. And, all this has been acting as constraint to the real sustainable development of N.E. India.

The 'hi-fi' life styles regularly projected in cable and local T.V. programmes normally are taken more as substance than as a shadow. Their electrifying effects are forcing the people here to have sky high aspirations, and for their achievement all sorts of dubious means are taken. As a result we find less generation of savings and conconmitently less private investment. If the ratio of bank deposit (per capita) to par capita income is taken as reflection of per capita saving then the following figures of 1989-90 then give us some idea on saving-generation in this region. They are 32.99, 24.49, 13.41 and 32.34 in Arunachal Pradesh, Assam, Manipur and Tripura whereas the respective figures of Gujarat, Maharashtra, Punjab and Tamilnadu are 47.65, 67.91, 61.24 and 57.95.

Again the wide gap between goals and achievements leads to scapegoating syndrome. This gets further compounded when the source of frustration arising out of non-achievement of goals is projected towards wrong object. Sadly this anomic situation is ruling roost in the society of N.E. India resulting in unsustainable (inflated) development here.

Going a step further one can say that the highly anomic social milieu leading to easy access to money is not creating motivation for the formation of, what may be called, calvinistic work cultures concomitants of entrepreneurship. It is found that the immigrants in this zone living under heavy constraints normally are the suppliers of entrepreneurship. In this connection one can recall the following words of Harvey Leibenstein. '. . . . outsiders are restricted from some economic opportunities, (so) their opportunity costs as entrepreneurs are likely to be lower than the other portions of popuiation, and hence they more readily engage in entrepreneurial activities compared to 'insiders' whose opportunity costs are higher.' ("En..epreneurship and Development" *American Economic Review*, May, 1968). Hagen's theory on entrepreneurship also is pertinent in the cotext of the development of N.E. India. His theory—psychoanalytical intergenerational theory of personality formation—*inter alia* states that the personality of a society receptive to developmental activities like innovation takes several generations to grow. In the light of the above views one looks at awe when he finds that immigrants in N.E. India are not in the good book of insiders. Racent trend of the slow and steady outflow of immigrant-entrepreneurs will prove obstructive to the development of this zone in as much as the fact that there will not be their replacement by insiders in the near future.

All said and done sustainable development of N.E. India in the very near future is bleak. After all, social constraints take several generations for their removal. What is of utmost necessity now is the enforcement of healthy law and order. And the doling of fund from the Centre must be in tune with the utilisation capacity of the different states here.

7

IMPEDIMENTS TO INDUSTRIAL DEVELOPMENT IN NORTH-EAST—SOME SOCIOLOGICAL ISSUES

— S.K. Agnihotri

The Government of India and the major financial institutions have recognised the North-East Region of India as industrially backward and a large number of concessions are available to the Region. These include concessional finance, subsidies for capital investment and transport, excise duty exemption, income tax holiday, establishment of specialised institutions to accelerate the industrial development in the North-East etc. In spite of these incentives, the industrial development in the Region has not been up to the mark. This is due to various constraints—institutional, political and sociological. In this chapter an attempt has been made to identify the sociological constraints impeding the industrial development in the North-East.

The North-East Region of India is an open region except few states. It has been experiencing heavy and continuous influx of population from Bangladesh and Nepal, apart from in-migration from various parts of the country. This has led to ethnic conflicts and consequent law and order problems. Another result of this migration has been the requirement of large investment package to offset the depressing effect on income of explosive population growth.

Major Issues

Some issues in this regard are discussed below:

(1) Regional dimension of industrialisation of North-East India has not been treated at all the levels as an integral part of the national plan

due to difficult terrain, distance from the heartland, nearness to the international borders and inadequate infrastructure. Down-stream industries have not been established in this part of the country to the required extent. Some measures in this direction have been taken only after social movements.

(2) Like in the other parts of the country, the current emphasis in the North-East Region also is on achieving financial targets. It often results in the culture of wasteful and infructuous spending. This aspect is of special importance in view of loose financial accountability in the Region. There are built-in deficiencies in the planning strategy, lack of integration in planning at the strategic levels and want of synchronisation of inputs and complementary activities in the vital areas of development. In spite of these deficiencies, there is little public awareness in the society.

(3) There are four major deficiencies in implementation of industrial projects in the Region:

(a) Absence of systems approach in decision making and judicious delegation of decision-making authority.
(b) Inadequacy in required quality, competence and motivation of administrative man-power.
(c) The socio-political environment in the region is responsible to a large extent in leakages and wasteful expenditure.
(d) There is often deficiency in planning process due to lack of awareness on the part of the decision makers at different levels of the intrecacies of the problems and the failure to visualise the repercussion effects of their decisions. In addition, there is often an absence, at the implementation stage, of the knowledge of the related aspects of the projects and their mutual interactions, on the part of those charged with the implementation of the decisions.

(4) Not all the income generated within the region is available for regional saving and capital formation. This is, sometimes, due to lack of perceived security. Most of the economic activity is guided by outside systems and often the income generated is leaking out of the region.

(5) Considerable part of its economic activity centres round subsistence agriculture and household-crafts generally in an extensive tribal economy.

(6) In addition, there are also cases of mis-location of industries on political considerations. These industries get congenitally handicapped.

(7) The land and the land tenure system are a big impediment to industrial development because of social customs, inheritance and land laws.

(8) In most of the North-Eastern societies there are traditional means of reaching culturally defined goals. Some of these means have since been institutionalised. The accepted ways of achieving success through education, talent, hard work, drive, determination and ambition have sometimes given way to a new culture of achieving goals without following the generally accepted "rules of the game". The emphasis now is to strive for success by any available means. When rules cease to operate in a society, a situation of normlessness or "anomie" results. In the situation of "anything goes," norms no longer direct behaviour and deviance is encouraged to achieve success. There are five possible ways in which members of a society respond in such a situation.

(a) *Conformity*: The members of the society conform both to success goals and the normative means of reaching them. They strive for success by means of accepted channels.

(b) *Innovation*: This response often rejects normative means of achieving success and turns to deviant means in particular to crime. In the traditional societies members at the bottom of the social structure may accept this position since they do not crave for mainstream (urban) success situation.

(c) *Ritualism:* The pressure to adopt this alternative is greatest for the members of the lower middle-class. Compared to the members of working class, they have been strongly socialised to conform to social norms, This prevents them from turning to crime. Typical lower middle class ritualist can be compared to the large population of service holders in the North-East, ultra-respectable but stuck in a rut. He is a *strickler* to the rules, follows the book to the letter, clings to red-tape, and conforms to all the outward standards of middle-class respectability. He has given up striving for success.

(d) *Retreatism*: This response generally applied to psychotics, pariah, outcast, vagrants, vagabonds, tramps, chronic drunkards and drug addicts. This group strongly desires to achieve cultural goals by the institutionalised means yet is unable to achieve success. They resolve the conflict of the situation by abandoning both goals and means of reaching them. They are unable to cope and drop out of the society, defeated and resigned to their failure. They often reject both the cultural goal and the institutionalised means.

(e) *Rebellion*: It is a rejection of both the success goals and the institutionalised means and the replacement by different goals and means. Those who adopt this alternative wish to create a new society. Often terrorism and extremism are adopted to reach their goal. It is typically members of a rising class rather than the most depressed strata who organise the resentful and rebellious into a revolutionary group.

In the region, the societies have reacted in all five ways in different states. There have been cases of insurgent movements some of which are still current. There are also cases of drug addicts which are a menace to the society in some states in the region. Further, except for Assam, the societies are generally inward looking and apprehensive of major industrialisation moves as these may change ethnic balance. This is a major constraint to industrial development.

Possible Solutions

For accelerating industrial development in the region, it is necessary to increase the number of people who conform to the cultural goals and the institutionalised means and to work out strategies to reduce the last four categories from the society. This effort coupled with the creation of conducive infrastructure will help the region to develop. In addition, following points will/may improve the situation.

(a) Total quality control.
(b) Major attention to irrigation and power.
(c) Development of resource based industries.
(d) Due importance to be given to thrust areas–agriculture and allied sectors, horticulture, sericulture, fishery.

(e) Improvement of quality of human agents by way of establishment of institutions entirely oriented to regional needs and aspirations and to create local expertise to successfuly deal with major regional problems and cater to high level manpower needs in the field of regional development.

(f) Actual participation of the people in the planning and implementation process.

8

RELATIVE CONTRIBUTIONS OF ECONOMIC AND NON-ECONOMIC FACTORS TO INDUSTRIAL BACKWARDNESS OF THE NORTH-EASTERN REGION

— P.R. Bhattacharjee

Theoretical Background

In recent decades growing dissatisfaction is evident with economists' "hegemony" in the analysis of the problems of development and underdevelopment. Scholars of other social science disciplines have been entering the field of economic development offering interpretations of the situations with non-economic tools of analysis. Even the economists feel that the "borderline between social sciences are becoming blurred today."[1]

The concern for discovering and specifying the non-economic factors of economic development has given birth to a host of theories some of which are presented by Benjamin Higgins in his celebrated work under the caption, "Cultural Determinism".[2] A look at these theories may help us in understanding socio-economic reality in the North-Eastern Region.

The most prominent example of non-economic interpretation of industrial or economic backwardness is provided by Boeke's theory of Socio-cultural Dualism. According to Boeke, social dualism is the clashing of an imported social system (Western) with an indigenous system of another style (Eastern). The socio-cultural divide makes the Western theory inapplicable to underdeveloped areas and so, efforts to develop them along Western lines are bound to fail.

David C. McClelland, a psychologist analyses interactions among social organizations, individual behaviour and economic development in his work on "Achieving Society". According to McClelland, a society with generally high level of "n-achievement" or achievement motivation will produce more energetic entrepreneurs, who, in turn, produce more rapid economic development. His theory isolates certain psychological factors which are generally important in economic development. When these psychological traits are present, people are capable of taking risks necessary for establishing and managing enterprises. The policy implication of this theory is that there is need for strong ideological movement in order to overcome resistance to modernisation in underdeveloped areas.

Everett Hagen makes an effort to construct a general theory of development based on a nexus of sociological, anthropological and psychological factors. He insists that in order to understand why some traditional societies enter into the stage of rapid economic growth sooner than others, we must understand the internal structure and functioning of the societies as both barriers to growth and the causes of growth seem to be largely internal rather than external.

The traditional society consisting of peasantry and other simple folk, the elite classes and the trader-financier leads to a particular type of uncreative and non-innovational individual behaviour. Consequently, traditional society is generally resistant to change. The change comes about if and when members of some one social group perceive that their purposes and values are not respected by groups in the society whom they respect and whose esteem they value. Such social disaffection is most readily apparent when a group migrates to a new society. Such a social group is often found to lead the development process by starting new enterprises.

Anthropologist Geertz is of the opinion that a wide range of cultures is capable of generating entrepreneurship and economic growth. Innovative economic leadership (entrepreneurship) occurs in a fairly well-defined and socially homogeneous group which crystallyzes out of a larger traditional group which has a long history of extra-village status and interlocal orientation. The innovative group experiences a fairly radical change in its relationship with the wider society of which it is a part; and this group conceives of itself as the main vehicle of religious and moral ecellence. He also stresses the fact that the innovational problems are more organizational than technical.

Anthropologist Charles Erasmus believes in the dominance of economic factors in development and possibilities of adopting cultures to the needs of economic growth. He lays great stress on the significance of demonstration effects in inducing technological change. He also points out that people's non-acceptance of change in methods of production may appear to be cultural at first; but a deeper analysis would often reveal that such a behaviour also reflects economic calculations. Citing the example of failure of irrigation systems introduced in Mexico, Erasmus remarks that the refusal of the local population to use apparently superior techniques was mainly due to relevant technical factors ignored by the western experts.

It goes without saying that in determining society's ability to effect or except economic change, political environment plays a very important role. Economic development will not take place in areas where political power elite is resolutely opposed to it. Moreover, now-a-days state is no longer viewed as an exogenous agent influencing the course of development but an endogenous element of the socio-economic framework.

Neo-classical political economy, which is a significant development in economic literature of the present time can throw light on the interaction between public policies and private lobbies and interest groups thus explaining why some economies grow faster than others.[3]

In this theory the state is seen to be pushed and pulled by lobbies and interest groups that are mostly interested in redistribution rather than growth and development. In this situation state intervention intended to improve the efficiency of resource allocation and channel it in socially desired directions may end up diverting resources to a significant extent from production to "rent seeking".

The North-Eastern Scenario

In order to examine the relative importance of non-economic factors in inhibiting the growth of enterprises in the North-Eastern Region we may begin from the socio-cultural dualism.

The dominance of the tribals and other backward social groups in the demography of the North-Eastern Region is a known factor. The technological gap between the tribal economy with its characteristic dependence on shifting cultivation and the modern industrial sector is too large to be bridged easily. When commercialisation of agriculture in modern lines is still a far cry and marketable surplus is low, it is extremely difficult to spread the entrepreneurial culture among the indigenous population. Therefore, the indigenous groups have not been able to participate in the process of entrepreneurship development. Traditionally, the tribal crafts have been part of the rural semi-selfsufficient socio-economic framework.

Of course, it would be grossly incorrect to describe the tribal community as a community outside the exchange nexus. They have been found to be exchanging their agricultural products with the traders from the outside for non-agricultural products without, of course, developing a tertiary sector in their own society. The first step in entrepreneurial development in the tribal society would be involvement in marketing and distribution of products—both wholesale and retail. The participation in this sector may emerge mainly from the literate tribals in urban, semi-urban and rural areas. Gradually, they may be expected to enter into other areas like transport operations, repair and servicing industries, ancillary industries etc. Of course, tribal youths with higher levels of education have still large scope of joining government and semi-government jobs, independent professions etc. and therefore, may not be attracted towards setting up enterprises to any significant extent.

But it must be noted that the tribal society in spite of backwardness, does not suffer from any insurmountable cultural obstacles to entrepreneurship development like the "Eastern" society mentioned in Boeke's theory of dualism. In fact, in many respects a substantial segment of the tribal society in the North-Eastern Region in urban and semi-urban areas is more "western" than their non-tribal counterparts owing to their contact with the missionaries and progress in education. It may be mentioned here that Mizoram, a predominantly tribal state has as high a literacy rate as 82.27 per cent according to 1991 Census. Nagaland, another predominantly tribal State has the literacy rate of 61.65 per cent. It is true that high literacy rate or even progress in general education is no indicator of growth of technical skill and enterprise, but it atleast indicates that the tribal society in the North-Eastern Region is not averse to change and that the cultural factor is not a stumbling block on economic development in general and entrepreneurial growth in particular.

The local non-tribals and the immigrants from the erstwhile

province of Bengal (the major part of which now constitutes Bangladesh) have their main participation in the primary sector; but they have been able to occupy a place in the tertiary-sector enterprises in the form of petty trade, transport operations and miscellaneous other activities. They are also coming up gradually in the small-scale sector of industries to a limited-extent. Their inability to participate in the process of industrialisation to a greater extent is mainly due to lack of entitlement to capital, technology and higher level of organisational skill. Given proper scope they will perhaps be able to develop enterprises in the ancillary industries. In recent time, infrastructural development has enabled them to participate in larger number in private services sector. The growing number of road-transport operators, transport-linked servicing shops, hotels, public call offices, XEROXING shops, beauty parlours etc. go to show that the educated youths of the North-Eastern Region are not averse to entrepreneurial activities of related infrastructure and capital are forthcoming. Their inability to develop enterprises emanates mainly from economic factors rather than cultural ones.

As mentioned by A. Sharma and A. Sahoo, the factors which facilitate or inhibit industrial development can be classified into two sets: One relates to supply side while the other to demand side.[4] While the supply-side factors like lack of infrastructural support, absence of right type of institutions, deficiency of human capital in the form of entrepreneurship and skilled labour, non-availability of credit etc. have attracted attention of the researchers, demand-side factors have not been adequately explained.

Actually a vicious circle formed by interplay of demand-side and supply-side factors have kept the North-Eastern Economy backward. On the one hand, supply-side factors have kept the productive capacity of the region at a low level and on the other, urbanisation, cultural changes and demonstration effects have made the demand for products more and more externally oriented to such an extent as to result in substantial income leakage.[5] The growth of the tertiary sector led by extensive development of public administration and other public sector operations have created a new middle class giving rise to a perceptible change in the level and composition of consumption baskets of a significant segment of population of the region.

The inroad of modern products into the region's consumption basket is a factor which is responsible for decay and dwarfed growth of cottage and small industries in this part of the country. While this phenomenon may be termed cultural in part, it is more economic in nature as it emanates mainly from integration of product market in India and a uniform pattern of administrative expansion in the country as a whole.

An important part of the population of the North-East consists of different groups of people coming from the rest of India in connection with various public-sector and private-sector activities. While the major protion of this segment are unskilled and semi-skilled labourers, professionals, government and non-government employees etc., a tiny portion has been associated with entrepreneurial functions in trade and industries.

This tiny group has the qualities of entrepreneurship described by Mc.Clelland and fulfil the conditions envisaged by Hagen in respect of leadership in industrialisation. They have contributed to industrialisation of Assam immensely.

But the very composition of industries has a limiting effect on the efforts of the entrepreneurs. For example, in Assam, the main industries are Tea, Petroleum and Gas, Coal, Fertilizer, Commercial Plywood, Matches, Sugar, Jute, Textile, Cement, Paper, Wheat flour etc. Of these the prominent ones i.e. Tea, Coal and Petroleum are resource-based industries. "The backward linkages of these industries are rather limited, while their forward linkages are with the industries located in big metropolises elsewhere. The result has been the emergence of enclave type economy, i.e. a few modern industries in the midst of traditional industries having very little or no interactions between the two."[6] Although Commercial Plywood, Matches and other wood-based industries have both high backward and forward linkages, their negative impact on the environment make their prospect limited in terms of sustainable development principle.

Therefore, we find that the North-Eastern scenario is more in conformity with the views of the scholars like Erasmus who explain apparently sociological phenomena in terms of techno-economic factors.

Among the non-economic factors the political environment can explain a good deal of industrial backwardness of the North-Eastern Region. The North-Eastern states have not been able to chalk out a clear policy on industrialisation. This can be explained in terms of tenets of modern neoclassical political economy. The ambiguity in industrial policy results from tug of war between the protagonists of local interests (e.g. advocates of preservation of tribal identity, fighters for regional autonomy, supporters of the son-of-the-soil priority etc.) on the one hand and those of fast industrialisation on the other, in between come the environmentalists who prefer a low pace of development in order to maintain ecological balance.

As a result of the pulls and pressures of these mutually opposed groups, the states in the North-Eastern Region have chosen an easy option viz. that of pressuring the Centre for greater resource transfer and spending them on relatively less productive welfare projects and administrative expansion. The consequence has been not only disproportionate growth of the tertiary sector to the neglect of commodity-producing activities but also a biased attitude in the mind of the youths of the region in favour of government jobs and against independent initiative.

It may be argued that this bias is inherent in the culture of the North Eastern people, but it must be remembered that necessity is the mother of invention and as Geertz points out, a wide range of cultures is capable of generating entrepreneurship and economic growth. Only appropriate environment has to be created by the power that be instead of succumbing to the lure of cheap popularity.

Conclusion

There are two real dilemmas faced in the North-Eastern region so far as the policy option is concerned. One is the conflict between industrialisation and ecological balance. The fragile ecology of the North-Eastern Region does not permit rapid industrialisation in the large-scale sector in the hilly areas as this is likely to lead to destruction of valuable flora and fauna, cause soil erosion and water pollution and affect the environmental balance. Secondly, when human resource development including entrepreneurial ability at the local level has not reached the required stage so as to make possible increasing participation of the indigenous people in the process of industrialisation, rapid growth of large and medium-scale industries may mean that geographical areas are being developed without uplift of the indigenous poor or even at the cost of the poor.

The conflict between rapid development of a geographical area and that of its backward people is the economic factor behind the insurgency problem in the North-Eastern Region, although it may not be the sole reason. It is also a fact that the insurgency problem and general weakness on the law and order front have been one prime cause of inadequate implementation of the development programmes in the North Eastern Region. This illustrates another vicious circle of poverty in social interaction.

The policy-makers have tried to solve the problem of insurgency by security arrangements on the one hand and by pursuing unproductive welfare economic policy on the other. The real solution, however, lies in resolving the conflict between development and environment on the one hand and between area development and uplift of the poor on the other. The problem of poverty has to be tackled by making the poor more productive and by protecting the environment.

For this, one has to give up the conventional idea of industrialisation. Even the attempt to rejuvenate traditional industries may meet with limited success owing to lack of support from the demand side which has changed drastically over the last few decades.

Industrial development in the North Eastern Region to be broad-based, has to be linked with modernisation of agriculture, animal husbandry and poultry, plantation on new lines (like rubber production) and forestry. This means that industrialisation will be concomitant of modernisation of the primary sector. It may be recalled here that the North Eastern Region has become dependent on the rest of India not only in respect of manufactured goods but also in respect of primary goods like rice, fish, and pulses. Unless productive ventures can be made in the modernised primary sector and the related processing and input-supplying activities, no big push initiative in growth of industrial enterprises may be successful or even desirable considering its "side effects." A gigantic effort for rural development alone can solve the dilemmas of development in the North-East and make development coterminous with increase in social welfare and social harmony.

What remains of the socio-cultural approach is the supreme importance of human resource development. There must be meaningful arrangement for training the youth for entrepreneurship in the emerging fields of industrial, commercial and services sector. The technology gap that exists in the region has to be bridged through spread of technical education relating to existing and prospective industries in North-East India. The unemployed youths running after the mirage of government jobs should be diverted to the area of self employment. If the area of self employment can be broadened successfully, there would be a great breakthrough in entrepreneurial development in the North Eastern Region.

REFERENCES

1. Higgins, B. (1968). *Economic Development*, Universal Book Stall, New Delhi, p. 224.
2. *Ibid.*, pp. 224-66.
3. Srinivasan, T.N. (1985), "Neoclassical Political Economy, the State and Economic Development", *Asian Development Review*, Vol. 3, No. 2, reprinted in Meir, M. (1990), *Leading Issues in Economic Development*, Oxford University Press, New Delhi, pp. 531-35.
4. Sharma, A. and A. Sahoo, (1992), "Zonal Planning in Industrialisation" in Adiseshiah, M.S. (ed.), *Planning Perspectives for the North Eastern and Eastern Zone*, Lancer Publishers Pvt. Ltd. & India International Centre, New Delhi pp. 108-38.
5. Bhattacharya, P.R. (1985), "Economic Base Analysis, Income Leakage and Regional Growth" in Ganchoudhury, J. (ed.), *An Anthology of Tripura*, Inter-India Publications, New Delhi, pp. 57-64.
6. Sharma, A. and A. Sahoo, (1992), *op. cit.*, pp. 118-19.

9

INDUSTRIALISATION OF NORTH-EAST INDIA—A NEW PERSPECTIVE

— Arunoday Saha

The process of opening up of the North-East India had its beginning early in the year of 1793 when a commercial treaty was executed between Raja Gaurinath (1780-94) of Assam and Captain Welse. In fact, Assam was truly opened and poised for development through trade and commerce when it came under the occupation of British in 1826. Tea plantation by the European planters in the mid of the nineteenth century gave filling to the process further. The boom in the tea market in 1860 in Europe encouraged the planters to plough back the profits and diversify the activities in the tea industries and the allied sectors. Oil was struck in Digboi first in India when the exploration of petrolieum started in the basin of the Brahmaputra. The tea plantation and the petrolieum exploration in the nineteenth century were the two earliest industrial ventures in India.

Assam, though an early starter in the industrial race in India is now way behind of many other states and it is yet to reach the take-off stage even after one-and-half century. Assam which is the leader and the trend-setter among the other states of the North-East India is endowed with the natural resources in abundance. It remains to be a big question to be addressed as to why the North-East India with so much abundant resources and even with early start could no yet be able to break the vicious circle of industrial backwardness. The reasons often attributed for the industrial backwardness of the region are mainly the lack of infrastructure, shortage of manpower and local entrepreneurship, weak market linkages and the dearth of institutional finances etc.

An indepth scrutiny, however, does not fully corroborate the finding for the non-industrialisation of the region. For example, the power/electricity is the key to starting any industrial venture. The North-East Region is abundant in hydel power which can be harnessed for changing the industrial scene not only of the region but of the rest of the country.

TABLE 9.1 : Hydel Power: Installed Capacity and Potential of NE India (1994)

(in MW)

State	Installed Capacity	Potential
Arunachal	21	26755
Assam	2	351
Manipur	3	1176
Meghalaya	187	1070
Mizoram	3	1455
Nagaland	3	1039
Tripura	16	10
Total	234	31856

Source : Basic Statistics relating to States, CMIE 1994. (Courtesy: The Tata Consultancy Services, 1996).

It is evident from Table 9.1 that only .03 per cent of the total potential hydel power is being utilized in the region. If the potential hydel power is harnessed fully, then the region can supply the surplus power to the other states and can serve as the "power-house" for the rest of the country. It is true that for harnessing the power potential, a huge amount of capital is required. But in today's context of globalization, there is no dearth of capital in the global market. Capital will come if the opportunity cost criteria certify that the project is economically viable.

The another factor responsible for the backwardness is the shortage of manpower and local entrepreneurship. This argument is not acceptable. The prerequisite of local entrepreneurship may be a necessary condition but it is not the sufficient condition. The U.S.A. is the most advanced country in the world, industrialisation there has taken place but it was certainly not by the indigenous people. In India also, industrial development of Bombay-centric region was not made by the local entrepreneurs of Bombay. So also is the case of industrial development of Calcutta and the adjacent areas. Industrious people from the other parts of India migrated to Calcutta and helped industrialise the area. While explaining the unabated flow and the trend of migration to the valley of Assam, Prof. H.K. Barpujari remarked: "Of the immigrants, the Marwaris constituting a minor segment of the population—sex ratio 360 females for 1000 males—are virtual controller of Assam's economy."[2]

In fact, industrialisation of any area does not depend exclusively on the local entrepreneurship or even on local resources. On what it actually depends is the comparative advantage of the region in one of the any indispensable factors of production. Japan's case is in point. Japan has comparative advantage in the field of entrepreneurship while she lacks in resources which are imported from the other countries. The shortage of her own resources never stand on the way of her supremacy in the industrial world today.

There is a common belief that the North-East India is the most backward area in terms of infrastructural facilities such as transport and communication. But facts tell otherwise. The region has 12.98 per cent of the National Highways of India whereas it covers only 7.76 per cent of the geographic territory of the country. Assam occupies the fourth highest position in the distribution of railway per 1000 sq. km. The Ministry of Finance, Government of India appointed a Group headed by Dr. (Mrs) I.K. Barthakur to examine the problems of industrialisation of the North-East Region in 1994 which made the following revealing observation—"The group felt that the basic infrastructure in the North-East Region was not as bad as generally believed. On the contrary the region was far above the most of other states of the country in terms of per unit population and per unit of geographical area served by the national highways, railways, communication and power. However, most of the facilities were under utilized."[3]

In a separate study, the Tata Consultancy Services also came out with the same type of conclusions. The TCS study has confirmed that Assam is "the best destination for investment." The TCS constructed the indices of Investment Attractiveness in the North-East Region for each of the Seven States. The following seven parametres were considered and an average 100-point was assigned to each of the parametres. The index turned out to be of 700 points when all indicators were added together.

Table 9.2 shows that Assam scores 526 out of 700 and has the edge over the other states in all categories except in the area macroeconomic indicator. Assam is hence considered to be the best destination of investment.

TABLE 9.2: Index for Investment Attractiveness for N.E. States

Parametre	Assam	Aruna-chal	Megha-laya	Mani-pur	Naga-land	Mizo-ram	Tri-pura
Resource	105	41	80	45	65	26	65
Infrastructure	68	60	60	83	60	68	30
Present Industrial-scenario	126	66	102	72	96	22	78
Human Resources	57	13	40	43	50	40	47
Financial Sector	80	35	75	51	87	45	60
Law and Order	60	105	90	30	15	90	45
Macroeconomic Indicator	30	37	40	43	57	43	30
Total	526	357	487	367	430	334	355

Source: TCS estimates, 1996

In view of the foregoing analysis, it is puzzling to note that Assam with its all favourable conditions and comparative advantages could not yet take off as a formidable industrial economy. One of the plausible reasons for the region for being not able to register itself as the industrially advanced economy is that the partition of India in 1947 virtually cut-off the whole North-East India from the rest of the country. The partition made the region completely isolated from the mainstream economy of India. Presently the North-East India is having its 90 per cent of borders with the international countries of Bangladesh, Myanmar, Tibet and China etc. and is annexed with the mainland of India through a "Chicken's Neck" only by 2 per cent of its borders. The possibility of the NE India to emerge as the industrially advanced economy continues to be ever elusive since the Independence of India. The vast market of Bangladesh which was earlier open was made closed after the partition. The time when India was planning for embarking on the massive industrial programme, the N.E. India suffered a set back due to its forced isolation thrust upon it.

Industrialisation presupposes that the economy must be an open economy, it must produce surplus and it must engage itself vigorously in export and imports. Unfortunately the North-East Region turns out to be a closed economy producing almost nil or no surplus and hence there is no export-import activities.

The North-East Region being the closed economy bounded by mostly foreign countries with no formal trade and commerce with them stands completely isolated. This complete isolation appears to be standing on the way of industrialisation of the region. If industrialisation is to take palce in this part of India, then the North-East Region must be integrated with the neighbouring countries breaking the isolation of economic barriers. Lessons from History confirm that Bombay and the region around of Bombay has become industrially developed only because the western coast had been integrated with the industrially advanced economies of the European countries. The Western part of India is ahead of other states of India since it has access to the higher technologies and the higher level of development of the European countries. By taking the advantage of the technology transfers from the old industrial giants like U.K., Germany and France, the Western part of India has been able to industrialise itself faster than any other region of India.

Now the situation has changed. The South-East Asia has meanwhile emerged as one of the industrially advanced subcontinent of the world. And the North-East India happens to be nearer to the region where the Asian Tigers have emerged as the formidable industrial force to recon with. The following table presents the GDP of the European Union and East, North-East and South-East Asia countries.

Table 9.3 shows that the GDP of the East and North-East Asia is alone higher than the GDP of the EU comprising of fifteen countries of Europe. The East, North-East Asia and South-East Asia together offer a vast in the subcontinent with total GDP of 99, 28, 278 million dollars. If this potential huge market is made open to the North-East India, the North-East India can take advantage of the higher technology suitable for its own development.

TABLE 9.3: GDP of EU and East, North-East and South-East Asia

(in million dollars)

Countries	
European Union	5575800
East. North-East Asia	8208122
South-East Asia	1720156

Source : Asian Development Bank, World Bank 1994, European Union & India 1995.

It thus becomes absolutely imperative for the North-East India to get itself integrated economically with the neighbouring countries for its development. When the doors will be open, the North-East India will be in better position to avail of the opportunities of export driven growth for its economy so long neglected and ignored.

It is now time for India to turn to the East through North-East India and catch up with the faster rate of development alongwith the Asian Tigers. Once given the opportunities to the North-East India by opening up its economy to the neighbouring economies of the South-East and North-East Asia, the North-East India will be able to make it by industrialisation. Asia's North-East is Japan, Taiwan and South Korea. They are the most advanced countries of Asia today. So there is every reason to believe that North-East of India like North-East of Asia can also become advanced provided the region is no more kept closed but made open and integrated with the rest of the world through the nearest South-East Asian frontier.

REFERENCES

1. Barpujari, H.K.: Presidential Address, Indian History Congress, Fifty-sixth Session, 28-30 Dec. 95, Calcutta, p. 17.
2. Barpujari H.K.: Presidential Address, Indian History Session, 25-30 Dec. 95, Calcutta.
3. NERC. IDBI Guwahati: Proceeding of the meeting dated Dec. 18, 1995.

10

CULTURAL ISSUES RELATING TO ENTREPRENEURIAL DEVELOPMENT IN THE NORTH -EASTERN REGION

-- Keya Sengupta

Introduction

The backwardness of the North-Eastern region is a fact which is beyond all debate. Almost all the indicators of development suggest the economic backwardness of the region, the vast potentiality for development notwithstanding. Developmental policies and programmes that have been the thrust of the efforts at achieving economic growth have met with very little success. In fact very little effort have been made to investigate into the causes behind the limited success of the various schemes that have been enunciated for the development of the region over the years. All debate and discussions relating to the development of the region have met with the usual lamentation that the region is a backward region and therefore needs to expedite its economic development. Consideration needs to be taken of the fact that wide diversity marks the various constituent units of the region which in its turn is vastly different from the rest of the country. Therefore any policy measure that meets with success in other parts of the country need not meet with the equal amount of success in this region.

The importance and role of agriculture for the development of this region need not be over emphasised. Significant proportion of the population is engaged in the agricultural sector both directly and indirectly, though the region is still way behind in terms of reaping the benefits of Green Revolution with the result that the productivity of the land is still alarmingly low, with wide disparity within the region itself.

For the region to attain any kind of economic development of a permanent nature, along with agriculture emphasis need to be laid upon industrial development. This is essential not only to tap the vast unutilised resources of the region, but also to improve the indicators of development for the region, as a whole. There is now no alternative, but to focuss attention to industrial development of the region, not only for its balanced development, but also for the development of the agricultural sector itself, because it is only an economy with strong industrial base that can provide a strong support to the agricultural sector. Industries have both a forward and backward linkage with the agricultural sector. Harnessing of the products of the agricultural sector by the industries which use them as raw materials will not only facilitate rumunerative prices to the producers, but will also encourage agricultural development on commercial lines. Income generated in the industrial sector will in turn raise the demand for the products of the agricultural sector. Similar dependence of the agricultural sector on the industrial sector for meeting the basic consumption needs of every day life and the need of the agricultural sector itself, such as the production of fertilizers, pesticides, agricultural tools and implements can be met only by the industrial sector. Therefore neither a total dependence on either the agricultural or the industrial sector can bring about desirable growth for the economy of the region. A proper synchronisation of the two sectors is what is called for, for any developmental effort to take shape.

The grim reality of the economy of the North-Eastern region is that even fifty years of planning has failed to record the emergence of the region in the industrial map of the country, the numerous policies, programmes and vast potentialities in terms of natural resources notwithstanding. The region is richly endowed with mineral resources such as petroleum, natural gas, sillimanite, chromite limestones and coal which are still mostly unutilised. The region is one of the richest in the country in terms of forest and water resources. High rate of literacy and strong and hardworking people of the region provide the manpower resources, which form the basic requirement for any kind of developmental effort.

Steps Undertaken to Uplift the Industrial Base of the Region

The prolonged backwardness of the region, has necessitated the setting up of the North-Eastern Council in 1971, with the main intention of focussing special attention to the developmental needs of the region keeping in view its developmental priorities. The main thrust of the Council are planning, funding and the balanced development of the region. Formulation of plans, in addition to the ones formulated by the respective state governments has been undertaken for the speedy development of the region, with particular emphasis to the backward and remote areas of the region.

Realising the importance of industrialisation for expediting the course of economic events of the region, the Central Government has announced a five years tax concession in the New Economic Policy for the purpose of setting up new industries in the region. In addition to that the Central Government has also constituted the North-Eastern Development Finance Corporation Ltd., with the main purpose of providing credit and.other facilities for the promotion, expansion and modernisation of industrial enterprises as well as infrastructural projects, in an attempt at heralding a new era of progress for the region.

Keeping in view the low level of local entrepreneurship the NEDFi, attempts to familiarise the local entrepreneurs with the complex banking procedures. The Corporation with this in view, proposes to provide assistance in the form of term loans, direct subscription/underwriting of equity and/or debt instruments provide financial guarantees. It further proposes to encourage and promote private capital both internal and external.

To bring industrial development to the centre stage of all developmental process the NEDFi, intends to build up a data bank for helping industries in identifying new technologies and market trends in the economy and other relevant informations. It will also compile profiles of projects with sound research for the benefit of entrepreneurs. For encouraging the growth of small units the Corporation will also consider providing the entire working capital requirement of the project till the year it is expected to reach the optimum level of operation.

Recognising the lack of entrepreneurship in the region, the Industrial Development Bank of India has conducted several entrepreneurial programmes, skill and technology upgradation programmes and industrial awareness camps. Till September 30th 1995 it supported 300 Entrepreneurial Development Programmes benefiting 7600 persons. The IDBI in collaboration with the NEC had originally conceived the Indian Institute of Entrepreneurs in Guwahati. It has also undertaken setting up of Training-cum-Developmental Centres (TDC) in all states of the region.

Formation of two Technical Consultancy Ltd. and the North-Eastern Industrial and Technical Consultancy Organisation Ltd. were the other means of promoting industrialisation of this region. These agencies were constituted mainly with the purpose of providing low cost consultancy services to medium and small scale industries and other services relating to industrial development.

In addition to the favourable investment environment in terms of natural, manpower and financial resources coupled with the effort made by the different financial agencies and developmental councils, the North-Eastern Region provides a very favourable market enabling the industrial products to be absorbed within the region itself. Increase in the income of a certain section of the people of this region in recent years can provide a tremendous market without which no plan of industrialisation can be sustained. Consequently, marketability of industrial products too does not seem to pose any serious problem for industrialisation of this region.

Entrepreneurial Scenario in the Pre and Post-Liberalisation Period

It would therefore be pertinent at this stage to make an analysis of the progress of industrialisation in this region against the backdrop of industrial climate drawn above. The chapter attempts to make an investigation into the total investment made by the private entrepreneurs in the region as well as the number of entrepreneurs responding to the various incentives both in the pre and the post- liberalisation period of the Indian economy.

Table 10.1 and 10.2 reveal the entrepreneurial scenario of the North-Eastern region. Table 10.1 shows that the percentage of the Letters of Intent and Industrial Licensing granted in the region is alarmingly low by the all-India standard. Examination of the pre-liberalisation period reveals that wide dichotomous traits characterise the entrepreneurial scenario of the North-Eastern states. Though the position of Assam is slightly better than the rest of the states of the region, yet by the Indian average Assam occupies one of the lower most position, the percentage of new entrepreneurs forth coming barely rising above one per cent. The other hill states of the region is marked by almost a total absence of entrepreneurs. The overall conclusion which one can draw from this table is that the region is far behind in terms of entrepreneurship, which could therefore be identified as a possible reason for the industrial backwardness of the region.

TABLE 10.1: Letters of Intent and Industrial Licences Issued in the North-Eastern Region

	Pre-Liberalisation Period						Percentage of all India Fig			
	1981		1982		1983		1984		1985	
States	LOI	IL	LOI	IL	LOI	IL	LOI	IL	LOI	IL
Arunachal Pradesh	.11	-	.096	-	.66	.186	.187	.331	.068	.609
Assam	.764	.84	.479	.231	.285	2.04	1.37	.88	.823	1.22
Manipur	-	.21	-	-	.094	-	-	-	.069	-
Meghalaya	1.2	-	-	-	-	-	-	-	.069	-
Mizoram	-	-	.383	-	.379	-	.752	-	-	-
Nagaland	.655	-	.096	-	.284	.186	.094	.220	-	-
Tripura	-	-	-	-	.094	-	-.	.110	.068	-

	1986		1987		1988		1989		1990	
States	LOI	IL	LOI	IL	LOI	IL	LOI	IL	LOI	IL
Arunachal Pradesh	.088	.162	.101	.211	.092	-	.0846	.239	-	-
Assam	1.76	.809	1.21	.635	1.11	-	.423	.717	.484	.516
Manipur	.088	-	-	-	.277	.277	.423	-	-	.258
Meghalaya	.088	.323	.101	-	.092	-	.169	.239	-	-
Mizoram	-	-	.101	-	.092	-	-	-	-	-
Nagaland	.354	-	.101	.211	-	-	-	-	.242	-
Tripura	-	-	-	-	.092	.277	-	-	-	-

Source: Computed from the Handbook of Industrial Policy and Statistics 1995.

Since the success of the New Economic Policy is expected to evolve around industrialisation and special policies and programmes for the North-Eastern region was undertaken by the government, with the hope of shaping the course of events in the region through industrialisation, it is relevant at this stage to review the entrepreneurial response in the post-liberalisation phase in the region. It is surprising to observe that not even a single entrepreneur has responded in any of the states, Assam being a marginal expeption, with just about 2 or 3 entrepreneurs coming up during the entire post-liberalisation period.

The region being a backward one, it is relevant to examine the number of entrepreneurs particularly in the backward areas of the region, who have responded to the new policies. Table 10.3 reveals that the entrepreneurial scenario in the pre and post-liberalisation era in the

TABLE 10.2: Letters of Intent and Industrial Licences Issued in the North-Eastern Region

	Pre-Liberalisation Period				Percentage of all India Fig			
	1991		1992		1993		1994	
States	LOI	IL	LOI	IL	LOI	IL	LOI	IL
Arunachal Pradesh	-	.39	.16	-	-	-	.37	-
Assam	.50	-	.65	1.42	.57	-	.37	-
Manipur	-	-	-	-	-	-	-	-
Meghalaya	-	-	-	-	-	-	-	-
Mizoram	-	-	-	-	-	-	-	-
Nagaland	-	.39	.16	-	-	-	-	-
Tripura	-	-	-	-	-	-	-	-

backward areas of the region are almost synonymous with the total number of entrepreneurs coming up in the various years.

An examination of the number of entrepreneurs forthcoming in the region, also prompts us to investigate into the percentage of investment made in the industrial sector as a proportion to the all-India investment made in the industrial sector. Low level of entrepreneurs results in disturbingly low level and almost insignificant percentage of industrial investment both in the pre and post-liberalisation period, in all the states of the region.

The grim reality of the industrial scenario of the region is that the New Economic Policy has not only failed to have any impact in the

TABLE 10.3: Letters of Intent and Industrial Licences Issued only to the Backward Areas of the North-Eastern Region

	Pre-Liberalisation Period				Percentage of all India Fig			
	1987		1988		1989		1990	
States	LOI	IL	LOI	IL	LOI	IL	LOI	IL
Arunachal Pradesh	.19	.52	.18	-	.18	.57	-	-
Assam	2.23	1.56	2.17	-	.90	1.71	1.05	-
Manipur	-	-	.55	.65	.180	-	-	.59
Meghalaya	.186	-	-	-	.36	.57	-	-
Mizoram	.186	-	.181	-	-	-	-	-
Nagaland	.186	.52	-	-	-	-	.524	-
Tripura	-	-	.181	.65	-	-	-	-

TABLE 10.4 (i): Letters of Intent and Industrial Licensing Issued only to the Backward Areas of the North-Eastern Region.

	Pre-Liberalisation Period				Percentage of all India Fig			
	1991		1992		1993		1994	
States	LOI	IL	LOI	IL	LOI	IL	LOI	IL
Arunachal Pradesh	-	1.03	.311	-	-	-	.81	-
Assam	.887	-	1.24	4.25	1.25	-	.81	-
Manipur	-	-	-	-	-	-	-	-
Meghalaya	-	-	.	-	-	-	-	-
Mizoram	-	-	-	-	-	-	-	-
Nagaland	-	1.03	.311	-	-	-	-	-
Tripura	-	-	-	-	-	-	-	-

Source : Same as in Table 10.1

TABLE 10.4 (ii): Industrial Investment in the Post-Liberalisation Period in the North Eastern Region

(Percentage of all India Fig)

State	1.8.91 to 31.12.91		1.1.92 to 31.12.92		1.1.93 to 31.12.93	
	Total	Backward areas	Total	Backward areas	Total	Backward areas
Assam	.166	.377	.049	.122	.303	.0369
Meghalaya	.0065	.0148	.0034	.0085	-	-
Nagaland	.0013	.0029	-	-	-	-
Tripura	.473	1.069	.584	1.45	-	-

Source : Same as in Table 10.1.

North-Eastern region, with the slight exception of Assam and Tripura, but the growth rate has actually slackened down causing grave concern to policy makers and planners. The vast potentiality for industrial development in terms of natural, manpower, financial resources and the special lucrative policies and schemes for industrialisation of the region notwithstanding, the North-Eastern Region has totally failed to respond favourably to industrialise herself.

Role of Entrepreneurs for Industrialisation of the Region

A serious and thought provoking matter is that insufficient entrepreneurs seems to be one of the most crucial factor responsible for the slow pace of industrialisation, since the region is potentially rich in terms of all other factors needed for industrialisation. Industrialisation and entrepreneurship are inseparable factors, and the crucial role of the entrepreneur needs to be highlighted in any study relating to industrial and economic development. The entire process of industrialisation evolves around the role of human factor in organising material and financial resources in the most profitable manner under the shield of various governmental policies and schemes. The crux of the problem which every policy maker should therefore take into consideration is to match facts with theoretical proposition. Resources by themselves, may make a nation potentially very rich, but for this richness to manifest itself into reality there has to be an agency or an organisation in the form of entrepreneurs who can through their initiative and motivation organise these resources for the successful implementation of industrial development. In the absence of any such initiative all resources may lie untapped and unorganised and may serve no useful purpose for industrialising a nation.

It is now increasingly maintained that entrepreneurs play a pivotal role in any process of industrialisation and the availability of entrepreneurs is one of the most important factor determining the growth and development of a region. Keeping this in view various measures particularly in the post-liberalisation period has been undertaken by the government, so as to appeal to the emerging entrepreneurs of the region to take up industrial projects on their own, unfortunately with very little success. Quantity and quality of entrepreneurs available in a region which is a pre-requisite for industrialising a region still remains a far cry.

Evidence suggests that one of the most important factors contributing to the slackened pace of industrialisation of the region is the failure of entrepreneurial development. Time is mature enough to examine the possible reasons for the lack of local entrepreneurship. Various training programmes have been organised for the development of the local entrepreneurs, the region is rich in almost all types of resources, in addition to the rich potential market which can cushion off the bulk of the industrial products, yet what could be preventing the growth of local entrepreneurs? The reasons for this is to be sought elsewhere, and appropriate measures has to be taken to alleviate the same.

Entrepreneurial Scenario of the North-Eastern Region

The North-Eastern region is a special region which does not have any history of local entrepreneurship. Realisation has now dawned upon many that economic factors alone canot help the emergence of local entrepreneurs, social factors need to be equally stressed upon. The North-Eastern region lacks entrepreneurial culture. Experience of entrepreneurial development of various underdeveloped regions reveal that entrepreneurial development is the outcome of not only physical and financial incentives, but more important, especially for those regions without any tradition of entrepreneurs, are the various aspects associated with the personality of the entrepreneur himself. The prospective entrepreneurs of a region should be dominated by a need for achievement and be driven by a high degree of motivation, in the absence of which even the highest degree of the opportunities may remain unexploited. Consequently, the same amount of facilities and opportunities may result in different types and degrees of entrepreneurial response in different regions. The personality traits of the entrepreneur, characterised by a sense of motivation and achievement is the result of social environment which have certain norms and values. Norms and values in turn are determined by the tradition of the society and its culture as well as the economic environment of the region concerned. The North-Eastern region especially the hill states do not possess any entrepreneurial tradition. The young potential entrepreneurs have never seen their elders take up any major entrepreneurial activity, as a result of which they themselves are a little apprehensive and perhaps unsure of themselves to undertake any major entrepreneurial risk, despite the existence of numerous facilities that are currently prevalent in the region.

An attempt to surperimpose an industrial culture on a non-industrial society may not establish any permanent and successful root unless and until the society itself gears for an industrial culture by changing its outlook towards life, its values and also its awareness to meet the challenges of a new industrial culture. Delineating the broad contours of growth of entrepreneurial culture is therefore an additional and in fact one of the most important determinant of entrepreneurial development in the North-Eastern region.

What needs to be highlighted at this stage is the meaning of entrepreneurial culture, because culture is the result of a number of complicated factors that determine human activity. "Culture is the language in which past events are interpreted, future circumstances are anticipated and plans of actions are formulated'' (Lovoie). The society of the North-Eastern region being marked by the absence of any past entrepreneurial experience their interpretation for any course of future events by formulating plans of actions becomes a very difficult proposition. Importance of culture consists in transmitting from one generation to another values and knowledge through imitation teaching and upbringing both by the family and the environment of the society.

Fortunately for policy makers, entrepreneurial culture is not frozen at a point of time and can evolve over a period of time however lengthy the time may be. This possibility is strengthened by the fact that, just as entrepreneurial development is the outcome of the tradition of entrepreneurial culture, the entrepreneurial culture itself can be shaped by many economic and social factors associated with entrepreneurial development.

Necessity arises in the North-Eastern region to strike the right balance between family rooted and society based values and cultures on one hand and the new challenges of entrepreneurship and industrialisation on the other. It is only when an individual is able to strike the right balance between the two, that enables him to make a rationale choice. Incentives and facilities in the absence of entrepreneurial culture will always remain underutilised, just as motivation without the support of material and non-material benifits will make the development of entrepreneurship extremely difficult. Dichotomous behaviourial traits nurtured by the different ethnic groups of the North-Eastern region make policy implementation for entrepreneurial development extremely difficult, since this warrants varied response from the different ethnic groups to the existence of similar potentiality of growth and uniform incentives. Lack of entrepreneurial culture in the hill states of the region necessitates the setting up of motivation camps to inculcate a sense of achievement and awareness to the growing competitiveness in the world around them. Though an extremely difficult proposition, yet there seems to be no other alternative to entrepreneurial development at present for the region, which in turn is the only means for the rapid industrialisation and economic growth for the North-Eastern region.

The above analysis therefore focusses attention to the fact that the mere presence of natural, financial and manpower resources along with various incentives are not enough to bring about industrialisation of a region. Absence of human factor in the form of entrepreneurship may fail to gear the economy into the desired path of industrial growth.

The crux of the problem for the North-Eastern region is the insignificant entrepreneurial development. What the policy-makers and planners need to pay attention is to investigate into the measures to mitigate this problem, in case any serious attempt is made to uplift the economic condition of the region.

REFERENCES

1. Berger, B (1991): *The Culture of Entrepreneurship*, Ed. Pub. McGraw-Hill, New Delhi.
2. Deshpande, M.U.: *Entrepreneurship of Small Scale Industries*, Pub. Deep and Deep, New Delhi.
3. McClelland, D.C. (1965): *The Achieving Society*, D Van Nostrand Company Inc. New York, 1961.
4. Nandy, Ashis (1973): "Entrepreneurial Culture and Entrepreneurial Men" in *Economic and Political Weekly*, Vol No. VIII, No. 47.
5. Sengupta, K (1992): "Role of Industrialisation for improving the Economic and Social Health of Meghalaya "Seminar paper on 'Social and Economic Health of Meghalaya' organised by NEICSSR in March 1993, Shillong.

11

INDUSTRIAL BACKWARDNESS IN NORTH-EAST: SOME BASIC ISSUES AND POLICY IMPLICATIONS

— V.S. Mahajan

While developing economies face social, economic and industrial backwardness (in fact these are inter-related), it is all the more so in their sparsely populated hilly and mountainous regions where there generally exist severe communication gaps. Not surprisingly, therefore, that much of North-East India which is still sparesly populated and faces difficult terrain in the shape of mountains and thick jungles has been victim of industrial backwardness and still countinues.

It is not that all the seven constituent states are at the same level of industrial backwardness, for a state like Assam which is far more populated per sq km as well as far more larger plain area and means of communication than any other state in the region, is also far more industrially developed comparatively. By and large all the states in this region do suffer from industrial backwardness and have a long way to go to enter into the mainstream of modern industrialisation.

It is also not true that hilly terrain faced by most of North-East states should become a permanent barrier in their industrialisation. In fact the experience of Western countries, particularly a country like Switzerland, which is mountainous and sparsely populated shows that if proper communication network is created as well the level of skills of local population developed, it is possible to bring about quick economic and social transformation even in a difficult mountainous terrain. And today Switzerland enjoys one of the highest per capita income in the world.

Why Industrial Backwardness?

Before we take up the issue of formulating suitable policy guidelines for creating a viable framework for industrial growth in the North-East, we have to pose the basic question how the current social and economic scenario existing here has proved to be hindrance in industrialisation of this region.

Here we take up the specific instance of a state like Mizoram which has population which is far more educated, skilled and socially forward looking than most other areas in this region. But then despite these plus points, it continues to be industrially quite backward. In fact this is the one state which still has the highest percentage of its population practising the outmoded system of agriculture, that is, *jhum* cultivation and has made little headway towards settled land-use, despite all the efforts made by the state in this direction.

In fact at one time, in the mid-1980s the government had shown great eagerness to close down all the *jhums* in Mizoram by the end of this century and beyond this practising of *jhum* cultivation was to be made legally punishable.[1] The idea behind this was to wean away farmers from this system of cultivation to alternative more viable and environment friendly system of settled land use which was also closely linked with agro-industries which enjoyed large income and job potential.

In a policy paper that I had drafted at this time for the Government of Mizoram,[2] I had clearly suggested how this 15-year period (1985-2000) should be split into three five years sub-periods and also spelled out how over time it was possible to put the affected population on alternative economic activities yielding sustainable income.

But then the subsequent experience shows that there has occurred little change in the mode of production and *jhumming* still continues to be practised extensively though we are reaching close to this century. Apart from social constraints, it also shows that without effective political and administrative will for closing down these *jhums* and even more importantly simultaneously ensuring better alternative employment avenues for the population thus affected, there are little chances of making much headway in this programme.

As conditions exist today, there is rigid compartmentalisation of growth mechanism in North-Eastern States, where one state hardly has any worthwhile trade, production and economic linkages with the neighbouring states—and this itself has been significant outcome of carving out economically non-viable separate states out of the earlier North-East, which in the days of British were a part of Assam province.

It serves no useful purpose, and least economic purpose, to keep these states isolated from one another, which only makes them more and more dependent on the Centre for resources and this, as the experience shows, does not go a long way in developing the economy of a particular state.

North-East as a Closely Knit Region

The policy framers would have to look at North-East as a closely knit region and not what we have it today, fragmented into seven separate states where even entry to outsiders is strictly controlled.[3] Thus while the Indian economy is being globalised with the far reaching recent economic and market reforms, it is unfortunate that North-East should be turning more and more introvert and not thinking in terms of becoming a part of the bigger family.[4]

Going back to Mizoram's experience, certainly if after 1985 determined effort had been made to develop close ties with the neighbouring state of Assam—which also is its major neighbouring partner and also proivdes it the only entry point into India—things would have a lot different and much of the difficulties faced today in creating viable alternative economic avenues for the people affected by closing down *jhums* would have to a large extent tackled.

Let me spell this out in detail. As we have observed, one of the major constraints by the hill and jungle locked area like Mizoram is its severe communication gap as well small population. Both these factors act as major hindrance to its industrialisation, which have to take the shape of agro-industries as well those industries which demand more human skills and less raw material inputs for the latter are neither locally available nor it is possible to import them because of heavy transport cost. Even when some key inputs are locally available for the setting up a particular large scale industry (say paper mill in Mizoram) it would not prove economically viable because of lack of local market as well as problems faced in hauling up other vital inputs from other areas and reaching the national market for the sale of final products.

Industrialisation Call for Different Set of Approach

Thus industrialisation in this region calls for a different set of approach which has to be thought in terms of encouraging close economic collaboration with neighbouring areas. For instance, Mizoram's inherent potential for the setting up of viable industry programme, say based on processing of ginger and fruits (like pineapple) where it is richly endowed with, as well creating a new set of production possibilities like coffee and rubber plantations as well as raising poultry and dairy products, are very closely related with its relationship with neighbouring state of Assam, with which it should develop close economic and commercial ties.

While I was posted in Aizawl and often moved into the long track of Silchar valley before entering into the hills of Mizoram, my mind would often think of turning much of this area, particularly that below from where Mizoram's winding track would begin into a rich industrial belt where joint ventures with the co-operation of both Assam as well as Mizoram governments could be successfully set up, for while Mizoram lacked flat and stable area so essential for creating base for large industry and this advantage Silchar enjoyed, on the other hand Mizoram could provide some key raw materials and more so its literate and skilled manpower as well as monetary resources needed for the success of these ventures.[5]

Thus a co-operative approach by both these government could flower into a model industrial town in this part of the valley which was close to rail, road and air network and thus enjoyed easy access to a large market which in fact is a major hindrance in industrial development of Mizoram.

Need for Developing Transparent Industrial Policy

This, in other words, means that industrialisation of this region (like Mizoram) where vast natural potential does exist as well there are comfortable literacy rates and local people have natural inclination to learn modern skills, we have to shun the current economic model of self-sufficiency of individual state, which would just not work because of several constraints faced, and instead encourage entry into industrial collaboration arrangements with neighbouring areas to take advantage of larger production facilities as well as communication and market access.

Similarly, the development of modern electronic and allied industries, where it is possible to sub-contract the manufacture of several small items to households in remote areas and thus create large employment avenues, would itself call for large assembly, managing and controlling units which could only be located in areas accessible to national as well as international markets. And this is again quite conveniently possible to achieve through close economic network of different states in this region.

Policy Issues

Thus unless we are able to tackle the existing isolation, that has further worsened with more compartmentalised industrial policies followed by different states after their creation and which as a matter of fact has resulted in near industrial stagnation and rise in employment particularly among the educated youth.[6] There is likely to be little progress made in industrialisation of this region. Here the major sufferers would be those states like Mizoram, Nagaland and Arunachal Pradesh—all of them practice rigid entry permit system and thus follow isolationist policy as well are lost in most difficult terrain. The policy framers of these states would have to soften such isolationist tendencies and try of enter into the national (even international) mainstream by looking at the whole North-East as a single unit for industrial growth.

Such united (co-operative) approach to industrialisation would also help to improve the means of communication in this region where there is need for according a top priority. There is also urgent need for vast improvement of the existing network of roads and making them all weather—currently most of them are lost to cummunication purposes in the prolonged monsoon period thus causing major losses to the economy of individual state.

Let me close this attempt on industrial backwardness in North-East again by referring to Mizoram where we have seen that in the last over a decade attempts at modernising its agriculture as well introducing structural changes in its mode of production and especially trying to take this state into the field of modern industrialisation, have met with little success. Meanwhile its population problem has further worsened and so has its employment issue. Thus long term solution before this state—and the same applies to other states as well—is to emerge out of the existing situation where *jhums* are still dominating the economy with all their negative effects and particularly creating high environmental pollution,[7] —lies in developing industrial and marketing programmes in close collaboration with neighbours which would bring it long term gains as well assure rising income opportunities to its youth.

REFERENCES

1. See the document of *Mizoram Government's Land Use Policy,* reproduced in *Economic Development of Border States of India* by V.S. Mahajan, Deep and Deep Publications, New Delhi, pp. 102-107.
2. See pp. 79-96 of *Economic Development of Border States of India, Ibid.*
3. This restricted entry is a hangover from the British period who were mainly interested in keeping these tribals out of bound to the Indian society, for lacking as they did in past tradition, culture, language of their own (unlike in other parts of the country), it became easier to convert them into Christianity. No surprise that the maximum percentage of population converted into Christianity it to be found in North-East. But the British at the same time were not interested in the economic development of these people, and thus situation got worse, as argued in this chapter, after creating seven separate non-viable states. Thus there is urgent need to think over this permit system.
4. Strangely we continue to practice dual approach to our industrialisation. While on the one hand we are keen to become integral part of the world economy by allowing multinationals and foreign investments by offering all possible facilities, on the other when it comes to North-East we even do not permit our own entrepreneurs to invest in these areas because of several restrictions laid down. It is no surprise that under such circumstances the hiatus in industrial development in North-East and rest of the country should have further widened.
5. This has been further spelled out in Chapter 12 "Need and Problems of Industrialisation in Mizoram" and Chapter 13 "Further Notes on Industrialisation in Mizoram", in the book *Economic Development of Border States of India, Ibid.*
6. Surprisingly while quite a few states like Mizoram, Nagaland and Meghalaya in particular, have a high literacy rate and youngsters are now exposed to higher education in good number, simultaneously we do not have sufficient opportunities to absorb this emerging youth, who are thus tempted to join forces of terrorism and political turmoil, so often witnessed in North-East. The best solution to get over such a state is to industrialise the region.
7. Continuous burning of forests for a very long time now has destroyed a good part of the greenery as well as made such area barren and exposed to periodic storms that often invade Mizoram and cause much damage.

12

LIMITS TO ECONOMIC DEVELOPMENT OF NORTH-EASTERN REGION: AN ANALYSIS OF CONTRADICTIONS BETWEEN ECONOMIC GOALS AND SOCIAL CHOICES

— Gurudas Das

Peripheral Limits to Structural Change of Development

The scope for and the nature of economic development of a particular area, irrespective of its development potentialities in terms of resource availability, is limited by its spatial location within the political geography of a country in addition to its own physiography. The 'Location Theories' have shown that the nearer a place to the market centre, the greater is its scope for development, the farther a place the remoter is its scope. The scope for the economic development of the North-Eastern Region (NER) located far away from the national market centres cannot be unlimited. Understanding this limit to economic development of a region which has become a periphery in the national geo-political map, not by choice but an act of history, would be helpful for the disillusionment with the idea of rapid economic development through industrialisation. This will perhaps also provide an explanation to the much haunted question as to why does the region remain economically/industrially backward in spite of being rich in resources? As the periphery being an area depended on the core/ centre, the peripheral economic structure develops as a complementary to the core, not competitive and hence remains exposed to the exploitation by the core. The nature of development at the periphery is largely determined by the dictates and needs of the core. Thus the peripheral locational existence of NER puts in itself a limit to her own prospective economic development.

Social Limits to Economic Development

The concept of 'economic development' is neutral in the sense that it does not take into account the social identities of the agents who play the leading role in bringing it. And it is not this secular theoretical concept of economic development that the region is striving for. The question of the role of the 'sons of the soil' is always entangled with the goals of economic development. Economic development as a goal is desired but under the condition that is should be brought by, and directly beneficial to, the sons of the soil. The tribal land ownership structure and the legal as well as social barriers to the entry of outside labour in the hills of the region have contributed to the growth of group monopoly in the factor market. The idea of 'ethnic identity' has been misconstrued with the ethnic group monopoly over the resources. Developmental measures that affect this group monopoly and ethnic hegemony which dictates the socio-political terms will hardly find any social sanction. Thus, while the tribal social structure rests on the ethnic group monopoly over the factor markets, the industrial development requires the elimination of all restrictions in ownership, factor mobility etc. As a result, economic development is sought without allowing economic laws to operate unhindered. Social choice acts as an obvious limit to economic development.

Limits to Growth of Agriculture

The physiography of the region with two-third mountainous and one-third plains does not allow agriculture to be a leading sector for the overall economic development. The scope for the development of agriculture is limited only to the two river valleys of Brahmaputra and Barak along with Manipur and Tripura plains. The valleys and plains are already over populated leaving a little scope for extensive agricultural practices. Intensive methods can hardly be applied in its full vigour in view of the fact that there is little space to accommodate the surplus labour force which will be generated in the process. The over saturated tertiary sector and the immature secondary sector have created a condition for primary sector to continue in traditional lines. As a result, economic development through agricultural improvement can hardly be a viable model of growth for the region.

Economic Development through Industrialisation: Limits to Growth of Small-scale Sector

More often than not, the planners, politician as well as researchers suggest the development of the small scale sector as a means towards industrialisation and overall economic growth of the region without realising the limits upto which this sector can grow. They look back to the past when there was a handloom in every house and women remained busy in making cloths for the members of their family. When villagers used to practice pottery, blacksmithy, carpentry, cane and bamboo works, metal and ivory works, etc. When they used to process tea, salt, rice beer, etc at home. That is when every home was a cottage industry. This past experience has led many of the researchers to see the future of industrialisation of the region embedded in the development of the small scale industries.

Although the villagers still do practice many of these manufacturing activities, the extent of such activities have largely declined following the integration of the region with the national market network. Not only the large industrial products have replaced the goods produced traditionally at home, there has been a complete change in the taste and preferences of the people living even in the remotest areas Individual preferences are now shaped through electronic media and everybody wants to buy the best and the latest within his reach. The markets of goods having cultural brands like Naga shawl, Assamese Mekhela, Khasi Ryndia, etc. where the small scale sector hardly has any competitor from large producers, are getting squeezed following the change in mass culture. Many of these cultural goods which were in regular use in the past are now used only in occasions and rituals. Thus the changes in demand following the changes in taste and preferences have largely reduced the market space for the small scale industries to grow. Except certain areas like agro-forest based processing activities, non-durable products, spepcific demand based products, servicing activities, etc. small scale sector does not have much scope to grow.

Limits to Growth of Medium and Large Scale Sector

Industries are often classified into two broad types, i.e. demand based industries and resource based industries. The demand based industries usually locate themselves near the main market centres. The NER located far away from the national market centres offers little scope for the development of any large scale demand based industries. Even the segregated regional market cannot generate sufficient stimulus for the growth of demand based industries in the medium scale sector. Thus, in absence of any well organised regional market, the very small size of the local markets has made such industries commercially unviable.

Unlike demand based industries, the resource based industries are usually located near the sources rather than the markets. While resources located in the periphery are being exploited to cater the national demand, these industries usually became extractive in nature, i.e. after initial processing the intermediate products are sent to the national market centres for final production. Most of the middle and large scale enterprises like plywood units, saw mills, paper mills, sugar mills, cement factories, oil refineries, etc. already established in the region are resource based. And the major commercially viable resources are already being exploited to the scientifically permissible extent leaving little scope for further growth of resource based industries in the region. Even in certain areas like wood-based industries the over-exploitation of resources has already generated negative consequences not only for the industry concern but also for the eco-system in general.

Whatever scope is left for the development of resource based medium and large industries in the interior hills could not be appropriated because of the avowed policy of the sons of the soil as well as ethnic monopoly in the factor markets. Industrial and trading licences in the hill states are issued only to the local tribal entrepreneurs. But the conditions of tribal society are hardly compatible for the growth of large scale enterprise. Tribal societies are small and social field is smaller. As a result members of the society are tied by personal relationship. The smallness of the social field necessitates multiple roles to be played by the same set of people. But the medium and large scale economic operations require functionally specific roles as well as impersonal interpersonal relationship based on performance and achievement rather than on an individual's personal ties with other individuals in the enterprise. Thus, the size of the society and the social relationship stand on the way for the growth of medium and large scale industries in the hills of the region.

Plantation—The Plausible Leading Sector and its Limits of Growth

The only commercially viable sector is the plantation for the hills of the region where large scale private investment is possible. In view of the fact that this sector is facing acute shortage of land for its further expansion in the areas considered to be its traditional domains, the hill states of the region having large tracts of lands with relatively small population and congenial climate for plantation will be the natural choice for the planters. However, in spite of commercial viability, plantation sector could not grow in the hills because of factor immobility. The tribal land ownership structure, land regulations as well as social resistance do not allow the entry of the outside private capital. As the development of plantation even under public sector involves large scale immigration of outside labourer on permanent basis, it does not get social sanction either. As a result, the potentialities remain unutilised as the social choice gets precedence over economic dictates.

13

A SOCIOLOGICAL VIEW OF THE MULTI-FACETED PROBLEMS OF INDUSTRIALISATION

— Sanjib Kr. Borkakoti

In this chapter, I will try to approach the problems of industrialization both as an academician and an entrepreneur.[1] Very often the analysts discount some major factors in the context of industrialization as they approach the whole issue either too theoretically or too empirically. A balanced approach with equal emphasis on both theory and practice only can take us to the heart of the problem. Otherwise a pure theoretician without any understanding of the ground realities might suggest that small scale sector has no scope in North-East India. Again an entrepreneur might go in for launching a consumer good, the preference for which is likely to decline in near future among the consumers. So the need of the hour is to have an extensive interchange of thought between the social scientists and the entrepreneurs if we really want to find a way out of the present backwardness of the North-East resion, regarding industrialization.

An important feature of the modern industrialization is that it is an alien process to most of the developing countries and areas thereof. While it has become an organic process in the United Kingdom, where the industrialization had originally taken place, the situation is entirely different in an average developing country. The problems of North-East India can be viewed accordingly. The problems of industrialization in this region is therefore a matter of acquiring socio-economic values required for an industrial society as well as of developing socio-economic institutions suitable for an industrial economy. Another important point is that these changes should go in tandem with the actual industrial programme. Otherwise, it might lead to social tension and thereby halt the whole industrialization process itself.[2] The present social unrest as well as extremist movement in the North-East also can be traced to such a mismatch between institutional development and industrial development.[3]

Any strategy for industrialization must necessarily take into account all these issues. Industrialization is not an already worked out formula that can be implanted or made to take root in any place. It is necessarily an inter-disciplinary process. A whole range of institutional set-up including education, health, culture and so on have to be developed sufficiently for the orderly transition of an underdeveloped economy to an industrially developed one.

Very often it is said that the North-East is rich in natural resources and yet it is not having sufficient industrialization. When we say such a thing, we presume that it is the abundance in natural resources which mainly and necessarily leads to industrialization. But that is not the case. The Japanese instance has proved that industrialization can take place even without having natural resources at home. Emperor Meiji had worked that wonder with his political acumen. He had converted the Samurai's, the feudal warrior class of Japan into primary producers and brought all the shipping lines to under the nation's control. After that the society gradually turned to secondary activities, which were aided by a strong protectionist regime. An extensive land reform enabled the country to make this transition.

It is true that we cannot copy the Japanese example at this late hour of history when an aggressive consumerist culture as well as a new international trade pattern have globalised the economy. Moreover the strong nationalist sentiment showed by the Japanese cannot be easily emulated. People cannot be restrained from purchasing imported commodities any more. But when we go to the lower segments of the market, we see that people with less purchasing power generally confine their choice to the local products to a great extent.[4] So the market is there in some segments. Any entrepreneur must identify those with proper care if he is not to be swept aside by the great onrush of products from other regions or abroad. I think the criterion of comparative advantage can be the guiding principle here.

However, the solution of the paradoxical situation of the North-East cannot be acquired from Japan. The co-existence of abundant raw materials and very little industrialization is the paradox that we have to solve. Such a problem is also faced by the backward Jharkhand area. It is a striking similarity between the North-East and the Jharkhand area that the majority of the population in both areas arė from tribal stock. These people have some common characteristics. These are:

1. They are used to live in quietude, away from the urban hustles.
2. Their methods of productions are of pristine conditions and there is not much effort to upgrade those.
3. Their exposure to the outside forces is very low.

All these characteristics are detrimental to the cause of industrialization. But the important point to be noted is that the ethnicity of the people are of no importance; the Mongolian population of Japan, Hong-Kong, Singapore etc. have proved how industrious they can be. It is the socio-economic characteristics that I emphasize on. When I allude to the large presence of tribal people in the North-East, I refer to their socio-economic character only. The people of the above mentioned three countries have long ceased to be tribal as defined by those characteristics. Almost no one lives there on pristine methods of production. Added to that, all of them have had suficient exposure to external influences from time immemorial. The landlocked North-East has always been insulated from outside world. Thus my hypothesis is that the presence of tribal people as defined socio-economically can only explain the paradox mentioned earlier. If and when the people of North-East come out of their tribal characteristics, the problems of industrialization in this region will be half over. Unfortunately the socio-political factors are taking the things in the other direction. The cultural revivalism in the region have made the people lukewarm to the socio-economic changes as the pristine methods of production have now become cultural symbols for the people.[5]

The implication of what I have said above is that the insufficient growth of entrepreneurship is a major problem we have to reckon with. In the present socio-cultural milieu the entrepreneurs seem to emerge only from those social groups who rank higher in the so-called caste hierarchy. It is because the high caste people have found the economic power as the alternative tool for social dominance. In fact a new social ordering has gradually developed where caste ordering has given way to class ordering.[6] I think this social change should be accelerated with some carefully structured plan which does not compromise the principle of social equality. The fact that more and more jobs are being reserved for the backward castes and communities makes it even more imperative to open new options and avenues for the social groups belonging to the high castes. Otherwise, the problem of unemployment and social unrest will become more intense thereby vitiating the atmosphere further.[7] Some people may misconstrue this suggestion as an attempt to give an elite bias to the industrialization. But the multiplier effect will take the benefit to all the classes.

The aloofness of the North-East youths to hard work and entrepreneurial activities is often referred to in any discussion on problems of industrialization. It is observed that most of the youths are attracted only to white collar jobs. But they cannot be faulted alone for this attitude. Their entire upbringing is done in an atmosphere where risks are always averted. It is therefore that they prefer to give bribe for a job than invest the same amount in some self-employment venture. There are so many allegations all around us now-a-days of massive corruptions. We forget or ignore the other side that to every corrupt official there are many more youths who are co-operating with him and are therefore equally guilty of curruption. It, therefore, becomes an issue of morality and ethics also. We are now living in a period where ethical values have taken a strong beating. All these must be changed. A revision in the education system will be required for that.

The salient points and the corrolaries of this chapter can be summarized as given below:

1. It is necessary to have an exchange of thought between the social scientists and the entrepreneurs about the problems of industrialization.
2. A new pattern of socio-economic values have to be developed to assist the process of industrialization.
3. The institutional requirements of industrialization should be carefully planned and implemented with the exactly required speed.
4. The commodities where the region enjoys comparative advantage should be identified for probable entry of entrepreneurs. The lower segments of the market can be monopolised by the indigenous producers.
5. The underdeveloped methods of productions prevailing almost

everywhere in the North-East should be phased out with modern production methods whereby more surpluses can be generated.

6. The exposure of the north-easterners to the new developments in science as well as uses of these in the sophisticated production methods is extremely necessary.
7. The dynamic youths having no job opportunities should be attracted to the secondary sector. Such a talent search can be done among the high-caste groups.
8. The merit of risk taking and the importance of industrial activities should be inculcated among the youngsters right since their childhood. The educational curriculum may be changed to incorporate these things.
9. The present decay of moral values must be curbed with due emphasis on ethics in the curriculum.
10. The rampant curruptions in the country must be checked if the attraction of easy money is to be curbed.

REFERENCES

1. The author did Ph.D. on the topic of industrialization. He also set up an S.S.I. unit and ran it for eight years.
2. Borkakoti, Sanjib Kr., 'An optimum strategy for industrialization in a landlocked and subsistence agriculture economy: Assam a case study', Unpublished Ph.D. thesis of the University of Gauhati, 1991, pp. 10-11.
3. Many technically skilled men produced by the educational institutions have remained unemployed or under-employed due to lack of absorption capacity in the existing industries. It is no wonder that several leaders of the extremist outfits have been found to be technical diploma holders.
4. This is seen in the case of products like snacks. If we consider national Vs. international products, we find that people with low income buys national products in case of cosmetics, apparel, etc. The costly products of multi-national producers cannot be afforded by people with low income.
5. Borkakoti, Sanjib Kr., 'Alternative plan for *jhum* area development' in *'Shifting Cultivation in N.E. India'* (ed) by D.N. Mazumdar, New Delhi, 1990.
6. Borkakoti, Sanjib Kr., "Caste definition and caste conflict," *Assam Tribune*, Guwahati, July 1, 1994.
7. Assam saw a massive flight of capital from this state during the hay-day of 'United Liberation front of Asom' in the eighties. The author was then informed by the spokesman of the business community that the amount was about Rs. 3,000 crores. The value of such outflow rose to about 10,000 crores in the nineties. This proves how an incongenial atomosphere can play havoc with the economic activities. The difference between the levels of industrial activities in West Bengal in the seventies and in the nineties also highlights the importance of social stability.

14

INDUSTRIAL DEVELOPMENT NEEDS ENTREPRENEURIAL DEVELOPMENT IN NORTH-EAST INDIA

— Pranay Jyoti Goswami

Introduction

The North-Eastern region of India is known for her immense natural resources with vast potentialities for developing various resource-based and demand-based industries. But the pace of development in that respect has not taken place on a scale commensurate with the possibilities and as a result except in certain sectors like petroleum, coal, tea and forest, other potentials have by and large remained untapped. For example, the region's hydel power potential is estimated at about 30,000 MW and deposit of natural gas at 23 million cubic mts. But the per capita consumption of electricity (1992-93) is as low as 159.4 KWH in Meghlaya and 83.9 KWH in Tripura as against 330.6 KWH for the country as a whole, Even though the region has an estimated deposit of about 928 million tonnes of coal, 2998 million tonnes of limestone and abundant resources in the forest, having ideal agro-climatic conditions, it is deficit in the almost all items of daily consumption and capital goods.[1]

Status of North-Eastern Region (NER) in Country's Industrial Scenario

In the industrial field, the region contains only 1.8 per cent of the registered factories providing employment to 1.7 per cent of the factory employees of the country. Table 14.1 shows the number of large and medium scale industries in North-Eastern Region. Table 14.1 reveals that

74.8 per cent of large and medium scale industries of NER is located in Assam. There is no medium and large scale industries in Mizoram. The condition of Tripura is also very bad i.e. 0.6 per cent. Table 14.2 shows the trend of development of SSI in different states of N.E. Region during the period 1971 to 1988. The table shows slow growth rate of SSI in this region during the period mentioned above. Table 14.3 compares the position of some of the North-Eastern states with that of some industrially developed states like Maharashtra, Gujarat and India as a whole. Table 14.3 reveals that in case of indusrrially developed States, gross output per employee is nearly Rs 3 lakhs or more whereas in case of NE States it is less than 1 lakh. In case of fixed capital per employee, it is less than one lakh in this region but more than 1 lakh in case of other developed States. However in case of net value added to output the condition of Manipur is very good.

TABLE 14.1: Large and Medium Scale Industries in North-Eastern Region (As on 31 March, 1994)

State	No. of Units	Percentage
1	2	3
Arunachal Pradesh	17	5.8
Assam	118	74.8
Manipur	6	3.9
Meghalaya	7	4.5
Mizoram	1	0.0
Nagaland	16	10.4
Tripura	1	0.6
Total	166	100.0

Source: Journal of NEC, 1995.

The growth rate of small scale industries in NE Region during the period 1980 to 1988 was lower (125.90%) than the average growth rate of ten states viz. Maharashtra, Gujarat, Tamilnadu, U.P., Bihar, M.P., Karnataka, Andhra Pradesh and Punjab (163.35%). Growth rate for the country as a whole during this period was 158.75 per cent. While SSI Units of NE States formed 1.75 per cent of the Indian units in 1988, the ten states had contained 78.69 per cent of the total.[2]

TABLE 14.2: Trend of Development of SSI in different States on N.E. Region (1971-1998)

States	1971	1981	1985	1986	1987	1988*
1	2	3	4	5	6	7
Arunachal	-	189	262	213	278	374
Pradesh		(1.9)	(1.9)	(1.3)	(1.8)	(1.8)
Assam	809	4,153	6,[illegible]43	7,362	8,727	10,210
	(81.6)	(42.3)	(47.4)	(44.8)	(44.1)	(50.1)
Manipur	8	3,422	3,157	4,220	4,830	2,892
	(0.8)	(34.8)	(12.9)	(25.7)	(24.4)	(14.2)
Meghalaya	-	233	571	643	762	1,000
	-	(2.4)	(4.1)	(3.9)	(3.9)	(4.9)
Mizoram	-	298	826	1,191	1,566	1,866E
	-	(3.0)	(6.0)	(7.9)	(9.2)	(9.2)
Nagaland	-	345	395	431	471	509
	-	(3.5)	(2.9)	(2.6)	(2.4)	(2.5)
Tripura	174	1,183	2,062	2,392	3,136	3,523
	(17.6)	(12.0)	(14.9)	(14.5)	(15.9)	(17.3)
N.E Region	991	9,823	13,816	16,452	19,770	20,377
	(100)	(100)	(100)	(100)	(100)	(100)
All India	2,39,128	5,23,180	8,54,843	9,50,334	10,48,253	11,58,765

Note: Figures in brackets indicate percentage, *= Provisional. E = Estimated

Source: Journal of NEC, 1995.

TABLE 14.3: Selected Ratios to the Industrial Sector (1989-90)

	Gross output per employee Rs. (in Lakh)	Fixed capital per employee (in Rs. Lakh)	Net value added to output.	Fixed capital to output
Assam	.87	.99	.17	.53
Manipur	.50	.57	.71	1.14
Meghalay	.70	.13	.36	.18
Tripura	.36	.36	.18	1.57
Gujarat	3.01	1.23	.17	.41
Maharashtra	3.22	1.21	.21	.38
All India	2.38	1.15	0.19	.48

Source: Basic statistices ralating to North-Eastern (Region (1995)

Objective of the Study

From the foregoing analysis it reveals that the industrial development in this region is very low. One of the main problems of this low rate of industrialization is lack of entrepreneurial development. In this connection this chapter seeks to analyses the problems and prospects of entrepreneurial development in this region.

Entrepreneurial Development in North-Eastern Region

The industrial backwardness of this region is the result of the operation of the combination of various factors—economic political, technological and sociological.

Inadequacy of transport and communication system, non availability of cheap and adequate power, the virtual non-inflow of institutional finance, dearth of skilled labour, problems of marketing, unstable law and order situation and insurgency are some of the factors that stood on the way of industrial development of the region.

There has also been unfortunately lack of initiative and enterprise within the region. Most of the few medium and small scale industries outside the corporate sector are owned and managed not by the children of the soil but by immigrant entrepreneurs. In other words, entrepreneurship is not emerging from among the indigenous group. In other words, there is a dearth of entrepreneurs in this region.

It is the entrepreneur who discover economic potentialities and opportunities in new commodities, markets, resources and organisation of production. The entrepreneur initiates varieties of enterprises, introduce new ideas and techniques of production, management and distribution of goods and services. Such kind of activities accelerate the process of economic development. According to Schumpeter, entrepreneur is not a man of ordinary managerial ability, but one introduces something new.

Two Survey Reports—Gujarat and Assam

The importance of socio-cultural variables as partial determinants of the supply of entrepreneurs, is emphasised by many development economists like Higgins and Kindle Berger. Other economists like Arthur Lewis (1955), Bauer and Yamey (1957), G.M. Meir (1970) also stressed the point. The eminent sociologists viz. C.E. Black (1966), B.F. Hoselitz (1961), S. Tax (1951),Lucy Mair (1963) also stressed on the importance of socio-cultural factors for economic development.

Mehta and Bhatt[3] explains differential growth rates of 100 S.S.I. units of Gujarat in terms of some useful sociological, economic and psychological variables like social castes, instiutions of joint family, occupational background of entrepreneur's father and entrepreneurs themselves along with risk taking abilities of the entrepreneurs. Their findings are as follows:

1. There is no significant relationship between social castes and remarkable growth of sample units.
2. The institution of joint family has some positive influence on the growth of enterprise.
3. The entrepreneurs who achieved high growth rates of their units had advantage of experience of their fathers in related sphere of activities.
4. Related working experience, trading backgrounds and training were important variable associated with entrepreneurs whose entreprises registered significant growth rates.
5. A desire to take moderate risk was associated with entrepreneurs of units with significant growth.

Bharati Sharma[4] also studied 200 entrepreneurs with varying background, took six socio-economic factors and tried to find out the effect of these factors on entrepreneurial development. The contents of her findings are:

> "It is obvious that for developing positive attitude towards business and industry, modern education, contact with relevant social groups, family and institutional support and particularly individuals own interest and initiative play a vital role."

EDP—An Assessment

Different organisations e.g. the National Institute of Small Industries Extension Training (NISIET), North-Eastern Industrial and Technical Consultancy (NEITCO), North-Eastern Industrial Consultancy Organisation (NECON), Entrepreneurial Development Institute,

Hyderabad etc. are the expert agencies helping NEC in her EDP programme. During Seventh Plan NEC has sponsored 152 EDPs benefiting about 3609 entrepreneurs. One crude index of evaluating an EDP is the success rate i.e. the percentage of successful trainees who have put up enterprise/industries. On the whole Seventh Five Year Plan the success rate was only 20.88 per cent. It also reveals that only 1/3rd of the trainees of 1985-86, EDPs could put up enterprise even after the lapse of five years indicates large time gap between training and starting of enterprise. Within one year of training nobody could set up any enterprises.

NEC since 1986-87 also sponsored training for women entrepreneurs. Generally because of traditional socio-cultural environment the women in general lag behind men in business and enterprise. But in the North-Eastern region due to matriarchal system prevailing in states like Meghalaya and due to higher women labourer participation and better social status of women, the entrepreneurial development programme conducted exclusively for women showed tangible results. The success rate of EDP for women was 63.4 per cent.[5]

A Note on Problems of Entrepreneurial Development in Tribal Hill Areas

A study[6] conducted by the NISIET during 1976-77 revealed that only 14.29 per cent of total entrepreneurs are tribals in North-East India. But in different states of North-East India there are variations of this percentage. It ranges in between .03 (in Assam) to 100 per cent in Arunachal Pradesh. The states where inner line permits prevails e.g. Arunachal Pradesh and Mizoram and/or which is inaccessible communicationally this percentage is very high. It was 100 per cent in Arunachal Pradesh and 98.88 per cent in Mizoram. The percentage of tribal entrepreneurs in other states of NER are as follows:

Meghalaya	-	35.02
Nagaland	-	16.79
Tripura	-	4.86
Manipur	-	35.61

In certain tribal areas, entry of outside entrepreneurs is very difficult as because of certain political restrictions (i.e. inner line permit) or because of resistance of local people. There is a feeling of economic exploitation by the non-tribals in tribal areas which has led to social tensions.[7]

Socio-psychological attitude towards industrial development in some tribal areas was not very helpful. As regards the problems of entrepreneurial development in tribal areas Dr. Mali said:

> "The problems are not similar and identical. These problems are individual, group and institutional in character. In enterprise launching ultimate decision is to be taken by individual concern. But he may lack motivation, he may not be aware of the entrepreneurial opportunities. He may not have required managerial skill, he may be afraid of procedural delays. He may not have finance for initial investment; he may not get family and community approval and support. In this way different problems act as hindrance in the process of enterprise launching."[8]

Conclusion

It is a matter of great hope that since 1985 NEC has taken up a comprehensive EDP programme. It is also trying to introduce an EDP component in the curricula at diploma and degree level of technical education. Government of India, more particularly since 1990 has been giving much stress for the economic development of NER. For encouragement of new entrepreneurs various types of incentives are also given to them in this region. It is a gratifying fact that as a result of all these efforts, even in some remote and inaccessible region the entrepreneurs are coming forward to take up industrial ventures. Tribal entrepreneurs also do not lag behind. Many of them want to set up industries which is something new for them.[9] These tendencies shows a ray of hope as regards entrepreneurial development in North-East India.

REFERENCES

1. Debey, H.S.: "Emerging Pattern of North-Eastern Economy", *Journal of NEC.* Jan-April, 1987, and Basic statistics of NER, 1995, p. 112.
2. Baishya, Prabin: "Industrial Development of the NE Region—A Study of Regional Imbalance". *Journal of NEC*, Jan-March, 1994.
3. Mehta, B.V & P.K. Bhatt: Analysis of factors Affecting Growth of Entrepreneurship (in) Gujarat Economy Problems & Prospects, Sardar Patel Institution of Economy and Social Research, Ahmedabad, 1983.

4. Gauhati University *Journal of Commerce,* Vol I, 1990, p. 66.
5. Phukan, S.D.: In Entrepreneurship Development and Present Industrial Policy. *Journal of NEC,* July-Sept, 1993.
6. Mali, D.D.: Development of Tribal Entrepreneurship in North-Eastern Region. *Journal of NEC,* Jan-March 1989.
7. *Ibid.* & other Journal of NEC.
8. *Ibid.*
9. Phukan, S.D.: *op.cit.*

15

UNDERSTANDING TRIBAL NOTION OF EXPLOITATION

— B.J. Deb

Tribal areas of North-East India are surcharged with the apprehension of exploitation from industrialization, a mode of development which necessarily introduces outside forces—technology as well as manpower into the society, more specially in a tradition bound one lacking the requisite know-how and entrepreneurial skill. Indeed, such a notion is playing a political role and the destabilising effect of industrialization on population structure and cultural identity in particular is projected by the political parties and pressure groups alike. No wonder, the resultant response is channelised in such a way as to claim an aura of legitimacy. Consequently, *socio-cultural identity has acquired primacy,* ascendancy over economic development and in the prevailing situation *primitive* economic methods continue in vast areas with unremunerative prospects. This resistance to change and development is evident in their opposition to layout of infrastructural facilities, extraction of soils and minerals, generation of electricity and setting up of medium and large scale industries.

This notion has seized the tribal mind in such a way that today, no political party, national or regional, does openly advocate industrialisation for economic development. The State Governments' industrial policy discourages the flow of enterprise from outside on the one hand, and the restrictive nature of employment policy acts as a scare-crow to potential investors on the other. In fact, there has hardly been any wothwhile interest by private industrialists in the development of North-East India, let alone the NRIS.

Against this background, it is necessary to examine the extent to which such a notion is analytically defensible. Apparently, a number of objections features tend to favour the apprehension of exploitation in the tribal areas. The insular nature of the society, the hangover of the colonial past, continuance of traditional economy, interaction of traditional and modern elements in polity; have all combined to provide sustenance to this apprehension. In fact, the very outlook of the people was inhibited by the Inner Line in certain places. Again historically, the tribal areas of the North-East fell into three categories—excluded, partially excluded and unadministered. In the post-Independent period, political extremism has come to stay as a method of inviting centre's resources to 'internal colonial' situation. These apart, geo-political factors have contributed to a feeling of alienation. The small size of the population also added considerably to their apprehension.

Numerous theories of exploitation have been advocated in social theory from time to time. In contemporary analysis, the notion of exploitation has been inseparably linked up with the existence of commercial or industrial society, or for that matter, with modern economic organisation. In a capitalist society, the charge of exploitation has been raised with respect to both the labour market and to exchanges of other goods. Exploitation is looked upon by Marx as a defining feature of a capitalist economic system. Although for Marx, exploitation was an inherent part of capitalism, he used the concept of exploitation with reference to labour market.[1] The nub of Marx's theory of exploitation is the view that exploiters are owners of the means of production who by definition take advantage of the exploited. "It is a necessary consequence of ownership of the means of production by a part of society and is necessarily eliminated when these resources are controlled by society as a whole."[2] It is clear that such a view does not explain tribal apprehension which is basically a question of 'we' *vs* 'they'. However to the extent Marx's theory of exploitation can be said to be normative and political,[3] the tribal notion bears some superficial affinity, just as the tribal perception generates opposition and hostility to outsiders, 'the insight provided by Marx might be employed in developing hostility to capitalism'. Again, if Marx's theory does paly a political role in restructuring society, the tribal perception can be said to be politically directed towards maintaining the supposed cultural identity.

Another theory that exploitation constitutes taking unfair advantage of someone in free-market transactions[4] may be generally true but it falls short of explaining tribal apprehension in the absence of free-market transactions in a tribal economy. It has been observed that exploitation is characterised by unequal possession of capital goods and private property.[5] David Miller however argues that although unequal access to natural resources, may be an important source of exploitation, exploitation can also arise in the course of market transactions between persons who were originally given equal endowments.[6] The idea of exploitation occurring through market transaction does not obviously explain the issue in question. Steiner centres his theory of exploitation on the violation of rights but Miller denies that exploitation is best conceives as a matter of rights violations. In the North-Eastern scenario, the issue of violation of human rights does figure in the discourse on exploitation, although in the context of industrialization the argument is not offered.

Goodin provides a more general theory of exploitation which distinguishes between exploiting a person and exploiting a situation.[8] The focus of his approach is that a theory of exploitation should not be parasitic upon a theory about the creation and distribution of valued commodities Fundamentally, exploitation involves violation of our duty to protect the vulnerable and that vulnerability could be, but is not necessarily economic. Such protection could be afforded by constitution and legal guarantees and more appropriately by democratic institutions and values. Even the liberal theory of exploitation allows identification of some transactions between persons as exploitative. However, tribal fear of exploitation is directed towards excluding others from economy and polity. It does not seek to ensure fairness or avoid wrongfulness.

As the prevailing theories of exploitation cannot explain the apprehension of the tribal people, the answer has to be sought outside the bounds of economic transactions. A meaningful approach would be to link such apprehension with ethnicity, an all-embracing phenomenon energising the perception of the tribal people and influencing political decision-making. From another angle, ethnicity is indeed an important resource, the mobilisation of which is noticeable in endless antonomy movements in the North-East various organisations which emerge in tribal societies become faced with the enduring base of ethnic ties and sentiments and use cultural symbols and emphasise the action on perceived threat from others to mobilise people, although various tribal groups are at 'different stages of ethnic formation'.[9]

REFERENCES

1. Reeve, Andrew (ed.): *Modern Theories of Exploitation*. Sage Publications, London, 1987, p. 2.
2. Carver Terrel, 'Marx's Political Theory of Exploitation' in Andres Reeve (ed.) *Modern Theories of Exploitation*, p. 71.
3. *Ibid.*, pp. 76-77..
4. Miller, D.: Constraints on Freedom, *Ethics*, 94(1), 1983, pp. 66-86.
5. J. Roemer, *A General Theory of Exploitation & Class*, London 1982, pp. 1-15.
6. Miller, D., 'Exploitation in the Market, in Andrew Reeve' (ed.), *Modern Theories of Exploitation*, pp. 152-153.
7. Hillel, Steiner, 'Exploitation, a liberal theory amended, defended and extended' *ibid.*, pp. 132-47 Liberty & Equality, *Political Studies*, 29, 198-1, pp. 555-69.
8. Goodin R., 'Exploiting a situation and Exploiting a person', in A. Reeve (ed.) *Modern Theories of Exploitation*, pp. 188-90.
9. Pakem, B., *Presidential Speech*, Third Annual Conference of NEIPSA, 1993, Arunachal University.

16

STATUS OF AND SOCIOLOGICAL CONSTRAINTS TO DEVELOPMENT OF NORTH-EASTERN REGION

— Anjan Thakur

The Backdrop

The North-Eastern Region of India, owing to its distinct culture, history, language and ethnic identity, often considered a homogeneous entity. Its geographical isolation from the rest of the country also gives vent to this categorization. Although we believe that any developmental model for the region to be formulated in a holistic perspective, that is taking the entire region into account, yet at the same time any socio-economic analysis which overlooks the diversity within the region would only render such approach meaningless.

The region abounds in flora and fauna. Study shows that about 80 per cent of the main species of flora is found in the region. It is one of the highest rainfed areas in the world. Assam specially, is full of rivers besides the mighty Brahmaputra. These rivers are ideal for generating hydro-electricity. Moreover most of the areas of the region being full of hills, the arable land is mainly confined to the valleys of the river Brahmaputra and Barak in Assam. Communication network of the region is under-developed. Recurrent floods and land erosion often results in the total collapse of the transport and communication system.

North-East, on the other hand is epitomised with regard to ethnicity, language, religion and culture. Accordingly the relation with the main-stream India varies from community to community. While this relationship is close in case of caste Hindus of Assam, in case of remote tribal community of Arunachal, Mizoram or Nagaland, Indian cutsoms and cultures are alien. As a matter of fact, baring Assam, most of the areas of the region had no cultural link with the rest of India in historical times.

It is the advent of the British to the region which brought NE Region to the political map of India. This too happen very late in comparison to rest of India (Assam went to British in 1826 and the other areas like Nagaland and Khasi Hills etc. went to the British only in the last quarter of the 19th Century). Still many areas of the region were outside British administration.

Although the region had great economic potentialities apart from its strategic significance, the economy and society of the region were rather backward while the British ventured into the area.

Apart from certain parts of Assam which came close to feudal economy and society other areas of the region can easily be characterized as tribal in so far as the socio-economic condition is concerned. *Jhuming* was the general practice. Many communities were still in the stage of food gatherers and hunters. Most of the groups lacked any geographical sense beyond their immediate territory.

Although latter the spread of Christianity a process encountered by the colonial people lent a common identity to many hill tribes besides infusing modernity among them, yet at another level the deliberate isolationist policy of the British has sentimentally alienated the tribal groups from the main-stream India which is mainifested in the secessionist tendencies so vibrant in the region.

As mentioned earlier that only Assam had trade and cultural links with the rest of India, there was a developed state form in Assam. But the trade relation was always a deficit one mainly due to the import of salt. Besides money economy was at a very low level of development.

When the British came to this region they suddenly introduced cash economy in the region. It resulted specially in Assam in a lot of suffering among the people and the peasantry rose against it for quite a few time. On the other hand, introduction of the cash economy in a traditional semi-tribal set-up compelled the peasantry of Assam to borrow money from outsiders in order to pay their revenues. It encouraged the usurious practices totally monopolised by the Marwari traders coming into the region from other parts of India. Moreover almost all the business and other entrepreneurial avenues generated went to the hands of the outsiders as the local people were hardly a match so far as skill and resources required for business activity is concerned.

This lagacy of this phenomenon still persists.

Without due consideration of this back-drop, any analysis of the socio-economic hindrances in the development of the region would only be a futile exercise.

Even a cursory observation of the yearly Indian economic survey would reveal the depressing state in which the economy of the region is touched.

The extent of commercial activity in the region is quite limited, capital formation is meagre and the performance of the government financial institution is also not at all upto mark.

Agriculture

We are using Assam as an yardstick of development as it is economically and commercially the most developed state in the N.E. Region. By assessing Assam's economic performance vis-a-vis other Indian states outside N.E. Region it would be quite easy to form a clear idea about the condition of the region. It does not require to re-emphsise that the regions economy is based on agriculture. If we look at the per capita foodgrain production in Assam it is too low in comparison to national average. But it is above Arunachal Pradesh, Mizoram, Nagaland and other N.E. Region States. Again the percentage of gross irrigated area to gross cropped area in Assam in 1986-87 was only 15 per cent against the national average of 30.4 per cent (Statistical Handbook of Assam 1994). Consumption of fertilizer is also very low in Assam. Other N.E. states do not even figure in the picture.

This indicates that agriculture which is the economic backbone of the region is quite fragile and characterised by an acute absence of commercialisation besides being quite vulnerable to the natural vagaries like flood, which takes away any entrepreneurial zeal on the part of the peasants. But the government's effort to control this perennial problem is quite negligible despite the fact that massive floods every year results in immense loss of human lives, and prosperity; each year, new areas get submerged in flood. Erosion also takes its own toll in an alarming rate in various regions.

There is no perceptible effort on the part of the Government to control this situation. This is notwithstanding the fact that the rivers in the region have tremendous potential to generate hydro-electricity, and provide irrigation facilities if duly harnessed.

Industry

In the industrial sector also the same situation prevails. The per capita gross industrial output of Assam, industrially the most developed state in the region was Rs. 807 in 1985 as against national average of Rs. 1592. In 1987-88, the industrial consumption of electricity as 31.2 KWH while the national average was 90.8 KWH. The condition of other N.E. states are far worse.

Transport and Communication

The network of transport and communication is also in a lacklusture state. Most parts of the region is still unconnected by railways. In Assam the British colonial administrator constructed railway for driving out resources like Tea, Crude oil, Coal, Plywood etc. Thus, barring areas yielding these items other important areas were deprived of railway network. Unfortunately by and large this situation still prevails.

It is but natural that without primary infrastructural facility like transport and communication any entrepreneurial initiative would be quite far-fetched.

All these amply demonstrate that massive governmental effort to develop the region is nothing but a myth. It is not that government has invested no money in the region. But due to the lack of transparency in its expenditure and the absence of well thought out policy the largest chunk of these investments go in vain and is only inflating the pockets of local elites including the politicians. This is partially true of the hill states.

Land Alienation

Land alienation is one of the most important issues in the region which has both socio and economic repercussions. It is mentioned earlier that total amount of arable land in the region is confined to the Brahmaputra, Surma and Imphal valleys. But even the available land area is also fast dwindling due to massive influx of outsiders. Forest coverage of region is also shrinking at an alarming rate. Tribals of the Brahmaputra and Barak Valleys are the worst victims of the phenomenon. Hence most of the tribals indulged in temporary *Jhum* cultivation. Moreover to avoid burden of taxation right from the British days the tribal people kept on shifting their place of habitation. As a result they did not get *patta* and against which they could have been provided credit from Banks. Again due to their peculiar social structure the tribals always prefer to live in isolation. Thus they kept on withdrawing to remote forest area as immigrants came and settled on their vicinity. Although in Assam the tribals in the Brahmaputra valley are no longer shifting cultivators, yet they possess insufficient land for cultivation. The result is an alienated, impoverished and disgrantled populace and this phenomenon is widespread in the region.

The people of the region complain that all socio-economic malady of the region is the consequence of a semi-colonial attitude of the Central Government towards the N.E. States. The indigenous people of the region feel that whatever benefit accrued from the development process is cornered by the non-indigenous people engaged in trade and commerce.

As a matter of fact it is not that no resource is being generated in the region. But this generation is meagre and the benefits of these resources have not percolated down to the people of the region.

Work Culture

It is customary in a section of the people to wholly attribute this phenomenon to the mindset of the indigenous people of the region. It is often alleged that the people of the region lack a work culture, that they are resistant to change and their attitude to the external environment is one of scepticism and their value system is geared to fatalism. Although there is truism in the allegation, they need to be examined in the contextual reality. Besides they do not represent the entire truth. Quite a few indigenous entrepreneurs are doing quite well although in a relatively low scale.

In Assam, a good number of Assamese entrepreneurs initially ventured into the tea industry. But it was not possible for them to stand the onslaught of the big industrial houses from outside who were also interested in tea industry. This phenomenon is also applicable on various other spheres. Many point out that the geographical remoteness of the areas and lack access of the local people to the external market have adversely affected the entrepreneurial zeal of the indigenous poeple of the region. This however gives rise to the question as to why the local people are not exhibiting entrepreneurial ability even in producing goods for which raw materials are available in the region besides a ready market. This can be attributed to several factors.

- Dearth of capital
- Underdeveloped transport and communication
- Precarious power situation
- Competition from the non-indigenous business houses.

Hence we should not underscore the crucial role of the Government in generating infrastructural facilities and in giving due encouragement to the budding entrepreneurs. Because we believe that it is these material obstacles that are inhibiting the growth of work culture and entrepreneurial activity in the region much more than any mystic psychological factors.

The Approach

It is already mentioned that the region is marked by a great extent of diversity in respect of economy, society and culture. Therefore, a single and homogeneous socio-economic development plan for the entire N.E. Region will not serve any purpose. This implies that we need to formulate such policies which suit the material and cultural milieu of respective communities. Consideration must be given to availability of raw material, capital skill and mind set of the people i.e. whether the policies for development of the community is acceptable to them or not as per their social and cultural heritage. All these do not undermine however the need to simultaneously instill new work culture and entrepreneurial spirit in the people. But it has to come gradually at a sustainable pace.

Priority Sector

Handicrafts and Handlooms

It is generally seen that in all the states of the N.E. Region, handicraft is a traditional practice. The handicraft items of the region have lot of demand even outside the N.E. Region. The NE people possess the requisite skill. But this household industry is being plagued by lack of marketing facility, absence of improved technology and dearth of capital. In many cases we observe the penetration of middleman between the producers and the market. As a result the profit generated from the product also do not reach the actual producers. It has negative effect on the zeal of the actual producers too.

In Assam *muga* and *endi* cloth are produced in many households. But here also the technology involved is obsolete. Considering the fact that *muga* and *endi* cloths are produced only in Assam in the whole world. Assam could have played a monopoly role in *muga* and *endi* products. But traditional production process along with old technology is halting the process of development of this industry.

Same situation applies to many traditional household industries like brass-metal, ivory craft and so on which are facing extinction due to lack of modern technology and marketing facilities.

This sector therefore, needs immediate attention and encouragement.

Horticulture, floriculture, fisheries, animal husbandry are other sectors which should be developed on priority.

In short both Agriculture and Horticulture industries possess potentialities and do not need high technology. The geographical climate i.e. rain and soil of the region is also suitable. Secondly the fishery potentiality in the region is largely untapped specially in Assam, where there are innumerable rivers and rivulets. The fishery industry reveals high economic potential. It is an irony at Assam and the whole N.E. Region is a fish importing zone. Development of these industries will not act as a cultural stock to the people of NE.

Development of Ancillaries

Assam and couple of other N.E. states like Arunachal Pradesh and Nagaland have vast resources of crude oil. Besides there are three refineries in Assam. But there is hardly any industry based on petroleum or its by-product like gas, paraffin etc. Examples may be given of a good number of industries based on petroleum by-products.

We intend to contend that small scale industries based on petroleum by-product would be able to change the entire economy of the region to a great extent. Therefore the area should be identified on priority basis.

Experienced Organisation can be entrusted plans, train entrepreneurs, building their leadership/management skills.

Agriculture

It is not to be reiterated that agriculture must serve as the basis for the designed development to take off considering its preponderance in the economic life of the people. But agriculture has to be turned into a productive industry if its economic viability in the long run is to be sustained. Experience of the developed countries demonstrate that the factors that contribute to high agricultural productivity were (1) mechanisation, (2) use of fertilizer, (3) bio-technology, (4) land management and tissue culture, (5) water management.

The last two among others have high prospects for increasing agricultural productivity of the N.E. Region. In fact growth dynamism demands that for agriculture both these should receive top priority which is yet to be experienced in the N.E. Region.

Development of Infrastructure

The two most important infrastructural facility namely transport and power must be developed within a short time frame. Water transport also should be given due importance in this regard. River transport in a big way can boost the economy by reducing the transport cost to a considerable extent. This is more applicable in case of Assam as the river Brahmaputra flows through out the State.

Power

It can easily be contended that the precarious power situation of the N.E. Region is a very significant bottleneck.

In view of enormous water resources in the region, scientific water management in the region will provide answer to several problems. With this objective, multipurpose hydel projects can be initiated which will bring forth substantial benefit to the region from power generation, flood control, irrigation and water transport. Hydro-electric projects can be instituted even at micro levels in remote areas.

Conclusion

After giving a outline of a development model for the N.E. Region we want to contend that as the region is marked by a plurality of ethnic, religious and linguistic groups who are again at different levels of development, therefore such model must devise policies to avoid creating more division among the people.

Uneven development would automatically give rise to antagonistic relationship between different communities i.e. economic disparities may take communal form which will push the region to the vicious cycle of political uncertainity which we are experiencing till now. It is but natural that all these people are not equally adapt in responding to the process of development. Therefore, planned human resource development must be undertaken so that various groups of people can equally participate in the development process. It will wither away the scepticism and instill confidence in them.

Moreover there are many traditional institutions among the tribal communities which are engaged in productive, religious and juridical activities within the respective communities. The strength of these traditional institutions should be utilised whenever possible. Their special capacity lies in mobilising collectively for productive purpose. In many areas even in Assam, these institutions are seen to be mobilising people in counstructing roads, canals for irrigation, embankments etc. This collective approach can be described as a tribal legacy. This may be one reason why in the N.E. Region individual entrepreneurial spirit is not very encouraging specially among the tribal communities. But instead of treating it as a negative aspect in orthodox manner and attempting to liquidate the same, developmental strategies should regard the collective undertakings as a strong point and incorporate it within the scheme of things.

17

SYNOPSIS: GRASS-ROOT ENTREPRENEURSHIP

— T. Cajee

It is indeed gratifying that NEICSSR is devoting this Seminar to the study of a question that has intrigued so many people, especially since the re-organisation of the North-East with many new States some twenty-five years ago. Visitors often ask why there is so little industry in the North-East and why of the little in evidence, the local indigenous people are so conspicuous by their absence. Yet, as many foreign tourists observed when they saw the so called "bazaar jeeps", till recently of World War II vintage, the indigenous people are "born technicians" who could maintain fifty-year old vehicles in perfect working order. Many ask how in a city where foreign missions have poured in experts from Europe with a very latest in Western technology for over a hundred years to keep the local youth abreast of what is happening in the field of technology in Europe, and with a vast reserve of trained manpower, there has been so little application of that knowledge in actual practice. Tourists, visitors and even local people ask why this is so. Last year even an IDBI team also asked why and how in an educated population, with wide acceptance of Westernisation and a high status for women, there is hardly any industrialisation in our own capital city of Shillong.

Social scientists and cultural anthropologists may be able to throw some light on the cultural and social issues involved. Living in the North-East as we do, in transitional indigenous societies, with the local indigenous cultures battling on two fronts; both with the mainstream national culture as well as with the technological Western culture, it would be interesting to explore how the so called "cultural bar" or "cultural divide" is working in indigenous societies to obstruct the spread of Western technology and thereby the process of development. Another interesting aspect would be the effect of the cultural struggle on the process of development. Does the deep seated cultural conflict develop an inertia in which development suffers as a result. To quote an example, Bhattacharya (in "Bureaucracy and Development in Meghalaya") found that cultural conflict as reflected in the bureaucracy in that "outsiders" posted in indigenous cultures as well as divisions among local bureaucrats into pro-modernist and conservative elements reflect the cultural conflict resulting in serious setback to the machinery's ability to act firmly or quickly.

Another interesting aspect is the cultural background of the local societies in the North-East. Does the local culture support the idea of entrepreneurship. David MacLeland, a Harvard psychologist (in the "Achieving Society") has dwelt upon the deep connection between the ways an individual hopes to develop personally and the economic resilience which the entire culture displays. Some cultures encourages their members to struggle hard to achieve success in spite of all odds i.e. they encourage the spirit of entrepreneurship while others are fatalistic and do not at all encourage the development of such qualities. In the early years of State hood there was a great amount of discussion on the disadvantages which an entrepreneur faces in the North-East situated as we are away from the centres of marketing in the Metro cities and the national mainstream. But even after an attempt at making a "level playing field" in the way of a subsidy by the Central Government on the transport of raw materials and finished goods between Siliguri and the entrepreneur's factory in the North-East. There has been little response from the indigenous people. It is indeed surprising that in spite of Thomas A. Edison's fame, even U.S. culture does not encourage the individual entrepreneur. Like their American counterparts, our own prestigious graduates from the Indian Institutes of Technology/Management (IITs/IIMs) rarely turned entrepreneurs as inventors were regarded as low prestige, there were no guarantees and they were outside normal channels by nature. Their image as persons creating gadgets in garages was not a model for yuppies who preferred risk-free well paid jobs.

Shirley Pessler, a University of Standord researcher found that in recent years American culture turned receptive to Computer entrepreneurs. Young men building gadgets in garages quickly turned millionaires and soon Silicon Valley had almost twelve thousand millionaires. Famous names like Mewlett and Packard, Steve Jobs and Bill Gates all became 'crorepatis' in record time. But U.S. models did not affect our own North-East. Even the delegations of young millionaires in their thirties under the banner of "Businessmen for Christ" visited the Metros only (Delhi, Bombay, Calcutta, Madras and Bangalore) to inclulcate entrepreneurial values among youth but did not reach our distant homeland. A. Gupta (in "Indian Entrepreneurial Culture") found that entrepreneurs like the Tatas were effective role models in the Metros where a well established corporate culture exists but had no such effect in rural areas. Perhaps also in the North-East where corporate culture is unknown outside Assam.

A. Kanitkar (in "Grass-root Entrepreneurs") found that micro industries were isolated from the formal sector. On the media, a Chamber of Indian Industry (CII) spokesman said that only ten per cent of the small industrial units were industrial units in the real sense of the word as the remaining 90 per cent were merely husband-wife teams on self employment ventures. It is these micro units which have a great future in Shillong. In Kanitkar's study, 86 units were covered with an average investment of Rs. 16,000 and ranging from only Rs. 5,000 to Rs 70,000 which an ex-serviceman got as a rehabilitation loan to start a Xerox copying shop. He found that one-third of the units were self-employed but the rest had become employers with an average of three employees each. The units started by the new entrepreneurs ranging from tea shops and *dhabas* to bangle shops, pot shops, farm equipment and transport business are all well known in Shillong and are not expected to arract criticism. Kanitkar found that the small capital required was raised within the family circle by the wfe selling her jewellery or as in the case of Uttam Biswas of West Bengal by a loan of Rs. 7,000 from his uncle who happened to hear of the project. Krishnan Kutty of Kerala was an ex-serviceman who was one of the exceptional cases of a formal loan. By and large, the new entrepreneurs were unaware of Bank schemes and were wary of formal banking centres. Outside their own family circle they looked to the local money-lender for financing the shortfall in capital.

Gupta and Kanitkar found that Western cultural values do not apply in our different culture. Entrepreneurs in the advanced West are motivated by the desire of being their own boss, job satisfaction etc. while in India the grass-root entrepreneurship venture is "the last resort of the desperate unemployed." An experiment in inculcating entrepreneurship in the Ranchi area of Chota Nagpur some years back among the indigenous people involved an umbrella organisation to support the new entrepreneurs in their 'teething problems' as well as to exert peer pressure in repayment of Rs. 5,000 loan. A novel and very successful initiative was taken by a Harvard trained economist, Dr. M. Yunus who found that formal Western-type solutions did not suit the economic problems in Bangla Desh. As the United Nations' recent report disclosed, women and children composed as much as 70 per cent of the 2.3 billion people living below the poverty line world-wide. Dr. Yunus found that women in the rural areas needed a tiny amount of capital to raise their standard of living and improve the food nutrition of their children. The women had their own schemes for micro projects such as raising poultry and eggs, weaving, making pottery etc. Dr. Yunus was persuaded to lend Taka 1,000 (Bangla Desh) i.e. about 30 Dollars U.S. to village woman, the repayment of which was to be made through a local pan shop-keeper, before returning to Dhaka. In this way was born the unique informal Banking system now called the Grameen Bank where the villagers themselves own the Bank through their own contributions to its capital and in turn borrowed funds from the Bank. In the Grameen Bank as well as Women's World Bank and similar ventures in South Asia, Bank credit is done on a group basis and not individually, thus utilising peer pressure for generating savings to contribute to the bank as well as for repayment of borrowings. Last year the Chairman, Central Social Welfare Board evinced interest in starting an informal Bank in Shilllong. This would greatly facilitate credit to needy weaker sections, mostly women and thereby improve their standard of living, health and nutrition of their children.

Whatever may be the problems facing the entrepreneurial ventures in what CII spokesman call the "real" Small Scale Industries (SSI), there appear to be few in the Micro industries sector where projects are so familiar and are not likely to attract controversy. No one is likely to object to such familiar projects as a tea shop or *dhaba,* a poultry or duck farm, a pottery or weaving shop etc. Capital requirements are also within the capacity of the family or kinship circle, ranging as they do from Rs. 5,000 to an average of Rs. 16,000 (if we include the costlier Xerox shops) but the introduction of informal banking would definitely make capital formation easier and also sideline the local moneylender.

Meghalaya is still among the least urbanised States in India but United Nations projections show that at the turn of the century as much as half the world's population would live in the cities and by the middle of the century, about two-thirds of the global population would move to the cities. Following world trends, we may expect Meghalaya's cities like

Shillong will expand greatly in the next few decades. The German town-planner, Dr. Otto Koenigsburger, who planned Jamshedpur and Bhubaneshwar, conceived the idea of the city as a self-sufficient unit, both economically and socially, even extending to the city producing its own food. Micro units can, therefore, be said to have a great future in making Shillong a self-sufficient city.

Kanitkar has noted the problems faced by the micro entrepreneurs—the grass-root entreprises. These are the need for training in entrepreneurship to be included in the syllabus for ITIs and under TRYSEM. The other is the need of advisory services to help grass- root entrepreneurs to diversify as the market may be faced with overcrowding of too many similar units come up one after another in the same area. As the micro units are always short of cash, units supplying goods and services to Government Departments face acute hardship owing to the time taken to obtain payments. In Assam, an Act and rules have been introduced for ASIDC to make an immediate payment of 85 per cent leaving only 15 per cent to be collected from the buying Department. We may to our advantage follow Assam's lead in this matter.

A few years ago, Haimendorf on a visit to the North-East advised the people of Nagaland to step up productivity in the way of goods and services for export to the national and global mainstream in order to pay for the manufactured goods which the people now required in their new higher standard of living. Cable TV arrived in the North- East some five years back coinciding with the liberalisation and globalisation of the national economy. This has created a widespread desire for more income required to meet the requirements of the new consumerist society brought in by the Cable TV whose consumerist message influences all sections of society but most of all the younger generation. An indicator of this consumerist trend is the recent proliferation of archery (betting) shops and lottery counters in the capital, which many authorities (in the B.B.C. programmes "Can Tribal Cultures Survive?", September 1983) identify as the obvious route for many aspiring for a higher standard of living in a backward society where the lack of educational (professional) qualifications as well as avenues of high income employment poses constraints to the indigenous population. As consumerist pressures build up in society, there appears to be no alternative but to accept Haimendorf's advice to step up industrial activity in the "real" small scale sector. On the other hand, acute unemployment pressurises the people into "grass-root" micro industries.

18

SOCIOLOGICAL CONSTRAINTS IN DEVELOPMENT OF AGRO-INDUSTRIES IN NORTH-EASTERN REGION OF INDIA

— D.N. Chakravarty

In every human society culture plays a prominent role in shaping and maintaining the society. It is embodied in customs,traditions, thoughts and insitutions of the social group throughout the ages. In India village is the actual domestic, agrarian and socio-cultural arrangement within which the largest part of the people of the country lives. The culture of the village is its socio-economic arrangements like land ownership, caste and religious stratifications, customary and ritual practices. By and large, the attitudes and identity of the contemporary Indian people are still strongly rooted in tradition and myth, influenced by cultural and historical conditioning. But in this process as time passes, science and technology which emerged as material culture find it difficult to retain its equilibrium with the non-material culture, customs, values and norms that exist in the society. This cultural lag is much more prominent in tribal communities, particularly in the primitive and shifting cultivators than in the non-tribals in the NE region. Therefore, the social level of acceptance of developmental activities is still a major problem.

Even now the tribal and peasant societies of Assam and the neighbouring states are under the grip of black magic, witchcrafts, polytheism and other traditional beliefs, values and norms and these non-material and irrational cultures are the main hindrance in the development of agriculture and agro-based industries.

The underdevelopment of economy of NE region, despite its rich resource endowments, is a matter of serious concern, which calls for a thorough investigation with a view to identify the inhibiting factors. A number of factors which can be mentioned are historical, socio-cultural, psychological, economic, political besides the topographical and other physical factors, The sociological aspects of this region are intimately entangled with the economic aspects and all the economic persuits are controlled by sociological customs in a primitive society.

Industrial development in general and growth of small scale sector in particular has been tardy because of weak tradition of enterprise and inadequate entrepreneurial and managerial inputs.

Social customs also lead the character of agricultural holdings, scatteredness and fragmentation of which have reached a point that they jeopardise the efficiency of agriculture and make cultivation costly and management difficult.

Agriculture is the oldest and most elemental form of agro-based industries. The origin of this industry in the history of mankind has given rise to many speculations among the anthropological investigators. Our Vedic literatures are full of references to established agriculture. The plough found a most glorified place in our Epics. But as the economic motive of the rural people of NE region is largely dominated by social customs and traditions, the development programmes and reforms in agriculture have not yet been able to root out the fifth century socio-economic basement. The methods of cultivation are as primitive as ever particularly in remote areas of plains and hills. A large section of the cultivators are not using improved methods of cultivation due to various reasons including the unwillingness to part with the age old system. Rural indebtedness and small holdings are the effect of age old subsistence nature of farming influenced by social customs. The tragedy is not only poverty, backwardness and misery alone but also helplessness and despair that renders the rural problems so difficult.

Some of the social customs still prevalent by and large in plain areas of Assam include no ploughing practice in the afternoon part of the day, number of non-ploughing days as per astronomical norms, no ploughing by Brahmin community, no cultivation practice after Magh Bihu for so many months and passing of time visiting relatives, no aftercare of crops after transplanting and many such other practices as a part of substantive nature of farming. This self-sufficient self-content nature does not allow them to think of profit-making surplus and to go for any kind of agro-industries.

The paddy husk, rice bran and many other by-products from other crops are generally not utilized for any economic purpose except for few areas like mulching turmeric and ginger, as a source of fire and sometimes as a cooking material, but most of these practices are also gradually eliminated. Instead of burning or spoiling these byproducts can be utilized for a number of small scale agro-industries. In Kerala any part of a coconut tree is converted into a flourishing industry. But due to absence of entrepreneurship movement this has not developed to a large scale except in some pockets where people are conscious and could be motivated by development programmes.

Practice to let loose the cattle after Magh Bihu does not only destroy vegetation but cause heavy damage to the *rabi* crops and willing farmers cannot go for a second paddy crop. Erecting fencing is also costly. This type of social customs in NE region is peculiar in the country and cause reduction in total production.

The craze for easy money and the tendency to grow rich overnight is a new culture developed very recently in the NE region, which is detrimental to the cause of economic development. This tendency is rampant not only in Assam but also throughout the NE region. Young people aspire to become petty contractors, office material suppliers, rather than entrepreneurs. It is only by creating more entrepreneurs rather than creating more contractors or commission agents or political brokers that economic development can be pushed ahead.

In the society there are various practices that involve heavy expenditure in ceremonies and celebrations which cannot be igrnored. For observance of socio-religious festivals in tribal societies huge quantity of rice is used for processing rice bear for entertainment of guests which aggravate their poor economic conditions. Cash money of tribal people is also drained away in village market by unscrupulous gamblers and traders of cheap fancy goods.

In the Karbi society a poor family which can hardly arrange two square meals a day can go to well-to-do Karbi family of the same village and have daily share of food till the stock of food of the second family is exhausted. Such a social system rather retards the progress by making people dependent and lethargic although social value of such a system is of very high order.

The system of Zeme Nagas of NC Hills to move all the young members of a village along with the married girl of their village and work in the *Jhum* land of her husband in another village for one season and in return getting only a pot of rice and a pig, has become an unavoidable social obligation but without any economic gain for the youths. Such social customs retard economic development of the family as well as of the community.

The shifting cultivation in the hills have a peculiar system of shifting the village to a new *Jhum* site. If the medicine man declares that a particular village is haunted by evil spirits, that village is shifted to a new site under the leadership of Gaonbura. As the village sites are not permanent, development works of permanent nature cannot be undertaken. This system of communal ownership of land prevent any capital investment of permanent improvement of land and is detrimental to development of agro-industry. In *Jhuming* land is the only factor in collaboration with labour that produces the output. There is practically little or no use of capital in agriculture operations of such an economy.

In Karbi Anglong the Karbis in the plain areas have a system of allowing their lands to be cultivated by non-tribals for a certain period on advance payment (Pikas system). In a sample survey it was revealed that 18.8 per cent of Karbi families having 145 hectares of land 26.4 per cent are given as Pikas and 66.7 per cent as *adhi* totalling 93.1 per cent. It has become difficult to remove this social system, because generally there is no written document and Pikas fearing detection declare as *Kamlas*, *Adhiars* or share croppers. This system is injurious for a Karbi family as it hardly gets sufficient money and remain half-starved.

Before 1926, the economy of Assam was partly feudal and partly tribal. In plains Ahom rulers had the ownership of all lands and in hills ownership of land belong to the community. The community ownership of land in the hills provided little incentive to the cultivators to produce surplus, since each village was self-sufficient having minimal inter-village exchange relationship. Profit making motive in economic dealings being generally absent which is replaced by sense of mutual obligations, sharing and solidarity. In plains agriculture was characterised by and large, by subsistence production. Many of the characteristics of tribal economy such as subsistence production, absence of surplus, predominance of food production, strong community solidarity, absence of profit motive in economic dealings were present in plains, some of which are present till today. This was why the caste barrier are not so rigid in Assam. The remoteness of the entire NE region from the main body of the country coupled with transport and communication difficulties was responsible for retaining the peasant and tribal characteristics of the regional economy.

The industrial development after British rule like tea plantation, oil refineries, coal mining, plywood factory, paper mill did not alter predominant rural culture of the society, because of very little linkage with regional economy in terms of employment, reinvestment of profit in other sectors etc. The recruited clerical staff from Bengal in tea gardens used to remit whatever savings they had made and labourers could hardly make any savings. The entire profit from tea industry was repatriated home. So Assam became a classic example for a dual economy with little interaction between the two sectors—modern and traditional. After Independence Assam and neighbouring states inherited the British legacy of dual economy as influenced by social system. So there was a lack of transition of larger sections of the regional economy from primitive to capitalist and a class of enterprising persons with sufficient surplus funds in hand did not emerge to grab the few opportunities thrown open after Independence.

The existing social system with its own cultural norms and values, ethics and customs prevalent amongst the rural people, particularly in the tribal areas, are not conducive to savings and investments. Whatever savings might be having, it is not further invested for further prduction. Savings enhance the prestige and social status of tribal family in the eyes of the community and lavish entertainment of feast to the community members enhance the social image. But this drains the savings in non-productive or consumption oriented activities which actually negates economic development.

In Assam there are about 25 lakhs of tribals (1/6 in hills) 95 per cent of whom are agriculturists but majority of them are agricultural labourers. Out of about 18 lakh hectares of winter rice area about half of which are cultivated by tribals most of whom are agricultural labourers or *adhiars*. The tribals belong to the poorest strata of the society who are having average holding size below 2 hectares. One cannot think of development of agro-based industries with such a occupational hazard. Once tribals of Assam were good sericulturists and 85 to 90 thousand tribal families were connected with sericultural activities. This flourishing industry is now gradually diminishing. Adoption of various traditional persuits like piggery, poultry, brewing etc. are gradually diminishing due to lack of adequate infrastructure and having no knowledge to keep pace with time.

However, the level of socio-economic development differ from region to region on the basis of which the tribals of NE India are divided into primitive, shifting cultivators, communities changed to settled agriculture and communities living in the vicinity of towns. Improvement in the socio-economic status of the first two followed by the third one is the main concern. Perhaps by providing basic facilities and only local or specially trained officers may persuade them for any kind of development.

In tribal areas resources are mostly owned by the community and so the decision for use of resources is made by community under the leadership of Gaonbura. Though reasonably well balanced the tribal economy is basically a subsistence economy. It spreads over forestry, horticulture, animal husbandry, poultry, piggery, brewing and some staple crops. Forests are important part of tribal life. They get food, fodder, fuel, manure, timber and oil from forests. The skill in tribals, which are not highly specialised and sophisticated, but being developed over centuries, are suitable to particular environment in which they live, over a wide spectrum, such as, hunting, weaving, basket making, fruit picking, agriculture etc. and given the traditional skill endowment, the tribals are slow in accepting new skills. Most of the tribals having egalitarian ethos, show great concern for the community, attach great importance to their traditional values, morals and institutions. Because of these sociological aspects individual oriented development programmes are not appreciated and desired impact cannot be achieved. Moreover, inadequate modern institutional infrastructure are generally not attuned to specific local situation. The fertile lands are not in possession of tribals. Most of them occupy undulating, sloping and rocky areas where only low value crops or forest can be grown. These tribals resort to shifting cultivation because it is the only appropriate method that can be used under such adverse topographical condition and due to non-availability of other suitable methods within their economic means.

However, it is not always the sociological constraints that hinder the progress of NE region. Though development programmes have been spread over both plain and hill areas, absence of proper infrastructure like market, communication etc. most of the tribals remain deprived of due price for produce. Non-availability of easy finance for purchase of inputs compell the tribals to approach money lenders or businessmen and are exploited. Total failure of the co-operatives in tribal areas is unfortunate.

Surplus generated in agriculture, particularly in plain areas, has not been negligible. Even then the process of reutilizing the surplus for profit making enterprise has not taken place generally due to lack of proper knowledge, guidance, training and encouragement. As a result there is transfer of capital from rural sector and rural labourers are migrating to the already congested urban areas. Statistics shows that labour engaged in agriculture and allied works in the country was 83 per cent male and 89 per cent female in 1973 which is reduced to 73 per cent male and 84 per cent female in 1988 due to migration to service and industrial sectors in urban areas.

As the population increased in the plains and in the towns of hill areas environmental degradation assumed an alarming situation in many places it has passed the carrying capacity of the environment.

It is apparent that primitive agriculture alone is entirely inadequate for sustenance of the rural people and revival of village industries for the purpose of providing additional employment and income for them is essential. For example, weaving has been a special agri-based industry for NE region but it has faced competition of synthetic and mill products. There is a loss of equilibrium of occupations in the economic organization of the villages.

There are ample scopes foı developing agro-based cottage industries in NE region. The state of affairs are still deplorable in the sense that no efficient organization is developed to suitably assemble available resources and encourage the local people to come out from age old sociological tangle to consider agriculture as a profession and develop agro-based industries to improve their economic condition.

The economy of NE region being predominantly rural, the overall development is very heavily dependent on rural development. However, this is entirely in the hands of the bureaucrats. The rural people in general are yet to be motivated well and the non-involvement of the people themselves or their grass-root level institution in the development process amount to a negation of development. These institutions like GS and GP have to be vitalised and involved in the rural development programmes. These are the proper institutions which can work for removal of sociological and religious dogma from the society. These hidden constraints demand more attention.

The socio-political aspects are so important that to a certain extent the problem of why some areas have remained underdeveloped might be answered by merely putting that they lack socio-political prerequisites for development.

In the present context education should have been enterprise-oriented rather than white colour job-oriented. The conventional education that is being imparted in our churches, mosques, schools, colleges and universities does not necessarily provide the types of skills and competence required for a developed economy in modern agricultural and industrial sectors. We have also not effectively attempted to revive the talent potential of the traditional cottage industries through appropriate training of artisans and proper research for the same. To produce right type of manpower for small industries including agro-industries separate institutions in this area or introduction of such courses in polytechnics/higher secondary schools of the region are necessary. Recent introduction of some relevant courses including agriculture and animal husbandry and some technical courses in higher secondary level of Assam is a welcome step. Agricultural universities and related institutions may think of introducing optional courses on small-scale agro-industries with small units as models by establishing a linkage with related industries.

Development is both material and spiritual. It is worth examining the continuity between tradition, myth and reality. A better understanding of the power of tradition and its hold on the society's collective consciousness is required. The change agents must understand the psychological hold of tradition on the people and try to influence them continuously and gradually.

For a holistic approach and to get from the people the conscious participation we must utilize our natural resources judiciously without hampering the eco-system to provide scope for a job-led economic growth strategy through a system approach in farming on mutually reinforcing blend of farm and off-farm enterprises. All these will call for a proper planning as per agro-ecological situation, topographical position, catchment area, demographic pattern, sociological status etc. with national, regional and state level policies. For this adequate investments in rural techno-infrastructure alongwith proper linkage with the production-marketing-consumption chain will have to be established.

If the technologies are relevant, economically viable and conform to the farmer's need and aspiration it is sure to click. Once the farmers accept the technology an effective approach would be to locate possible agro-industries for processing the output, byproducts or surplus into more value-added products, reducing the net wastage and increasing profit margin to the farmers. The agro-industries should be located in rural areas where production of particular raw material is highest to ensure remunerative price to the farmers. In the development process this point needs no over emphasis.

It must be admitted that we have failed miserably to develop, mobilize and deploy our human resources in proper way because we are facing a serious crisis of leadership and character. The idealism, value-base and inspiring vision as driving force of our motion are missing in many areas and are being occupied by unrestrained pursuit of parochial privileges and sectional interests.

Only through our own collective energy, intelligence, abilities, value consciousness and vision and also dedication we can shape our society to solve our internal problems and move forward .owards a leading position in the arena of wider competition.

19

COMMUNITY AND ECONOMIC DEVELOPMENT IN ASSAM: THE EXPERIENCE OF THE 1980s

— Samir Kumar Das

The isolation of the local economies in the North-East is now rapidly breaking down as they are increasingly being inserted into the burgeoning network of global economy. The process has received a new fillip as a result of the new economic reforms vigorously pursued since 1991 in India. Three major objectives of these reforms have been (a) to neutralise the regime of control over both incoming and outgoing investments; (b) to reduce the authority of the state in directing, regulating and coordinating the economy and (c) to drastically curtail the scope of state's interference by imposing stringent limits on on-schedule budget deficits.[1] All these obejctives hinge on the assumption that an economy left to itself, that is to say, market forces and untrammelled by state's interference can perform better than the one under its strict supervision.

While globalization is the current trend of the Indian economy there is no denying the fact that the phenomenon of ethnic assertiveness has also grown in both intensity and extensity over the recent years. This is evident not only from the quantitative increase in ethnic killings and losses of private and public property but also from certain disconcerting trends of highly qualitative importance. If Ted Robert Gurr is to be believed, for the 1945-1989 period, more than 200 groups "openly resisted the terms of their incorporation in states, controlled by other groups. Their grievances about discrimination and threats to group identity . . . motivated hundreds of protest movements".[2] One wonders whether Gurr has taken the north-eastern India into his consideration: The number would surely then be higher than what his estimate says. Indeed, there is reason to think that ethnic killings since 1971 have acquired a mass and anomic character.[3] Besides, there are two complementary trends—noticeable in recent years which in their combination, have made any easy solution to the problem of ethnic assertiveness almost impossible: First, the growing tide of ethnic assertiveness has also resulted in a considerable erosion of the trust reposed on the state as the ultimate arbitrating agency for resolving inter-ethnic conflicts.[4] it is true that most of the ethnic communities are up in arms with each other. But, they would, with minor exceptions however look upon the Indian state as the ultimate agency vested with the responsibility of resolving their conflicts. The credibility of the Indian state was never so seriously at stake before. Corresponding to the erosion of the credibility of the Indian state, ethnic assertiveness has acquired in recent years, what may be called, a new legitimacy. The fight for one's community and if necessary, to lay down one's life at the altar of the community are the noblest of all virtues. There is in fact no other virtue--higher and nobler than this. We would do well to pause here a bit and try to explain how community prevails over its individual members in situations of ethnic assertiveness. It is for instance, argued particularly by the Marxists that the community prevails over its individual members—especially the subaltern sections of it, because its elite has successfully drilled it (the community) into their consciousness from without for achieving its essentially narrow and selfish ends. The process is so successful that the individual is ready to commit what in Social Theory is known as, 'altruistic suicide', that is to say, suicide in the larger interest of the community. It is of course foolish to discard such a possibility. But this view exaggerates not only the ability of the elite to do so given that it is willing to do it, but also its existence as a distinct entity--differentiated from the subalterns including the workers and peasants who constitute the bulk of the community.[5] When differentiation is not too sharp to warrant such a possibility it is reasonable to assume that the individual members within the given community will 'resemble' each other. The 'resemblance' may be so perfect that each individual member tends to be an illustration of what Emile Durkheim would prefer to call, 'psychological type' of society.

> . . . under these conditions all members of the group are not only individually attracted to one another because they resemble one another, but they are also linked to what is the condition for the existence of this collective type, that is, to the society that they form by coming together. Not only do fellow-citizens like one another, seeking one another out in preference to foreigners, but they love their country. They wish for it what they would wish for themselves, they care that it should be lasting and prosperous, because without it a whole area of their psychological life would fail to function smoothly.[6]

When the individual is merely an illustration of this 'collective' or 'psychological type of society', any infringement of this 'type' is taken to be an infringement of her/himself. She/he has no existence apart from her/his community. What is She/he other than the community? Death for the sake of community becomes the other name of self-preservation. Thus, to cite an instance, Asom Sahitya Sabha, the supreme literary body of Assam providing much of the intellectual leadership to the movement, exhorted on 'the Assamese' to prepare for 'supreme sacrifice' way back in 1980: ". . . the Assamese as a race (perhaps a milapproprism, SKD) . . . have a right to survive with dignity and self-respect and not as second-class citizens. They also have a right to place under the sun that they can call their homeland. This they are determined to preserve even with supreme sacrifice."[7] The phenomenon of ethnic assertiveness has acquired a new legitimacy in the Durkheimian sense of the term.

The problem is that the globalization of Indian economy is incompatible with the phenomenon of ethnic assertiveness recently experienced in different parts of India--especially in the North-East: First, ethnic assertiveness presupposes that the scope of the economy remains confined to the locality supposed to be the homeland of the asserting ethnic community. Ethnic assertiveness in most cases, is expressed through autarkic demands, that is, demands for 'excluding others from the majority economy, polity and society'.[8] On the other hand, the package of economic reforms facilitating globalization is centred on the assumption that the economy can perform better if it becomes an integral part of the global economic network. An economy remaining confined to the bounds of locality is deprived of many of the strategic advantages that the global economic network confers on itself. Secondly, it would however be wrong to suggest that an economy remaining confined to the bounds of locality is unaware of these strategic advantages. But the point is that it operates according to an axial principle that is at variance with the one governing the operation of a globally-linked network. Their respective axial principles are divergent. A globally-linked economy for instance, holds that higher productivity and even a more equitable distribution of economic resources are possible under present conditions, only when the economy gets integrated into the global economic network. An ethnic community that asserts itself, on the other hand, argues that since there is no value higher and nobler than its survival as a distinct and autonomous body and since group autarky is central to its survival as such, it prefers its survival to higher productivity and a more equitable distribution of economic resources. When globalization in spite of its many strategic advantages is considered to be detrimental to its survival as a distinct and autonomous community it trades them off for the latter. As Hardin observes: ". . . linguistic groups may strive to be more broadly autarkic than many other kinds of social groups. They have to be merely in order to sustain their communities. But the costs of social autarky, when the autarky includes economic separatism as well as linguistic and social separation, can be massive."[9] As we have said, no cost is as 'massive' when the very survival of the community is put at stake. Thirdly, globalization and ethnic assertiveness cannot go hand in hand for their operations leave mutually adverse impact. First, when an ethnic community asserts itself, it is in opposition to another community that its assertion acquires a social character. Viewed in this light, ethnic assertion is invariably oppositional by nature. But that a community is opposed to another does not necessarily mean that the opposition breaks into violent conflicts and thereby produces law-and-order problems. These are often held to be responsible for a sudden decline not only in incoming investments but also prevailing rate of investments. However, it must be admitted that the estimates concerning the panicked flight of capital appear to be exaggerated.[10] It seems that the industrialists and businessmen are slowly learning how to live with such violent conflicts and law-and-order problems in the region. In Anthropological terms, this situation is called, 'violent normalcy'. Secondly, forces of globalization demand that the state's regime of control established since 1947 with remarkable fluctuations of course, is reduced to the absolute minimum--if not, completely neutralised. It is believed that the market forces can serve as a great balancer --a role that was hitherto assigned to the state. But, market forces--especially their unfettered nature requires a kind of social relationship that may not coincide with the ones that ethnic communities have set for themselves, and choose to be guided by. We may say that when there is a conflict between market-required social relationships and ethnically-preferred social relationships, there is always a tendency on the part of the people to follow the second. If I am a seller in this age of globalization, I cannot discriminate between an Indian and a Pakistani buyer—let alone, a Bengali and an Assamese on nationality grounds, provided they are ready to pay the price at which I am willing to sell the product. Ethnic discrimination in transactional relationships may take on any of the three forms: (a) refusal to sell goods and services to people belonging to an alien ethnic community; (b) refusal to buy goods and services from people belonging to an alien community; (c) manipulating prices for either buying or selling in cases where members of an alien community are involved in the transactions. Thus, it may be that I sell goods and services to an alien at a price higher—sometimes forbiddingly so, than what I might have charged from the members of my community. Ethnically-specific pricing is an instance of how supposedly unfettered market relationships characteristic of globalization are vitiated, violated and turned aside.

Economic discriminations bear out two-fold impact on us: On the one hand, even globalization requires state regulation especially in these matters in a country like ours. State regulation of this nature does not soring from the imperative of correcting economic imbalances that is to say, imbalances intrinsic to the economy as it did during the era of welfarism, but from the imperative of keeping social constraints at bay. But once again the state faces a dilemma in this regard. To the extent it starts regulating the intrusion of social constraints, to that extent it allienates the asserting community/ies that do/es the discrimination. State's credibility and economic development through globalization do not go hand in hand. There are scholars like, Jyotirindra Das Gupta who would argue that state's credibility defined as its ability to elicit obdience from its citizens and economic development and positively correlated in the sense that the more there is economic development, the higher the state's credibility will be. In fact, Das Gupta's notion of 'functional authority' is one in which the authority of the state depends on the functions it performs for ensuring economic development.[11] In a region like the North-East, such assumptions have to be taken with not just a pinch but a sackful of salt. Economic development *per se* may not add to state's credibility. It may in fact be counter-productive. Secondly,

Ferdinand Tönnies once made fundamental distinction between transactional relationships characteristic of *Gesselschaft* and non-transactional relationships characteristic of community or *Gemeinschaft*. Ethnic relationships, according to him, are restricted to the community implying thereby that they do not touch upon the society's transactional, market relationships.[12] In fact, ethnic politics takes a serious turn as a result of the intrusion of ethnic relationships on the sphere of economic transactions. Ethnicity becomes a problem inscfar as it extends itself beyond its realm, into the so-called non-ethnic sphere of market.

Ethnicity hence, is not the anti-thesis of market relationships. It is only when ethnicity has gained a political currency and prevails over other non-ethnic idioms (like, class, gender etc.) of social interactions, it is seen to make preferences for certain types of social relationships including market relationships even at the cost of economic efficiency. The exact cost, however, is far less easy to calculate. For one thing, any attempt at calculating economic efficiency is always a counterfactual exercise as it presupposes the question of what it could have been had there been no ethnically-preferred market relationships believed to be constraining it. For another, it also delves into the question of value. If ethnically-preferred market relationships or what we call, autarky are central to the survival of an ethnic community as a distinct and autonomous entity then sacrificing economic efficiency may be gleefully accepted as its necessary cost. The argument against smaller states on grounds of economic inefficiency loses much of its weight on this count. What our protagonists of globalization interpret as 'constaint' may be viewed as a necessary cost by the members of an ethnic community.

From the above exercise it is apparent that any talk of globalization in its pure and unadulterated form is bound to be vacuous. Instead, it would be more meaningful to look into the market relationships in so far as they are affected by the phenomenon of ethnic assertiveness. How are market relationships affected by inter-ethnic relationships? This calls for a look into what we call, ethnically constituted market in North-East India. We will confine ourselves to only one illustration of this market—how it gets ethnicized as result of an almost incessant influx of outsiders/foreigners who are ethnically divergent from the natives of the region. In order to illustrate the point, it draws heavily from the experience of Assam during the 1980s. The prevalent analyses of ethnically constituted market portray what we call, a simple model. At the end we have made a plea for outlining a more complex model.

The simple model harps on two major premises: On the one hand, the factors contributing to large-scale migration and displacement especially of the labouring people are taken to be *compelling* in the sense that neither the sending country/region nor the receiving one is seen to do anything to stop it. Thus, it is argued that the production process in all the South Asian countries is such that it has a tendency of displacing them. As a commentator has recently pointed out:

> . . . the pattern of homelessness, displacement, eviction and migration of the rural poor is uniform in South Asia. The pervasiveness of structural adjustment programme in countries of South Asia is the backdrop against which the displacements and migration continue apace. Pakistan, Bangladesh, India, Sri Lanka—all these countries are witnessing frantic construction of dams, thermal plants, tourist resorts, transport and cargo terminals. Waterbodies are facing pressures from tourism or industrial expansion. Within India the Narmada project is not alone in creating uncertainty in the lives of people. Similar plans are afoot elsewhere threatening or causing displacements.[13]

In simple terms, the roots of displacement and migration including trans-border migration are to be located in the very model of economic development that the South Asian countries have been following since the beginning of 1990s. On the other hand, it is true that in the receiving countries/regions, migrants are most unwelcome. Yet, they do not or cannot do anything to stop the alarming inflow. The experience of Asom Gana Parishad during 1985-90 is a case in point. While none of the estimates during the Assam movement (1979-85) has put the figure of illegally settled foreigners below 8 lakh and the party came to power with the promise of detecting the foreigners, deleting their names from electoral rolls and deporting them, the actual number of deportees during 1985-88 was not more than 170.[14] It is true that the party leadership has accused all the preceding governments of acting in collusion with the vested interests of the foreigners. Since they acted as captive vote banks politicians showed little interest in evicting them. But it is hard to believe that the party might be accused of doing the same. Whatever be the reason, the fact is that even a regional party finds it difficult if not impossible, to stop the alarming influx or to actually deport the already settled foreigners. On the other hand, that nothing is done either to stop the influx or to deport the already settled foreigners does not mean however that they are not unwelcome in the receiving region or country for they pose a threat to its economy, society and polity. The extent of the threat will determine the nature of the response. A more acute threat will obviously require a preparation for what Asom Sahitya Sabha calls, 'supreme sacrifice'. But a less acute threat is likely to elicit a more modest and mellower response. In fact, the simple model is simple because it establishes a direct and unmediated relationship between the threat and response. As Apurba Baruah in one of his papers concluded: "It is . . . clear that the fear of the 'outsiders' noticed in Assam today is the result of bitter conflicts over jobs, land and cultural hegemony."[15]

The simple model of ethnicized market outlined above has to be taken with utmost care in a region like, the North-East where the ethnic heterogeneity and its articulation into the market relations and vice versa are too complex to be accommodated into the simple model. It is not possible to offer a detailed critique of the simple model. But we may restrict ourselves to an analysis of only two premises that make the situation highly complex: First, the autarkic demands and the movement inspired by them are supposed to be detrimental to the evolution of a national market—let alone a global market.[16] Neo-Institutionalists under the leadership of Mancor Olson point to the need for obliterating autarky to make the way for globalization. Hardin also seems to be at one with the Neo-Institutionalists when he says that "there is no reason for opposition to social autarky for groups whose separation from the larger society has no negative effect on the larger economy or on the economic prospects of other groups." But what about those groups that have a higher 'negative effect'? Do they have to cease to be what they actually are? The simple model of the Neo-Institutionalists certainly underestimates the role of ethnic communities in responding—more often than not negatively, to the globalizing measures undertaken in the larger society. It has to be empahsized that since autarky is a means of establishing and maintaining community identity, it is unlikely that the community will be a pliant observer of those measures that seek to erode it. Or may we say that even if they do so, the agencies doing it will suffer from a tremendous credibility gap. The challenge in the North-East is however to ensure economic development without eroding the community identity in a way that prompts negative responses from it.

Secondly, the simple model assumes that since the immigrant poses a threat to the identity of the Assamese, he becomes a target of attack.

The immigrant and the Assamese are always viewed in oppositional terms. Such a simple oppositional view hides more than what it reveals. In fact, one has to keep in mind that the category of immigrants settled in Assam is not a compact and homogeneous one. For instance, there was always a perceptible difference between the Bengali immigrants and the non-Bengali ones—nonetheless in a minority. The threat from the non-Bengali immigrants was predominantly of economic nature while that from the Bengali immigrants—especially Bengali Hindus was predominantly of cultural nature. It is argued that an immigrant does not automatically become a target of attack provided he is assimilated into the Assamese mainstream. The more the immigrant is culturally assimilated, the less the possibility of his being the target of attack. But what about the Bengali-speaking Bangladeshi Muslims who have been culturally assimilated by way of returning Assamese as their mother tongue in several consecutive Census-operations? In an apparent sense, there was no reason why they should be attacked. In the case of Assam, it may be pointed out that the immigrant becomes a target of attack in those cases where the possibility of resistance is the least and the possibility of resistance is least when (a) the immigrants are small in number and live in isolation. Thus it is no wonder that the Bengali-speaking people of the Barak Valley have been far less the target of attack than their brethren in the Brahmaputra Valley; (b) they are not economically dominant. The Marwaris for instance have monopolized the business and trading sector. But the Assam Movement of 1979-85 have by and large spared them; (c) they represent—not the 'high culture' but what in Social Theory is called, 'mass culture'. Thus, it is not without reason that the Bengali Muslims and Santhals become the easy target of attack in the Bodo-inhabited areas of Kokrajhar.

In conclusion, we may say that it does not make much sense to regard community as a 'constraint' to be done away with to make the way for globalization. Whenever such constraints are forcibly sought to be done away with, they have provoked 'negative responses' from the concerned community. The solution perhaps lies initiating community-sensitive economic development.

REFERENCES

1. For a lucid appraisal of these reforms, see, Jagdish Bhagwati, 'India's Economic Strides' in *The American Enterprise*, March-April 1994, pp. 55-61.

2. Ted Robert Gurr, *Minorities at Risk* (Washington D.C.: US Institute of Peace Press, 1993), p. 92.
3. See, Samir Kumar Das, 'Bichchhinnatar Katha: Uttar-Purba Bharat-barsha' (*in Bengali*), in *Nandan*, 32(3), March 1996, pp. 41-46.
4. See, Samir Kumar Das, 'The State and the Middle Class: The Case of Assam (1979-90)' in B. Datta Ray & S.P. Agrawal (eds.), *Reorganization of North-East India Since 1947* (New Delhi: Concept, 1996), pp. 114-27.
5. Samir Kumar Das, 'Agrarian Question and the Assamese Community' in K. Alam (ed.), *Agricultural Development In North-East India: Constraints and Prospects* (Delhi: Deep & Deep, 1993), pp. 236-49.
6. Emile Durkheim, *The Division of Labour in Society,* Introduction by Lewis Coser & Trans. by W.D. Halls (New York: The Free Press, 1984), p. 60.
7. Asom Sahitya Sabha, *Eclipse in the East: An Analysis of the Present Agitation in Assam* (Guwahati: Publicity Cell, Asom Sahitya Sabha 1980), p. 8.
8. See, for an analysis of Group Autarky, Russell Hardin, 'Communities and Development: Autarkic Social Groups and The Economy', paper presented to a Conference on 'A New Institutional Approach To Development: Achieving India's Full Potential' organized by The Centre for Institutional Reform and Informal Sector, University of Maryland at College Park and Indian Institute of Management, Calcutta at Park Hotel, Calcutta during 15-16 January, 1996.
9. *Ibid.*
10. Samir Kumar Das, *ULFA--A Political Analysis* (Delhi; Ajanta, 1994), p. 75.
11. Jyotirindra Das Gupta, *Authority, Priority And Human Development* (Delhi; OUP, 1981), p. 3.
12. Ferdinand Tönnies, *Communities and Society,* trans. & edited by Charles P. Loomis (New York: Harper & Row, 1957), part one.
13. Ranabir Samaddar, 'Ethnicity, Fragmented Politics and Labour Market in South Asia--Issues in Transborder Migration', paper presented to a Seminar on 'Security in South Asia' organized by the Dept. of International Relations, Jadavpur University, Calcutta during 26-27 March, 1996.
14. Samir Kumar Das, *Regionalism in Power: The Case of Asom Gana Parishad 1985-1990 (Unpublished).*
15. Apurba Baruah, 'Assamese Middle Classes and the 'Xenophobic' 'tendencies in Assamese Society' in *Frontier,* 31 October, 1981, p. 5.
16. Samir Kumar Das, 'Jatiya Bazar Nei Bolei Ei Arthanaitik Biparyay' (in Bengali) *In Overland,* 8 August, 1993.

20

STATUS OF AND CONSTRAINTS TO INDUSTRIAL DEVELOPMENT IN NORTH-EAST INDIA

— N.N. Bhattacharyya

Introduction

Industrialisation has always been recognised as a major tool for economic development of a region. It is the principal component of the secondary sector and its main function is to provide work for the growing population to satisfy the demand for manufactured goods and to raise the standard of living by the per capita income of the region. It is responsible for converting raw materials into finished goods which in turn encourage the development of tertiary sector, like marketing, transport and servicing etc. The transfer of persons engaged in primary sector to secondary and tertiary sectors are generally visualised as social changes brought about by industrialisation.

India has been experiencing the acute problems of industrial development since long. In fact, there was no industrial policy of the government in the pre-Independence period. An industrial policy was first announced by the Government of India only in 1948. Accordingly the Government was responsible for the planned development of industries including their regulation and it was revised in 1956. Under this policy the industries were listed in either Schedule A (Central Government owned) or in Schedule B (state owned) and other industries which were not listed in schedule A and B were left to the private sector. The Eighth Five Year Plan (1992-97) with a size of Rs. 7,98,000 crores was launched on 1 April 1992. The plan targeted a lower growth of 7.5 per cent in industrial production as against 8.5 per cent achieved in the Seventh Five Year Plan period. But the Eighth plan stressed in achieving efficiency of production by relaxing the industrial policy framework. The current strides in the direction of a liberal industrial policy need to be viewed against the backdrop of the recent changes in the global economic and political order. The industrial policy of the government is now imbued with a spirit of liberalisation and openness which the business and industrial community welcome. The government has liberalised many of statutory hurdles to facilitate the flow of foreign and indigenous capital to industry.

Regional Personality

A little knowledge of the physical and cultural setting of India's North-East is essential for analysing the resource-base and the diverse nature of inter-relationship between the natural resources on the one hand and the men and their activities on the other.

The North-East India covers an area of 255,082 square kilometres and supports a total population of 31 million which accounts for 7.7 per cent of the total land surface of India and contains 4 per cent of the total population of the country. The northern and north-eastern border of the region are composed of highly folded and tectonically disturbed sedimentary rocks. The central plateau extending over Meghalaya and Karbi Anglong is composed of old Archaean basement rocks including some Tertiary formations. The plains and other hills of North-East India are composed of Tertiary formation. The landforms contain a variety of minerals, most of which are not yet commercially exploited (Table 20.1).

The North-East India is generously blessed by nature with its huge sources of water. The water resource of the Brahmaputra basin is 500 km^3 and that of the Barak basin is estimated at 91 km^3. There is considerable amount of ground water in the region and in most cases it is contaminated with high concentration of iron, dissolved acids, toxic substances etc. Supply of such quality water to various consumers like Public Health, Agriculture and Industry requires scientific treatment for better uses.

TABLE 20.1

Minerals	Reserves (million tonnes)
Coal	928
Limestone	1300
Fire clay	2
Iron ore	20
Rare earth	17
Quartz	2
Marble	72
Base Metal	0.11
Crude oil	70
Natural Gas	48

Natural vegetation and forests are called 'green gold'. These resources contribute to the regional and national economy and also ameliorate the regional climate and maintain ecological balance. The forest area, of the region comes to 48 per cent of the total area, of which 39 per cent is reserved forests, the rest being unclasified or within the ownership of District or village councils. The natural vegetation falls in several major types: broad evergreen type, sal forest, mixed deciduous, savanah, bamboo and cane, coniferous and miscellaneous varieties Thus the forests of the region are rich in timber, cane bamboo, agar wood and medicinal plants and provide habitats for various types of birds, reptiles, herbivorous animals and their predators. These forests and animals of North-East India may prove to be very good attraction for the tourists and there are very good prospects to develop forest based industries including tourist industry in the region.

The region is blessed with excellent soil condition of different types. A variety of crops like, rice, wheat, maize, sugarcane, jute, cotton and fruits such as pineapple, oranges, lime, banana, guava etc. are grown on different soil types of the region. The chief plantation crops grown in this region are tea, coffee and rubber. The area under tea plantation is about 2 lakh heactares, coffee 2000 hectares and rubber 5000 hectares.

The work participation rate in Assam is 36.37 per cent, Arunachal Pradesh 47.46, Manipur 41.51, Meghalaya 43.06, Nagaland 44.20, Mizoram 49.36 and Tripura 31.36 according to 1991 census and the national average is 37.64 per cent. Besides the rate of literacy is comparatively higher ranging from 41.22 to 81.23 per cent with a large number of educated men and women in all the states of Noth-East India. In spite of these advantages, the region is depending on foodgrains, pulses, mustard oil, sugar, other products like fish, eggs, building materials like cement, steel and hardwares, electrical goods and other items of daily consumption. Thus the region is yet to experience economic development on a scale achieved by many other states of India.

Constraints to Industrial Development

The process of production in North-East India is still for self consumption and not for market sale. For example, agriculture and allied sectors are still based on traditional techniques. The major industries like petroleum refineries, coal, fertilizers, cement, paper mill etc. established in this region have not generated employment of the local people. The region has only 1.8 per cent of the registered factories providing employment only to 1.7 per cent of the factory employees of the country. Except tea and petroleum industries, which were started and organised by Britishers in Assam, not much progress has yet been achieved in the industrialisation of India's North-East. The whole region is still industrially backward while other Indian states having the same industrial conditions have gone ahead. The main reasons for this state affairs are lack of infrastructure and negligence, inadequate finances, low level of local entrepreneurship and orthodox attitude towards industrial development.

The difficulty of transport and consequence lack of marketing facilities are the greatest hurdle to the industrialization of the region. The local entrepreneurs of North-East India are not familiar with complex banking procedures. So they have not been able to the take full advantage of the presence of various financial institutions and banks like IDBI, SIDBI, IFCI, ICICI, UTI, LIC, GIC etc. So an institution with special knowledge of the region and dedicated exclusively to its requirements is felt necessary. Besides industrialization also depends on the qualities of people, their ability and desire to learn and apply better methods of production to their enterprise and the removal of all institutional obstructions including red tape.

Present Status of Industries

The growth of industries in North-East India is very discouraging. Most of the large and medium industries belong to plywood and roller flour mills and there are about 94 large and medium scale industrial units of which 70 are located inAssam. Similarly the region accounts for only 2 per cent of the total small scale industrial units of the country and nearly 41 per cent of the total small scale units of the region are located in Assam. Nearly 50 per cent of small scale industries are based on locally available resources and technology oriented industries like electronics are absent in North-East India. Handloom Weaving is very important in this region and there are about 1.3 million handlooms and about 1.5 million weavers in North-East India. The total production of these looms is about Rs. 1060 million which accounts for 6 per cent of the national output. There are about 5000 handicraft units engaging about 40,000 craftsmen. The main items of handicrafts are bamboo and cane baskets, cane furnitures, mats, wood-carving, terracotta, dolls and toys etc. There are 22 industrial estates in North-East India and they are distributed 12 in Assam, 5 in Tripura, 2 in Meghalaya, and 1 each in Arunachal Pradesh, Nagaland and Manipur.

Conclusion

The above discussion has given an idea about the industrial base, constraints to industrial development and the present status of industries. The entire region is endowed by natue with abundant resources, but is still economically a backward and poor region. The whole region is characterised by poverty, untapped resources and under utilized manpower. The region's efforts towards industrialisation has not yet met with any outstanding success. It is very difficult to adopt the pattern of industrialisation in North-East India as found in rich countries. So the main thrust of the development strategy for a poor region like North-East India should therefore be to establish small and middle size industrial units in selected sites in rural and semi-urban areas. Such industries can be established without separate building for factory, a large group of hired labour and costly sophisticated machinery. The majority of population live in villages and over 70 per cent of the population depends for their livelihood on agriculture and primary section. So the development of the industrial sector should be related to agriculture and allied activities. The food processing industry has a bright future in the whole of North-Eastern region. Similarly the tea packaging may get a boost if the railway networks container services reach the region. There is a very important need for creating better transport and communication facilities for attracting investment by entrepreneurs in the states of North-East India.

REFERENCES

Alexander, J.W. 1958: "Location of Manufacturing: Method of Measurement". *Annals of A.A.G.*, Vol. 48, pp. 20-26.

Goswami, P.C. 1988: *The Economic Development of Assam*. Kalyani Publishers, New Delhi-Ludhiana.

Nugent, J.B. and M.K. Nabli, 1992: "Development of Financial Markets and the Size Distribution of Manufacturing Establishments: International Comparisons", *World Development*. Vol. 20, pp. 1489-1500.

Singh M.B. 1983: *Industrial Development Patterns and Potentials in Eastern Uttar Pradesh*. Lotus Publications, Varanasi.

21

SOME ASPECTS OF INDUSTRIALISATION IN NORTH-EAST INDIA

-- B.B. Kumar

The North-East region of the country is among the least developed and least industrialised parts of the country. The region was self-sufficient in the production of clothes. Practically every home had looms for weaving the clothes. Assam was famous for its silk cloths. The tribal used to weave beautiful cloths/shawls with rich designs. The village industries were equally developed.

The area is rich in natural resources with fertile soil, and perennial water sources.It is equally rich in mineral and forest wealth.The literacy rate is higher and the region does not lack in hard working skilled and un-skilled labour force.

Assam continues to lead the country in tea industry. The same is more or less true in the case of petroleum industry.The potential for the development of hydel power is unlimited in the region.The Assam tea not noly caters to the needs of the domestic market, but also feeds the needs of the international market. Other plantation crops, such as, coffee and rubber have substantial potential in the region and if developed scientifically, may meet the domestic demand inside the country, as well as ever increasing demands in the international market. It is not difficult to develop such industries and to produce quality products of coffee and rubber of international standards.

As stated above, the region abounds in forest wealth. However, the pace of deforestation is very high. The bamboo and reed reserve of Assam (including Meghalaya and Mizoram) used to be 42 per cent of the country's total output as per the Techno-Economic Survey of Assam conducted by NCEAR in 1959-62. The output of the same may not be sufficient to meet the needs of even Jagi Road Paper Mill in near future. The ever decreasing pine forests may not meet the needs of a few plywood factories for a considerable period. The resource is also depleting very fast due to the greed of the contractors and the suppliers. Huge developmental fund is pumped in the area but the demand of money is greater, mostly due to consumerian ethos and the glamour of the market. The forests are the easy prey. In spite of the rich forest wealth, the forest-bassed industries, specially, the medium and small scale industries, and the forest co-operative societies have not grown. The forests have failed to accelerate the industrial growth of the region. Some of the industries, such, Tuli Paler mill in Mokokchung District of Nagaland, are sick and are on the verge of closure.

In spite of the tradition of villaage and cottage industries, the number of small scale industrial units are not large. Most of the small scale units are in the big towns. The number of such units, only on paper, is very large and a large number of persons take the benefits of loans, grants, subsidies ets. without really starting the industries.

The extractive industry is mostly in the fields of petroleum, coal and limestone.A very powerful pressure group operates against the extraction of oil and natural gases in region.

Most of the organized industrial units in the states are in the State of Assam. Such units are mostly in public sector. Most of the industries are rich and incur heavy losses. According to Economic Survey, the net profit (after tax) of all non-departmental central public sector enterprisess declined from Rs. 3789 crores to Rs. 2368 crores during 1989-90. The trend continued in 1991-92 also. The Planning Commission envisaged the declining role of the public sector (Eighth Five Year Plan, Vol. I) due to the same reason. The question is, whether North-East is in a position to attract capital to fill the void?

Infrastructural facilities are inadequate and mostly substandard. This includes the social infrastructure also. It is very weak in the hilly areas, and even at district and subdivisional towns and is practically non-existent at lower levels. CMIE's index of relative development of infrastructure for 1992-93 (based on CMIE basic Statistics Relating to States, September, 1994) gives an idea about the same.

States	Index
Arunachal Pradesh	44
Assam	93
Manipur	81
Meghalaya	65
Mizoram	63
Nagaland	71
Tripura	63
All India	100

Thus, the Index of relative development of infrastructure is comparatively lower in all the states, specially in the hill states of the region.

The region has inadequate communication network. It is easily disrupted and is tortuous. The resultant transport and communication bottlenecks create problems in development of the area including the development of the industries. The average length of roads per 100 sq. km. is 20.96 km as against national average of 48.79 km. The proportion of surfaced roads to total roads is 6.46 per cent. The national figure is 18.96 per cent.

The states of Arunachal Pradesh, Manipur, Meghalaya, Mizoram, and Tripura had no railway even now and the student community of the state opposed the opening of the rail-link. However, the railway route length per 300 km in Assam was 31.45 km. as against national figure of 19.01 km. in 1992-93. The state moved from 7th to 4th position among the states of India between 1985-86 to 1992-93.

The percentage of population and the villages covered by the electricity is comparatively very high except in Arunachal Pradesh and Meghalaya. 98.8 per cent of the villages of Nagaland and Tripura covering 99.7 per cent population of the states were covered by electricity during 1989-90. 67.7 per cent of population and 95.4 per cent villages of Assam, 67.9 per cent of population and 61.8 per cent of villages of Manipur, 63.3 per cent of population and 44.3 per cent of the villages of Meghalaya, 69.9 per cent of the population and 56.5 per cent of the villages of Mizoram and 33.9 per cent of the population and 41.8 per cent of the villages of Arunachal Pradesh were covered by electricity uring 1989-90. The All India figures for the same period was 82.8 per cent and 81.3 per cent for the same period. The percentage of the villages covered by electricity increased in 1993. It was 98 per cent for Assam, 85 per cent for Manipur, 80 per cent for Mizoram, 49 per cent for Meghalaya and 54 per cent for Arunachal Pradesh as against All India figure of 84 per cent for the same period.

The consumption of energy is very low in the region in comparison to the all India figures. (CMIE Basic Statistics: State, 1994). The data for 1992-93 is given for perusal. The rank among the 24 consumer states is given in the brackets.

The electricity supply in many part of the region is very erratic. The region is rich in hydel and gas potential. The region suffers from endemic power shortage in spite of the same. Lack of political will and other negative factors comes in the way of timely completion of many power projects, such as, the Doyang power Project in Nagaland.

Infrastructural deficiencies adversely affect industrial progress of

State	Per capita Power consumption	Per capita consumption of commercial energy
Arunachal Pradesh	128.3 (18)	130 (18)
Assam	91 (21)	84 (22)
Manipur	40.4 (17)	88 (21)
Meghalaya	159.4 (16)	121 (19)
Mizoram	126.1 (19)	90 (20)
Nagaland	100.1 (20)	77 (23)
Tripura	83.9 (22)	55 (24)
All India	330.6	232

a state. However, it is not always the case. A sugar mill may not grow rich in place like Dimapur due to communication bottleneck, as the raw material for the factory as well as the market for sugar are not far away. The same is the case of many consumer industries. There is big market for processed food in the region. The raw material is also abundantly available. These positive factors have not prevented the industries from growing rich. Over-employment, financial indiscipline, mismanagement, political and bureaucratic interferences accelerate the process of industrial sickness. These factors need to be countered by the respective State Government.

The business community feel insecure in the present atmosphere of agitations and frequent bundhs. Violence, extortion and harassment of the outsiders further aggravate the problem. Thus, adverse human ecology is not conducive for attracting capital from outside. The atmosphere must change for the success of privatisation and the growth of the industry.

The region has the potential of producing a large number of consumer goods. The fruits and vegetables may by abundantly grown and preserved. The immense potential of the growth of horticulture needs harnessing. The examples may be multiplied. The net inflow of most commodities may be stopped if there is political and popular will to develop industries. This may ease the problem of communication bottle necking to a very large extent.

22

SOCIAL HINDRANCES TO ECONOMIC DEVELOPMENT OF ASSAM

-- P.C. Dutta and B.C. Pradhan

The North-Eastern Region comprising seven states viz. Arunachal Pradesh, Assam, Manipur, Meghalaya, Mizoram, Nagaland and Tripura has a total geographical area of a little over 2.5 lakh sq. km. inhabitated by a population of about 31.5 million. Nearly 90 per cent of the population live in village. The econonic structure of North-East India is similar to the general economic structure of our country as a whole. It differs from the rest of India only in kind and not in degree. But due to its physical geography as well as the social and political conditions prevailing in the region, North-East India has a relatively backward economy. While the region covers a bigger area of production than the national average, production per hectare is lower than that of India as a whole. Geographically, the area consists of hills and plains with different levels of economy. At the social and political plane, ethnic considerations sometimes came in the way of integrated economic development of the region. But since the economies of the hills and the plains are more or less complementary, the whole North-Eastern region may be treated as single economic unit.

However, our study is limited to Assam as it is the pioneer state of the North-Eastern region, whose economy is full of potentialities. Further, the economic backwardness and slow and lopsided industrial development of Assam, in particular, best deserves our attention, International events have recently drawn attention to the importance of this border state, where it is vital to enhance productivity capacity, and in particular to improve transport and communications. This is of course, in addition to Assam's role as producers of tea, oil and some other agricultural products. Yet, so far, Assam has hardly received its due share of encouragement and assistance under the different plans.

The present state of Assam, after several political dissections, consists of 78,523 sq. kms in area forming about 2.4 per cent of 3.29 million sq. km. of Indian union. It is bound on the north by Bhutan and Arunachal Pradesh, on the east by Arunachal, on the south by Nagaland, Manipur, Meghalaya, Mizoram and Tripura and on the west by Bangladesh and West Bengal.

In Assam about 70 per cent of the rural population depend for their livelihood in agriculture and allied sectors. In such a situation, the economic development of the region may be analysed in relation to agriculture and allied activities. If industrialisation is to have an impact on the living condition of the people, the programme of industrialisation has to be closely interwoven with the development of all other sectors of the economy, more particularly, agriculture.

Before coming the British, the people of this region were not so developed and were in no way a match with other states of India because modern science and technology was fully unknown to them or what Professor W. W. Rostow calls 'Pre-Newtonian Science and Technology'. The British after pushing up their administration to North-East India, did not help Assam in bringing about economic development for the benefit of the state, whatever industries they had set up, like Tea plantation, oil and other mineral extraction, were done only to further their own interests. Hence, although economic development took place during colonial period in the area, it was confined to the tea and oil producing areas of Assam plains and in some mineral producing areas of Assam hills. In the rest of the areas of the region, the traditional tribal economy or pastoral economy persisted.

The foundation of the economy of Assam is agriculture. Increased agricultural production satisfies the most urgently felt needs of the bulk of the population in an underdeveloped society and it is the most rapid and dramatic demonstration of progress for the overwhelming majority of population. The contribution of agriculture and its allied occupations like animal husbandry, forestry, fishing etc. to state's income is the largest among all sectors. The primary sector itself absorbed 77 per cent of the total working population in 1971 which was 82.3 per cent in 1951. But it is decreased to 74 per cent in 1991. At the same time, in the tertiary sector it is increased to 20 per cent from 12 per cent. The agricultural sector absorbs the major portion of working population in the state. Agriculture is so much basic to the state's economy that development of Assam would invariably mean development of her agriculture. Though Assam is endowed with ideal conditions of agricultural prosperity, there are many impediments in the way of its achievements. Agricultural production has not been able to keep pace with growing population and growing demand of the state. Even until the ugly years of planning, Assam was a food surplus state, but due to excessive growth of population the usual slow rate of growth in production turned it gradually into a deficit state.

Such fluctuations in the production of agricultural crops is mainly caused by inconsistency in the yields of food crops because the degree of oscillation in the area of non-food crops is much less.

As in the field of agriculture so also Assam is industrially very backward. Excepting tea, pertoleum and paper, industries are almost non-existent in the state. For long time Assam has been treated as supplier of raw materials and no attention was paid to the manufacturing activities of the state. Although the state has rich natural resources, industrialisation has not progressed. Since the state is a labour surplus economy having abundant raw materials, the only way to relief the over burden agriculture is to develop the small scale and cottage industries which are labour intensive. However, it is most unfortunate in the case of Assam that most of the small scale and cottage industrial units are sick and require huge patronage for revival and development. Hence, it is felt that the poverty of Assam in general and its backwardness in the fields of agriculture and industry are not only due to the lack of improved transpo.t and communication facilities and other infrastructural facilities but also due to several sociological hindrances. So, besides economic factors, attention must be paid to the sociological factors responsible for causing backwardness of Assam economically.

The different sociological factors responsible for the economic backwardness of Assam may be outlined as follows:

The population of Assam is composed of many heterogeneous elements. There are a number of tribes professing different rituals and beliefs and speaking different languages and dialects. The tribal people in Assam form an important element in her social life. Besides the tribals, there are many other sections of backward people in Assam. The Constitution of India has provided special treatments for all these special groups. They constitute nearly 45 per cent of the total population of Assam. The literate unemployed youths belonging to this category are dreaming about a job under either state government or Central

Government by availing reservation quota. They are not willing to work hard in fields as well as in sericulture, weaving etc. which are the traditional small scale and cottage industries of Assam.

In an undeveloped country like India where religous beliefs, social customs and taboos play an important role in shaping the economic activities of the people, a great diversity of these amongst the inhabitants affects the economic life profoundly. Due to the primodial loyalties of the people of Assam, they are unwilling to adopt the modern technology. Even if the peasants of Assam are largely guided by the traditional customs and traditions as a result of which the agriculture suffers heavily and that retards the economic development of the state.

Another social problem for the economic development of Assam is that although the men are generally hard working, the women have the dominating voice in all the affairs at home, which is most prevalent in some tribal areas of Assam. The daughters inherit the property to the exclusion of the sons and after marriage the groom comes in bride's house instead of bride going to the groom. As a result the male members of the family take no initiative in incentives for the economic prosperity. Long Assam social tension and unrest retard the economic development of the area.

The above study reveals that some social factors are also responsible for the backwardness of Assam alongwith other economic and political factors.

Firstly, as Assam is an agricultural State. Sufficient attention must be paid for the development of agriculture in Assam and its allied sectors. The technology of agricultural production has to be revolutionalised. The use of outmoded methods has to be gradually eliminated and replaced by modern methods. For the development of agriculture, literacy and education are to be given priority. Hence, government should take necessary measures to educate the farmers for the maximum utilisation of the factors of production.

As Assam is agriculturally based society and the infrastructure for large industries are yet to emerge, agro-based and forest based small industries can solve the problem of unemployment because these are possible with minimum amount of capital. The different financial organisations are to be set up by the Government to provide finance and encourage to the educated youths or job seekers to divert their attention towards agriculture and small scale and village industries. Further, it is impossible on the part of poverty stricken people of Assam to establish large industries with scarcity of capital. Again, to revolutionalise agriculture, modern technology with improved implements and agricultural machinery and repair and service workshops are essential. Most of these products are the output of small scale and cottage industries are complementary in Assam. Hence, only small scale and cottage industries of Assam can solve the problems. As India's heart lies in villages, the central as well as state government should start decentralised process of planning from the grass root level. The Panchayati Raj system in Assam is to be reformed and financial autonomy is to be given to the panchayats without any vertical interference. The new industrial policy of Assam is to be implemented sincerely for the real cause of the State's economy. Department of Health and Family Welfare should work in a devoted way to check the overgrowth of population. The age-old practice of shifting cultivation in the hill areas of the state has to be stopped and they are to be provided irrigation facilities, conservation of soil etc. for the purpose. The village money lenders should be banned and other intermediaries are to be replaced by government agencies.

REFERENCES

Statistical Hand Book of Assam, 1980, 1984, 1994.

D.D. Mali and P. Deka: *Industrial Development in North East India:* Omsons Publications, Delhi.

Pankaj Thakur (ed.): *India's North East:* Prakash Publishing House, Socio-Economic Forum for the North East.

D. Bharali (ed.): *Economic Development of the North Eastern Region:* Spectrum Publications, Delhi.

P.C. Goswami: *The Economic Development of Assam:* Kalyani Publishers, New Delhi.

R.K. Choudhury: *Economic Problems of Assam:* Kitab Ghar, Guwahati.

P.K. Dhar: *The Economy of Assam:* Ashomi Prakashani, Guwahati.

Census of India, 1991.

P.C. Dutta: *Certain Aspects of Consumer Behaviour in Assam: An Empirical Study;* unpublished Ph.D. Thesis.

Satistical Abstract of Assam, 1978.

23

SOCIAL CONSTRAINTS TO INDUSTRIAL DEVELOPMENT: THE ASSAM SCENARIO

-- Lipi Ghosh

Industrialisation is the cornerstone of economic growth. In our country the programme of industrialisation has been launched vigorously from the second Five Year Plan. It is however a recognised fact that the pace of industrial development is very slow in the whole of North-East India. Industrial backwardness of the region is reflected by the fact that there are less than 3 per cent of the country's large and medium scale industries and 2 per cent of small scale industries in the region. The region's share in value added by manufacturing is barely 2.5 per cent.[1] This chapter attempts to deal with the question of industrialisation in Assam itself and tries to identify the forces of social constraints which impede growth of industrial development.

To take into account an estimate about industrialisation in Assam, we can distinguish between large and medium industries and small scale industries. In Assam till 1980, there were about 70 industries in the large and medium scale sector.[2] However, with change in the definition of small scale industries, i.e. raising the investment limit to Rs. 20 lakhs and subsequently to Rs. 35 lakhs, some units have fallen into the category of small scale units. Hence by 1980, 62 units are found as medium and large units in Assam. It has been provisionally estimated that the number of permanently registered small scale industries (S.S.I.) units in Assam stood at 6,713 as on 31.3.85 Most of these units have their own accommodation.[3]

Assam thus presents a pleasant challenge to the planners for economic development. The State is now passing through one of the crucial periods of her industrial history. The North Eastern Council which was set up in 1972, is engaged in the task of helping the constituent units of the region including Assam in coming to grips with their complex problem of backwardness. In order to boost up industrial activities in the state, various efforts continued to be undertaken by the state and central governments.

Although Assam has immense natural resources, tea still occupies the dominant position in the industrial era. The industrial era in Assam began only with the setting up of public sector refinery at Guwahati and a fertilizer company at Namrup. The new industrial policy together with specific incentive scheme in the decade of 1980s have yielded encouraging results leading to setting up of a large number of small scale and tiny units in the state. Some of the important industrial ventures which came up in state in the decade were a polyester synthetic spinning mill of the Assam Polytex Ltd near Jagir Road, Namrup, III project of the Hindustan Fertilizer Corporation and an animal feed plant at Changsari. The Centre sector investment in the state in the period was however very meagre and State Government continued to move the Centre for a hike in her capital subisdy to 33.3 per cent, so as to attract more private capital to the state.[4]

It may be interesting to take up the history of industrial planning in Assam at this juncture. Assam did not have any full fledged Directorate of Industries for more than a decade after Independence. It was only in 1958 that a full fledged Directorate of Industries was set up. Besides the first systematic effort for the industrial development of backward areas was made on the basis of the recommendations of the Pandey Working Group and Wancho Working Group.[5]

In 1969, the Government of Assam announced its first industrial policy and offered a number of incentives and facilities for industrial development. But this industrial policy did not create the necessary climate in the state.

A number of fiscal and financial incentives were announced by the Central government and the All India Financial Institution in 1971 for inducing industrial development in backward areas.[6]

A new industrial policy statement was announced by the Union Minister of State for Industry in Lok Sabha on 23 July, 1980 with some objectives like--optimum utilisation of the installed capacity, maximum production and achieving productivity, higher employment generation, correction of regional imbalances through professional development of industrially backward areas and faster promotion of export oriented industries.[7]

In 1981, the Sivaraman Committee recommended the growth centre approach for the industrial development in backward areas. In the North-Eastern region, the committee emphasized entrepreneurship as a strategy for industrial development. The state government has also implemented a number of incentives and facilities for industrial development of the state. The Conference of Industries Ministers of State and Union Territories of the North-Eastern region in 1981 recommended a resource-based approach for industrial development.[8]

In 1982, another industrial policy was announced and this declared a number of incentives and facilities. The Government of Assam has set up a number of organisations for the promotion and development of different sectors of industries in the state. It had set up separate Directorate for Handloom and textiles and also for Sericulture. For looking after Khadi and Village industries, the government has set up many Corporation of Boards. For the promotion of the textile industries Assam State Textile Corporation was set up. For the development of electronics industry the Assam Electronic Development Corporation was set up in 1984.[9]

Another industrial policy was announced in 1986. This policy has been regarded as the most dynamic policy announced so far by the Government of Assam. This policy has announced a number of incentives and facilities for the indigenous entrepreneurs. The National Council for Applied Economic Research prepared a blue print for an estimated amount of Rs. 268 crores for the industrial development of the state during the Fourth Plan.[10]

It was till 1988 that the Government of Assam has made a total investment of Rs. 99.05 crores in 4 public sector units. To take the latest figure about capital investment, the following statistics is appropriate:

Capital Investment Subsidy Sanctioned

Year	Subsidy for large & medium IND		Subsidy for SSI Unit	
	No.	Amount ('000 Rs)	No.	Amount ('000 Rs)
1988-89	15	9162	285	49466
1989-90	10	4327	526	30707
1990-91	—	—	—	—
1991-92	10	36844	370	36844

Source: Statistical Hand Book, Assam, 1993.

Such being the broad outline history of industrialisation in Assam, it follows our task to find out the most prominent reasons which constrain industrial growth in the region. We can say that the forces which arrest self-reinforcing industrial growth have been held in check in the case of Assam by a number of factors like economic, political, historical, socio-cultural, psychological and physical. This study indentifies the factors and categories four most remarkable social constraints behind industrial slothness. These are--lack of entrepreneurship, lack of proper basic infrastructural facilities, low technology and inadequately trained manpower and finally inadequate financial support.

Absence of entrepreneurship is one of the major problems of economic and industrial development in Assam. If one takes Assam's underdevelopment in the historical context, one finds that till the arrival of the British, Assam's economy was partly semi-feudal and partly tribal. Following British rule Assam was gradually opened up and the capitalistic mode of production replaced subsistence economy. In upgrading economic enterprises, the British recruited 'Babus', mostly from Bengal for clerical jobs in government offices and industrial undertakings. Bengali Babus remitted home whatever savings they had and so a class of self-seeking enterprising Assamese persons with surplus of money did not emerge.[11] The situation continued even in post-Independent days. If the entrepreneur class would have been from the indigenous population, they would have probably ventured on new enterprises with their surplus funds, but unfortunately they were not. This would have raised the level of economic development and resulted in higher industrial growth.

Absence of entrepreneurship among the tribal people of Assam is also one of the major problem behind industrial developments. Although there are available resources in the tribal areas of Assam, innovative entrepreneurs with new ideas, drive and initiative from amongst the communities are absent. So potentialities for taking up production, distribution and marketing of new productions are not forthcoming at all. In fact the existing social system within its own cultural norms and values, ethics, customs etc. prevalent amongst the tribal communities of Assam in both plains and hills are not conducive to savings and investments. So subsequently there is lack of finance which is one major criteria of economic development. To take instance, whatever savings some well to do tribal families of different communities might be having, it is generally not invested for further production of goods and services. Savings enhances the prestige and social status of a tribal family in the eyes of the communities and at the same time the prestige of the family further enhances if it can entertain the community members in lavishly arranged and expensive entertainments like feasts and religious rituals.[12] It may be added that corporate life of tribal communities in Assam society also arrests financial investments and entrepreneurship. The tribal social system is based on their corporate life and maintained through the institution of kinship. Under such a system a family has obliging needs for other fellow members not only of sharing the economic activities but collective consumption also. To take instance, in Karbi society a poor family members can go to a well to do Karbi family of the same village and have a daily share of food till the stock of food stuff of the second family lasts.[13] From the point of view of economic development such a social system rather retards the progress by making people dependent and lithargic although the social value of such a system is of very high order. From the point of view of economic gains of the concerned families, the implication is negative although from the view point of social obligation the system appears to be all right.

Infrastructure for planned industrial growth is one of the major pre-requisites for industrial growth. In other words for a dynamic industrial growth of a region or state, the creation of basic infrastructure is highly essential. A programme for setting up industrial estates with infrastructural facilities like housing, allotment of land, power, communication, water and other allied facilities was initiated under the Growth Centre Scheme, but due to lack of proper implementation, it could not give any expected result and failed to meet the changing needs. Here again some of tribal social systems are important for impending growth. To take instance shifting of village system among some of the tribal communities retarded economic progrress. No good infrastructural network can develop within such shifting village pattern. If in a Karbi Anglong Village the medicine-man declares that a particular village is haunted by ghosts and evil spirits, that village site is also abandoned and the entire village is taken to a new site.[14] Such being the transitional character of village existence, no proper infrastructure can develop.

The prevailing technology in the region is also minimum. In the case of handloom-industry, the looms in use are mostly primitive. Therefore, need arises to popularise the improved tools and techniques. Manpower planning is also an important criteria. Man power planning which implies human resource development as well as its employment is beset with many complexities and it assumes crucial significance in the context of backward regions like the North-East India. Industrialisation, with the help of mass skilled workers from outside are done in the region, which is not advisable. Here the social constraint grows itself from the lethargic character of the people in the region. One important instance of wastage of man power is the existing gambling in weekly markets in and around many Assam villages, both in tribal and non-tribal areas.[15] The weekly markets in Assam villages are heaven for gamblers. On the market whatever amounts remains after selling the goods, the villagers are induced to take part in the gambling dens, which are usually installed in the vicinity of the market. Thus cash money is wasted and drained out in a scrupulous way. This indicates nothing but useless wastage of man-power and finance, which could be invested in the area's economic development.

Finally, one of the major causes of poor industrial growth is lack of finance, arising out of some second grade treatments on part of government to the North-East Indian states. This may be treated as an indirect social constraint. P.C. Goswami observes--"The percentage of loan sanctioned and disbursed to the North-East region in relation to all India figures was less than 1 per cent in 1983-1984, to the whole of N.E. India only 1.2 per cent of the total assistance from all India financial institutions have been flowing upto the end of March, 1987. On the other hand developed states like Maharastra has received 18.01 per cent followed by Gujarat 12.21 per cent, Tamil Nadu 9.81 per cent and Uttar Pradesh 8.71 per cent in the same period.[16] Even ten years after, the percentage remains lower for Assam as compared to the above noted other states:

State-wise Assistance Sanctioned by All Financial Institutions (AFIs)

State	Year	(Rs. Crores) Cumulative upto end March 1993
Assam	1992-93	909.7
Gujarat	1992-93	19061.4
M.P.	1992-93	7496.2
Tamil Nadu	1992-93	13310.4
Uttar Pradesh	1992-93	11874.5

Source: Office of the Economic Advisers, Ministry of Industry, Government of India, Handbook of Industrial Policy & Statistics, New Delhi, 1995

So, here attitude of government of India makes a kind of indirect barrier to industrial development to the region.

To conclude, it is evident that industrialisation in Assam is lagging for behind all India industrial growth is due to various constraints inside the region. A major part of the constraints may be termed as social constraints, whether direct or indirect. A concentrated efforts by various development departments with total support of the peoples will remove the constraints,--is the hope for the future. Such an attempt and resultant strength will place Assam at per with most advanced states of the country and it will undoubtedly be a glory for the Assamese generations to come.

REFERENCES

Shashi Ahluwalia (ed.): *Social and Economic Development in N.E. India*, Delhi, 1986, p. 55.

Directorate of Industries, Government of Assam, *Annual Report*, 1980, p. 55.

Ibid., p. 56.

Directorate of Economics and Statistics, Government of Assam, *A Brief Review of the Economy of Assam*, 1987-88, pp. 4-5.

D.D Mail, *Economic Problems & Planning in Assam*, Guwahati, 1989, p. 141.

Ibid.

D.D. Mali and P. Deka, *Industrial Development in North East India*, Guwahati, 1987, p. 57.

D.D. Mali, *op. cit.*, p. 141.

Ibid., pp. 142-143

Ibid.

P.D. Saikia and D. Borah, *Constraints of Economic Development in North-East India*, New Delhi, 1991, and P.C. Goswami, *Socio-Economic Research in Tribal Areas*, Jorhat, Assam, 1972.

Ibid., pp. 30-31.

Ibid., p. 32

Ibid.

Ibid., and P.C. Goswami, *The Economic Development of Assam*, Guwahati, 1976.

P.C. Goswami, Four I.F.C.I Lecture, Gauhati University, Guwahati, 1988 and Directorate of Industry, Assam, *Report on Industrial Development*, 1980 and 1990.

24

LACK OF ENTREPRENEURSHIP AND INDUSTRIAL DEVELOPMENT IN MEGHALAYA

— M. Banerjee

Introduction

Entrepreneurship is a purposeful activity indulged in initiating, promoting and maintaining economic activities for production and distribution of wealth and service (Baruah, 1987).

The facing of uncertainty is a unique function qualitatively different from other economic factors and represents as an essential mark of the entrepreneur. It is recognised as an essential ingredient of economic development and an integral part of socio-economic transformation. Various concepts and theories propounded by researchers seem to indicate that the emergence of entrepreneurs in a society depends upon closely interlinked economic, social, cultural, religious and psychological variables. Entrepreneurship as an economic activity emerges and functions in sociological and cultural set-ups (Baruah, 1987). In fine an entrepreneur is one who is qualified, venturesome, having possessed the concrete knowledge of result of his venture, who can skilfully organise the factors of production for economic development ready to face cut throat competition and last but not least who can take calculated risk (Senapati, 1995). Entrepreneurs are not only born but also can be trained and developed (Mali, 1995).

India lives in villages and its economy is based primarily on agriculture. Even since Independence, the Five Year Plans of the Government of India have been directly or indirectly stimulating industrialisation as a subsidiary economy of the country. In this programme for rapid industrialisation of a basically agricultural society the planners and policy makers have been concerned with two general social issues:

(a) Whether the norms of the traditional society will impede the process of industrialisation or
(b) Whether rapid industrialisation will bring about undesirable cultural disorganisation. The inadequate infrastructure, absence of indigenous entrepreneurship, public undertakings and private enterprises as well, traditional agriculture, non-availability of trained manpower, institutional finance, hostile attitude of the rebels, higher growth rate of population along with influx of migrants are some of the factors associated with slow economic growth of Meghalaya.

Keeping this idea in mind the author has made an attempt in this chapter to find out the causes leading to lacunae of entrepreneurship for industrial growth in Meghalaya in the socio-economic and psychological perspectives.

Area and People

To understand the development of entrepreneurship in the initial stage it is utmost necessary to know a brief account of the people and their economic standard. Meghalaya is one of the smallest state with an approximate area of 22,000 sq. kms. According to 1991 Census, Meghalaya had a population of 1,774, 778. Growth rate of total population of Meghalaya and India, since 1901-1991 is shown in Table 24.1.

From Table 24.1 it is noticed that compared to all-India feature after 1981 there is a rapid increase of population in Meghalaya.

In Meghalaya a majority of pupulation living in the villages treat the major economic activities be it agriculture, collection of minor forest produce or weaving as a way of life rather than any commercial propositions big or small and this underscores a mere lack of orientation of the rural people. There is no steady generation of marketable surplus and therefore minimal activities towards commercialization. The orientation of tribal settlements to produce whatever is required for consumption results in a lack of internal markets. There is thus an urgent need to forge an economic orientation amongst the rural population, in

TABLE 24.1: Decadal Change in Population 1901-1991: Meghalaya and India

	Meghalaya		India	
Census Decades	Total Population	Growth Rate (%)	Total Population	Growth Rate(%)
1901	340524		238396000	
1911	394005	15.7	252093000	5.8
1921	422403	7.8	251321000	-0.3
1931	480837	13.8	278977000	11.0
1941	555820	15.6	318661000	14.2
1951	605674	9.0	361088000	13.3
1961	769380	27.0	439235000	21.6
1971	1011699	31.5	548160000	24.8
1981	1335819	32.0	685184692	25.0
1991	1774778	32.9	836212161	23.6

Source: Calculated from Census of India, 1981 and 1991 Meghalaya, and Basic Statistics of NER, 1992.

order to increase the productivity of economic activities over and above the present subsistence level.

History shows that the Khasi-Jaintia Hills are particularly remarkable for agricultural and mineral products. Cultivation both by terracing and *jhum* (shifting) methods was extensively carried out in the past as it was still to-day. *Jhum* cultivation is more prevalent in the northern Bhoi region and Lyngngam area of the west. Terracing cultivation is often practised in valleys and flat lands raised on low level grounds. It was also mentioned by 'Gurdon' that Khasi-Hills may be made self-sufficient in respect of rice if extensive cultivation is undertaken (Barch, 1987). The Khasi and Jaintia Hills is famous for production of fruits like—mango, plantains, oranges, citrus, limes, pine-apples etc., all these varieties are still cultivated in the hills, in fact cultivation of best qualities of oranges, citrous and limes, pine-apples, jack-fruits is concentrated more largely in the Khasi-Jaintia Hills than anywhere else in erstwhile Assam. In the pre-British period, Khasi oranges with those of Garhwal and Sikkim varieties were sent to the Middle-East and transported as far as Central Europe. Colonel Lister, writing in 1853, estimated that 20,000 maunds of iron were exported from the Hills in the shape of hoes to the Assam Valley, and in lumps of pig iron to the Surma Valley, where it was used by boat builders for clamps. Dr. Oldhan, writing in 1863 says, 'The quality of this Khasi iron is excellent for all such purposes as Swedish iron is now used for' (Gurdon, 1990). It was also mentioned by Gurdon that rearing of cocoons and weaving was an important industry among the people of Sumier, Shangpung, Saipung, Mynso in the middle plateau and Umpanai, Um Mynso, Bhoi Lalu, Bhoi Khyrwang, Bhoi Ksi etc., in the Boi areas. The cotton produced in the Jaintia Hills on the banks of Kupli river in the large quantities in the pre-British era was one of the finest varieties in Assam (Durrah, Industries in Assam, p. 32).

So Meghalaya was supposed to be self-sufficient in agricultural as well as mineral production be it rice, cotton and fruits production and also in production of iron and other mineral products namely, coal, limestone etc. So there was no need of the people to go for any alternative economy. Table 24.2 indicates that cultivation is the main occupation in Meghalaya followed by other activities like agricultural labourers and a negligible percentage of population are engaged in household industry. As a result of increasing population leads to an increased pressure on agricultural land that again tends to lower the productive capacity of the land.

On the other hand enormous efforts on spread of education has created a literate workforce who do not prefer agriculture, instead, they look for easier means of earning large amount of money in short time, Table 24.3 shows the percentage of literacy in Meghalaya in 1981 and 1991.

Table 24.3 indicates that Meghalaya has a literate population of 39.15 per cent which is above the national average of 36.23 per cent according to 1991 Census. Due to increase in literacy rate and urban migration as well decrease in fertility of the soil, literate young folks want immediate earning avenue. Timber extraction permits and road contracts provide such an avenue of windfall earning and there is neck to neck competition for such type of contracts. Government employment is also regarded a highly white collared engagement. However, there is a saturation state in government services and in recent years Government potentiality to absorb the state unemployed work force has come down significantly. The young force prefer neither working in agriculture nor in industries in the private sector, instead desire employment in the Government sector. At present the ratio of the government employees to total population in the State is around 1:27. It is also observed that technical graduates in Meghalaya are currently unemployed. Hence it may be seen that skilled manpower remains underutilised in Meghalaya. The private sector has not come out as an alternative avenue for

TABLE 24.2: Occupational and Literacy Structure of Meghalaya (Proportion of Main Workers to Total Population and Distribution of Main Workers to Type of Occupation 1991).

State	Main workers		
	Persons	Males	Females
Meghalaya			
Total	40.32	62.83	37.17
Rural	34.44	60.62	39.38
Urban	5.88	75.76	74.24
	Agricultural Labourers		
Total	12.51	58.30	41.70
Rural	96.41	57.94	42.06
Urban	3.59	67.98	32.02
	Other Workers		
Total	14.75	74.43	25.57
Rural	48.83	77.51	22.49
Urban	51.17	71.49	28.51
	Cultivations		
Total	55.31	57.65	42.35
Rural	99.06	57.65	42.35
Urban	0.94	58.25	41.75
	Household Industry		
Total	0.40	56.64	43.36
Rural	77.57	55.18	44.82
Urban	22.43	61.66	38.34

Source: Basic Statistics of North-Eastern Region, 1995, North Eastern Council Secretariat, Shillong.

absorption of the employable workforce. The functional characteristics of almost all the towns of Meghalaya is such that nearly 60 per cent of the work force is engaged in tertiary sector activities. In absence of

TABLE 24.3: Percentage of Literacy in 1981 and 1991

Area	1981			1991		
	Rural	Urban	Total	Rural	Urban	Total
Meghalaya	27.45	64.12	34.08	32.60	67.68	39.15
India	29.65	57.40	36.23	29.65	57.40	36.23

significant manufacturing activities, job prospects for rural migrants appear to be limited. The situation thus is a vicious circle which, *inter alia* leads to growing uncertainty in society, social tensions and upheavals. So it is necessary to intensify activities in the private sector, specially creating value-added activities that are also remunerative for the local employable populace.

External and Internal Forces for Development of Entrepreneurship

After formation of the State 'Meghalaya Industrial Development Corporation' was set up by the Government which helped coming up some industrial enterprises in the joint sector. All round development of an area requires certain infrastructure facilities, e.g. electricity, transportation, land and natural resources etc. Meghalaya falls under the category of the 6th schedule of the Constitution of India. This constitutional provision provides protection to the ethnic identity, culture of the local indigenous people. The most prominent protective measure in this regard is the Land Transfer Act. In case of indigenous people they never face any problem related to transfer of land within themselves. The Khasi Hills District (Establishment, Management and Control of Markets) Regulation 1979, which prohibits anyone other than a local tribal resident of the district to carry on a wholesale or retail business except under a licence issued by the district council. These two factors prevent economic exploitation of the local tribal on one hand leaving a damaging effect in limiting factors in accelerating development through infusion of external investment on the other.

Meghalaya is one of the very few power surplus states in the country. Excess power generally is being sold to neighbouring States. The generation and sale of power in Meghalaya between 1990-91, and 1992-93 is shown in Table 24.4 below.

TABLE 24.4: Generation and Sale of Electricity in Meghalaya (in MKWH)

Years	Generation	Sale in Meghalaya	Sale in Meghalaya as % of total generation
1990-91	338.63	192.10	56.73
1991-92	421.08	217.67	51.69
1992-93	429.80	230.55	53.64

Source: Statistical Handbook of Meghalaya.

Power consumption in the state has been stagnant over the last few years. Only 37 per cent of the State power consumption is by the industrial sector. Further, per capita power consumption in Meghalaya is only 135 KWH. which is only 30 per cent of all India average.

Meghalaya produces large quantities of coal of very high calorific value with low ash content. This coal can be used for production of several precious chemicals and other industrial products. Meghalaya also has a very large deposit of limestone. So limestone based projects have a high prospect in Meghalaya. There are few cement manufacturing companies in the private and Government undertaking sector in Meghalaya, namely.

(1) Mawlu Cherra cements Ltd., in Cherrapunji.
(2) Jaintia Cements Ltd., in Garo Hills District
(3) Virgo Cements Ltd., in Garo Hills District.
(4) RKB Cements (P) Ltd., in Shillong.

Apart from electricity and natural resources, to accelerate all round development, Government has launched some special schemes for the indigenous people to give more emphasis on self employment of the unemployed youths. Besides this a series of specific incentives/subsidy is also provided for motivating quick generation of local indigenous entrepreneurship. These are as follows:

(a) For Large and Medium Scale Industries

(i) Cost of infrastructure for large and medium industries in Meghalaya.
(ii) Upto 75 per cent of the stamp duty on deeds relating to loans from financial institutions are exempted in Meghalaya.
(iii) Subsidies on Power tariffs for two years—30 per cent and 25 per cent for load below 2.5 MW and above 2.5 MW respectively upto a ceiling of Rs 5 lakhs.
(iv) 90 per cent subsidy (maximum Rs 2 lakhs) for the cost of preparation of project feasibility report, and
(v) Reimbursement of 10 per cent of the cost of infrastructure for electronics industry.

(b) For Medium Scale Industries

(i) 10 per cent subsidy (upto Rs. 3.5 lakhs) on the cost of infrastructure for large and medium industries in Meghalaya.
(ii) Upto 75 per cent of the stamp duty on deeds relating to loans from financial institutions are exempted in Meghalaya.
(iii) Subsidies on Power tariffs for two years—30 per cent and 25 per cent for load below 2.5 MW and above 2.5 MW, respectively upto a ceiling of Rs. 5 lakhs.
(iv) 90 per cent subsidy (maximum Rs. two lakhs) for the cost of preparation of project feasibility report, and
(v) Reimbursement of 10 per cent of the cost of infrastructure for electronics industry.

(c) For Small Scale Industries

(i) 10 per cent subsidy (upto Rs. 3.5 lakhs) on the project cost for industrial estate in Meghalaya.
(ii) 50 per cent reduction in rent for lands and sheds in industrial areas for local tribal entrepreneurs.
(iii) 30 per cent subsidy on the wage-bill for local tribal employees (upto 20 employees) if the investment of the unit on the plants and machineries is above Rs. 5 lakhs, and 50 per cent subsidy on the cost training of local tribal employees.
(iv) Reimbursement of Sales Tax for initial 5 years on the purchase of raw materials and sales of finished products.
(v) 4 per cent limit on the Meghalaya Finance Tax.
(vi) 50 per cent subsidy (upto Rs. 20,000 per annum) on the cost of drawing the power connection, in addition to 50 per cent power subsidy for units consuming minimum 500 units in the manufacturing process.
(vii) 100 per cent subsidy (upto Rs. 10,000) on the cost of preparation of feasibility studies.
(viiii) Subsidy (upto Rs. 25,000) on the cost of technology procured from NRDC and other national laboratories. Reimbursement (upto Rs. 10,000) of the cost of laboratory equipments and 30 per cent subsidy (upto Rs. 15,000) on the cost of fabrication of prototypes for important substitution.

(ix) 50 per cent subsidy (upto Rs. 50,000) on the pollution control measures for the unit.

(x) Full subsidy (upto Rs. 30,000) on the cost of infrastructure for horticulture development and for transportation of finished products of horticulture-based units.

(xi) Reimbursement of 40 per cent of the cost of infrastructure for electronic industry (Government of Meghalaya, Tata Consultancy Services).

The above mentioned infrastructure facilities are provided by the Government to generate the motivation of entrepreneurship among the local people to boost up their economy and own states as well. But the tribal people living in villages are reluctant to venture a new line of activity or get engaged in activities away from their villages. This has led to migration of outside labourers to the state resulting an increase in population and cost of production as well. The influx of external labour has made the supporters of protectionism to demand higher caution on entry of so-called foreigners into the State and thereby unknowingly inhibiting investors from outside the State. On the other hand wage rate in Meghalaya for both local and external labour is quite high and this along with the high cost of transportation makes Meghalaya products non-competitive in external markets. On the other hand Meghalaya does not have any railway network, the nearest rail connection being at Guwahati in Assam, road transport is the only means of communication available in Meghalaya. So the improvement of communication and at the same time it is equally necessary to generate marketing facilities for immediate disposal of products.

Another important aspect should be mentioned here that industrialists hesitate to invest in the State due to local disturbances. In order to give a push to the pace of industrialisation in Meghalaya banks have additional responsibilities to play providing financial assistance to the small scale industrial entrepreneurs. It is also to be pointed out that attitude towards repayment of bank loans has to be changed by the borrowers. Unless the Bank's dues are recovered there would be no recycling of funds and the genuine promoters of industry would be denied of loan facility from the bank. It is pertinent to mention that loan recovery position of entire Meghalaya is poorer in comparison to all-India picture.

Conclusion

From the above mentioned information it is found that even though the State offers considerable scope for industrialisation, Meghalaya still continues to remain one of the most industrially backward states of the country in spite of its enormous natural and human resources. Meghalaya suffers from a number of constraints, which have arrested the pace of industrialisation in the State. For an individual to emerge as a successful entrepreneur he must have full knowledge of opportunities available and the environment. He must also have knowledge of enterprises and technology. In addition to knowledge he should have skill to select a product or a process, prepare a scheme of a project report and establish and run an enterprise. But knowledge and skill alone will not make an individual an entrepreneur. In order to make the knowledge and skill operative one must have sufficient motivation, personal efficiency and self-confidence.

A majority of entrepreneurs in Meghalaya lack requisite experience in running business units. Almost all entrepreneurs lack formal education or exposure in management. In order to give a fillip to the nature of the state the quality and availability of scientific and technical manpower need be improved substantially. Knowledge of specific customer requirements and market characteristics on the part of entrepreneurs, happens to be very poor. Another important aspect should be kept in mind that family background plays a crucial role in shaping the destiny of an individual. It is the family setting that motivates an individual to achieve something new. Many a time interest of an individual comes in conflict with the expectation of the family. As a result many prospective entrepreneurs opt for wage earning career instead of an entrepreneurial career.

Besides the influence of the family, there is the influence of society, the caste and the religion which an individual belongs to. Individuals are generally status seekers. An individual will obviously like to take up that kind of activity which the society imparts status. In Meghalaya the existing situation is such that a person with a white collared government job with assured income commands higher status in the society than a person who is self-employed, even though both the individuals have similar level of income and standard of living. This sort of situation is not conducive for the encouragement of entrepreneurship rather frustrating.

Another most vital problem is the small size of local markets. While over 81 per cent of the state population is dependent on the primary sector, there exists no major agricultural surplus. Since the rural population has little to sell they do not possess substantial purchasing power. This lack of purchasing power on the part of the majority population lead to lack of effective demand for industrial product. Motivational training is one of the important direct measures that may be adopted for the purposes. Entrepreneurial education should form a part and parcel of the educational system, so that an orientation develops among the local youths right from the beginning.

Entrepreneurship is such a motivation that cannot be expected to grow overnight. In fact it is developed through the culture of the community. In Meghalaya the indigenous people those who accepted agriculture as main support of their living could not think of any big industry as their alternative occupation. Since Meghalaya has a high potentiality for growth of industries based on agricultural, horticultural and forest resources, the state needs to develop adequate facilities for the preservation and storage of such highly perishable goods. Hence Government agencies should come forward to highlight indigenous products of the people engaged in cottage industry which is the sapling of a big industry in future.

REFERENCES

Barch, H (1985): *The History and Culture of the Khasi People*, United Publishers, Guwahati, Delhi.

Baruah, A.R. (1987): "Developing Entrepreneurship in North Eastern Region: An Approach", Mali, D.D., P. Deka, (In) *Industrial Development in North East India*. Omsons Publications, New Delhi.

Gurdon, P.R.T. (1990): *The Khasis*, Low Price Publications, Delhi, (Revised edition).

Mali, D.D. (1995): Motivating the Youth for Entrepreneurial Career; Why and how. (In) *Core Problems of the Scheduled Castes* of Assam (ed.) Bimal Kumar Hazarika. Assam Institute of Research for Tribals and Scheduled Castes. Guwahati. pp. 9-16.

Senapati, G.C. (1995): Training of Scheduled caste youths for entrepreneurial motivation. (In) *Core Problems of the Scheduled Castes of Assam* (ed.) Bimal Kumar Hazarika, Assam Institute of Research for Tribals and Scheduled Castes. Guwahati, pp. 120-128.

Tata Consultancy Services (1995): Government of Meghalaya. Review and Impact Assessment of Industrial Policy, Calcutta.

25

RISK, TRANSACTION COST AND ENTREPRENEURSHIP DEVELOPMENT IN ARUNACHAL PRADESH

— N.C. Roy and P.K. Kuri

Introduction

One basic characteristic of organizational mode of production in the state of Arunachal Pradesh is its family centredness, the major part of the state income being generated by the production units whose operative loci are the families. The shift of production from the family-based organisation to the non-family based organization has not yet taken place to any significant extent. In fact, the corporate mode of production remains highly limited to a few enterprises developed only in recent years. To date, entrepreneurial activities have not got any environment to flourish in a self-sustained manner. However, with the growth of secondary and tertiary sectors of the economy some entrepreneurship has come into being, but a greater part of this entrepreneurship has been provided by non-locals or migrant people. Arunachalee element in the whole spectrum of entrepreneurship is insignificant. In order to highlight the factors responsible for the very low level of entrepreneurship in Arunachal Pradesh, it is necessary to consider the specific conditions of the state.

Till Independence, the economy of Arunachal Pradesh was purely agricultural; modern tertiary sector was almost non-existent and some handicrafts were produced largely for consumption at home. Agriculture was wholly traditional. It was based mainly on shifting cultivation using family labour and other traditional inputs having very low productivity.

With the Independence of the country, the government tended to prepare the institutional framework to launch the development programme in the state. The initial efforts of the government fructified into the development of different infrastructural facilities and administrative centres. This government-directed, newly-grown sectors came to take the lead and acted as a strong stimulus to initiate the development of agricultural and industrial sectors in the state.

The initiation of development programme in this state has witnessed the induction of new technology and new institutional mechanism in agricultural and industrial sectors. This development in the production frontier has been accompanied with the growth of a non-traditional mode of organization of production, the organization which has come to use the wage labour, modern inputs and often hired management services, and in the process some entrepreneurship has grown up. However, as mentioned above, in this state, the role of local element in the new organizational mode of production has not to date been significant. In this chapter our basic intention is to identify the factors which prevented the full flourishing of local initiative in the new organizational form of production. It is agrued in this chapter that high risk and transaction costs are the two factors which are mainly responsible for the slow growth of local entrepreneurship. We do not take into consideration the constraint imposed by inadequate development of infrastructural facilities in this state. The role of infrastructural development in the industrialisation and growth of entrepreneurship is universally recognised. The main limitation of this chapter is its inability to highlight the relative importance of infrastructural factors in the growth of entrepreneurship. For convenience this chapter is divided into two sections. In the first section, we develop an explanatory framework. Section-II explains why entrepreneurship has not yet emerged here on a desired scale. Suggestions and conclusions also appear in this section.

SECTION - I

The growth of entrepreneurship is usually associated with the gradual change in the organizational mode of production. This organizational growth is propelled by the efficiency derived from the use of better inputs and this is invariably linked with a number of changes such as technological improvement, flexible factor intensity and in general a rise in the scale of production. All these changes are shaped, among others, by two factors: behaviour of risk and transaction costs.[1] When the makret for different inputs is underdeveloped and more specifically when the market for risk is almost non-existent, the risk and transaction costs associated with production organized extra familially remian high and under such conditions family tends to be the main organizer of production (Pollak, 1985). In a typical tribal economy, transactions are limited within community and production is organized at home to reduce their cost.

One outcome of such a regime of production and exchange is the very low productivitiy of different inputs and a small quantity of surplus. In the traditional society the small surplus is not used in productive investment, rather it is used for purchase of insurance through the provision of this surplus to the families suffering a deficit in production. This constitutes a type of mutual insurance, (Roy and Kuri, 1995). The emergence of market for risk tends to reduce the utility of mutual insurance obtaining in the traditional society. The process starts changing with the emergence of market and specialisation. The expansion of horizon of market brings into the picture the possibility of earning profit and use of this profit in the purchase of better and more productive inputs. This way of disposal of surplus weakens the traditional mutual insurance mechanism. With the emergence of market insurance, the successful innovators and entrepreneurs depend upon the market insurance. The market insurance no doubt enables the entrepreneur to trade some of this risk, but the trading of all risks is not possible. Some of these non insurable risks, in fact bring the profit, for example, the risk associated with the fluctuation of prices. The entrepreneurial success depends upon how efficiently this type of risk is tackled by the entrepreneur through the mediation of different institutional instruments.

Another spin-off from the emergence of market is the reduction of transaction costs. Market tends to enhance the flow of information. Along with the emergence of market there comes the standardization and codification of rules and regulations guiding the exchange. The contract also becomes easier and contractual relations are enforced by the judicial system. Judicial enforcement of contract is cheaper than its

1. The concept of transaction cost originated with Ronald Coase (1937). It was further developed by Williamson (1975 & 1979), and others. Simply speaking, transaction cost is the cost of contract: the cost arising out of pre-contract negotiation, associated requirement of information and the monitoring of contract.
2. In Anthropological literature this is called reciprocity. Firth (1967) and others.

customary enforcement. The uniform legal system makes long term contract between people belonging to different communities possible and this leads to the reduction of the cost of different economic transactions. A person can now purchase the labour services or other inputs from people belonging to other communities without suffering the risk that prevails when uncodified, non-standardized and possibly different customary rules and regulations are practised. Thus, entrepreneurship grows through an evolutionary process involving structural and institutional changes. At the individual level it involves a steady learning of the process of risk management and reduction of transaction costs. The growth of market and better flow of information facilitate this learning process and make room for the growth of entrepreneurship.

SECTION - II

In the state of Arunachal Pradesh no modern industry was established prior to Independence; even administrative services of the government were largely non-existent. Trade was highly limited and localised. Inter-tribal trade was few and far between. The economy was thus highly primitive and was characterised by very low productivity. Transactions were mainly non-monetized. In such a condition, innovativeness in organization of production through the medium of entrepreneurship could not grow.

After Independence, with the growth of tertiary sector, there came into being modern trade and industry. Of course, the government initially tried to develop the local handicrafts through the development of different craft centres. Even measures were taken to protect the local market against the wholesale marketing of industrial goods especially of those types which were supposed to corrupt the indigenous taste (NEFA Administration). Another purpose behind such restrictive practices was to encourage the local entrepreneurs.

The achievement in this regard seems not to be very outstanding. In spite of government's efforts, the local industry did not grow much, and the local preference shifted towards industrial goods produced elsewhere. The local entrepreneurs have not grown in large numbers, and moreover, the local people have shown a tendency not to face the competition of the market aggressively. This tendency is found in their preference for collaboration with the outside entrepreneurs. In such collaborations, the local promoters play a passive role; often they hire out their licence, buildings, mechinery, etc. to the outside entrepreneurs and they collect mainly the rent and interest. In organizational matters they play no role in many cases. Only in few cases they organize the business hiring the managers and skilled labour from outside the state.

In a market economy, an entrepreneur can partly trade his risk originating in business and partly he has to carry the risk especially the type of risk which is not insurable. The rise of corporatism has no doubt reduced the risk of business venture, but it has not eliminated it. A potential entrepreneur can, however, through various institutional machanisms reduce his overall risk. When this institutionally developed business environment is compared with the traditional economic environment of Arunachal Pradesh, it is found that the people here could through traditional means trade almost all their risk. The mutual insurance mechanism that was operative in the traditional Arunachal economy protected the income and consumption of the autochthonous people. This traditional insurance is dysfunctional in the modern sector where different market based insurance mechanisms are operative to cover risk, and yield returns, the amount of which being dependent upon the efficiency with which one can cope with this risk. Many potential entrepreneurs in this state find the risk associated with modern business to be too high: this is mainly because some of these institutional risk-coping mechanisms such as the companies with limited liabilities, etc. have not yet been properly developed in this state. The underdeveloped state of the business-promoting modern institutions tends to encourage the local entrepreneurs to operate mainly in the protected market, such as construction, government supplies, etc. where business complexity and associated risk is low.

Another factor having deleterious effect upon the entrepreneurship in Arunachal Pradesh is the high transaction costs in the modern sector. In the traditional economy of Arunachal Pradesh transaction costs were minimized by organizing production in the family farm and limiting the exchange of goods and services and often this exchange hardly crossed the tribal and local boundary. Limited market where bartering was the rule and monetized exchange was the exception created a set of rules and regulations which were known to everybody. These rules and regulations varied from tribe to tribe. Technology was very simple and unchanging over the generations and this simple technology enabled the people to organise production efficiently in a family farm. In order to minimise the transaction costs trading and general economic relationship were mainly established with known persons preferably with those belonging to one's own community.

Modern secondary and tertiary sectors appeared in this state rather suddenly and the business venture in these sectors carried high yield in an expanded horizon of transactions and complex technology. One characteristic of the expansion of the modern sectors in this state is that the different service sectors such as administration, educational institutions, hospitals, etc. were opened in the initial stage, and this created vast job openings in this sector. Those who got education found it very easy to get job in this sector. When, after some development of tertiary sector, the problem of modernization of agriculture and industry arose, the people of Arunachal Pradesh could not exhibit much entrepreneurial abilities. This is because the operations in modern sectors are guided by a complex set of institutional factors incorporated in the standardized rules and regulations. These standard rules and regulations of modern sector differ significantly from the traditional rules and regulations which guided the transactions in the peasant agriculture of Arunachal Pradesh. In this state the people have been operating in different institutional regimes, the regimes which vary from tribe to tribe. These institutional regimes are highly localised and they hardly go beyond the boundary of a tribe. In this state the institutions especially the legal institutions guiding the economic contract of the all the major tribes have not yet been codified and standardized. Moreover, no effort has yet been made to bridge the gap between the traditional institutional system and the standard institution operative elsewhere in the country.

This lack of the growth of institutions especially the ones dealing with economic contract has kept the transactions costs too high in the industrial sector. A successful operation in this sector warrants that the operator be well equipped with all information relating to the market, the relevant technology and too many sets of rules and regulations guiding the transactions. The problem in this state is that the business information is limited and business education is not adequately developed. Moreover, the traditional rules and regulations are not standardized so as to make them transparent. All these factors seems to underline the high transaction costs of business in this part of the country. The entrepreneurial growth requires a simultaneous development of different factors such as technical and business education, standardization of rules and regulations, better flow of information, etc. The encouragement of public limited companies with local initiative is an efficient institutional mechanism to develop entrepreneurship. Since the institutional factors inverwoven in the market mechanism seem to have stood in the way of entrepreneurship development in Arunachal Pradesh by creating the hurdle of high risk and transaction costs, it is necessary to develop the market fully so as to make possible the better trading of risk and to evolve the institution in a way which would reduce the cost of transactions.

REFERENCES

Coase, R.H. (1937): The Nature of the Firm, *Economica*. NS4: p.p. 386-405.

Firth, R. (1967): Themes in Economic Anthropology: A General Comment, in : Firth. R. (ed), *Themes in Economic Anthropology*, London: Tavistock Publications, pp. 1-26.

NEFA Administration: Different Reports.

Pollak, R.A. (1985): A Transaction Cost Approach to Families and Households. *Journal of Economic Literature*, 23: pp. 581-608.

Roy, N.C. and P.K. Kuri (1995): Risk, Land Reform and Agricultural Productivity in Arunachal Pradesh, paper presented at the International Seminar on Environment, Bio-diversity and Sustainable Development in North East India. (NEHU: Aizawl, Mizoram, 26-27 Sept. '95).

Williamson, O.E. (1975): *Markets and Hierarchies. Analaysis and Anti-trust Implications*. New York: The Free Press.

Williamson, O.E., (1979): Transaction Cost Economics: The Governance of Contractual Relations, *Journal of Law and Economics*, 22: pp. 236-62.

26

INDUSTRIALISATION AND ENTREPRENEURIAL DEVELOPMENT: A STUDY OF ZIRO TOWN IN ARUNACHAL PRADESH

--- Amitava Mitra and Dani.Chobin

Industrialisation has a major role to play in the development of an economy. The industrial sector which process a relatively high marginal propensity to save and invest contributes significantly in the eventual achievement of self-sustained economy with continued high levels of investment and rapid rate of increase in income and industrial employment. Thus industrialisation is inseparable from a substantial, sustained economic development because it is both a consequence of higher income and a means of higher productivity. It can be fairly contended that economic development is almost synonymous with industrialisation. Rapid development and diversification is not possible without due emphasis in industrial development.

Arunachal Pradesh (earlier known as North East Frontier Agency) started the journey to development only after the Independence of the country in 1947. In fact at the time of Independence Arunachal economy was a monoeconomy characterised by subsistence agriculture and a few cottage industries. Even upto the sixties, whatever manufacturing activity there was, it was only confined to handicrafts, a few saw mills and a vaneer factory. Thus the state is extremely industrially as well as economically backward due to historical factors and due to her belated entry into the process of national development. Unfavourable topographical and locational factors have added to that situation. However after becoming a union territory in 1972, there was a major shift in the earlier policy of development inducing a number of steps taken by the Government for accelerating rapid development of the state. Arunachal Pradesh has achieved significant growth in her income, literacy and urbanisation.

However the pace of industrialisation in the state is very slow in spite of the fact the the state is blessed with abundant potential for development of resource-based and demand-based industries. For example, the manufacturing sector has contributed around 5 per cent of Net State Domestic Product (NSDP) at constant prices of the state in 1991-92 (Economic Review of Arunachal Pradesh, 1993). Not to speak of large scale and medium scale industries, even in terms of small scale industries, the share of Arunachal Pradesh is only 1.8 per cent among all the states of North-Eastern Region in 1991. Several problems relating to socio-economic, topographical, infrastructural, financial, lack of entrepreneurship etc. are working as barriers to industrialisation of the state. At present our emphasis is mainly on emergence of entrepreneurship as a factor for rapid industrial development of the state. It is widely accepted that the availability of entrepreneurship is one of the most important determinants in the process of industrialisation. Most of the social scientists agree that man stands at the centre of economic activity and he assumes various roles at the development process and out of these multiple roles, his role as the organiser of human and material resources is the basic one.

The local people of Arunachal Pradesh are good craftsmen. They have a tradition of artistic craftsmanship, which is manifested through the products they produce. For example, Elwin states that "The chief art of NEFA is weaving and it is on the handloom that the greatest progress has been achieved" (A Philosophy for NEFA, 1999). Similarly Prof. Haimendorf speaks of highly developed aesthetic sense of Apa Tani tribes that "They show excellent taste in their colour combination and pattern of their textiles." (The Apa Tanis and their Neighbours, 1962). So the tribal entrepreneurs may now take the challenge to organise small industries with local resources and skill. For this, they require some sources of the funds for capital investment and look for entrepreneurial qualities.

This chapter is a humble attempt to study the socio-economic origins of the entrepreneurs of Arunachal Pradesh, in general and Ziro Town of Lower Subansiri district, in particular. The study is expected to help in identifying the advantages and the constraints associated with the socio-economic background of the entrepreneurs. For this purpose, a sample survey of small scale industrial units of Ziro, the district Headquarters of Lower Subansiri was selected. The sample survey is expected to give a good picture about the emergence of local entrepreneurs, because Ziro town (declared in 1991 Census) is mainly inhabited by Apa Tani tribe. The Apa Tanis are generally regarded as keen traders among the different tribes of the state. They have sharp sense of business as has been pointed out by Prof. Haimendorf (A Himalayan Tribe, 1980). The socio-economic factors like high density of population in Apa Tani valley and a quick response to modern education have also pushed them to take up business challenge.

SECTION-I

The Sample Study

A sample survey of 27 small and tiny industrial units of Ziro is undertaken for the purpose of the study. Out of 27 entrepreneurs included in the study, all were males and there was no woman entrepreneur. The conspicuous absence of women entrepreneur is due to the fact that their entry into entrepreneurial role is somewhat determined by the traditions of the society and the level of literacy. The mean age of entrepreneur is 27 years. The industry-wise distribution of entrepreneurs is given in Table 26.1.

TABLE 26.1: Industry-wise Distribution of Entrepreneurs

Sl.No.	Industry	Number of units	Number of tribal entrepreneurs
1.	Automobile servicing and repairing	6	5
2.	Furniture making	6	4
3.	Printing	5	2
4.	Saw mill	2	2
5.	Trunk making	2	Nil
6.	Others	6	1
	Total	27	14

Note: The others include manufacturing of electrical accessories, making bakery products, black-smithy etc.

Source: Sample Survey.

Table 26.1 shows the industry-wise break up of tribal ownership in the Sample Survey is saw mills (100%), automobile servicing and repairing (83.33%), furniture making (66.67%). If we observe more minutely regarding the ethnic origin of entrepreneurs, it is found that out of 27 entrepreneurs, 14 (51.85%) are local tribals and the remaining 13 (48.15%) are non-tribals. Among the non-tribal entrepreneurs there are 6 Bangalees, 4 Assamese, 2 Biharis and one Nepalee. In this connection is is to be noted that since the non-tribals have no legal rights in land and they are not entitled to get trading licenses unless alloted by Government. It is found sometimes that the tribals are getting the license and giving it to non-tribals against some arrangement of payment. In such type of collaborations, the local entrepreneurs play a passive role and they mainly collect the rent and interest. In some cases they start the business with the help of hired managers and skilled labourers recruited from outside the state. In our study area, it is found that most of labourers recruited are from outside the state.

The educational standard among the entrepreneurs is shown in Table 26.2.

TABLE 26.2: Education of Entrepreneurs Included in the Study

Level of Education	Number of Entrepreneurs	Percentage
Illiterate	4	14.81
Less than Matriculate	12	44.44
High school pass	11	40.75
Graduate and above	NIL	NIL
Total	27	100.00

Source: Field Study

From Table 26.2 it is found that majority of them (44.44%) are less than matriculate closely followed by High School pass (40.75%). In our sample study there is not a single graduate entrepreneur and four entrepreneurs are declared themselves as illiterate. So, it can be safely said that the level of educational standard among the entrepreneurs in the sample study is quite low.

In response to a question of earlier occupation, it is found that 40.75 per cent of respondents have reported themselves as students. That means there is a direct entry from students to join as entrepreneurs in the study area. Around 25.93 per cent of respondent entrepreneurs have revealed business as their previous occupation. Most of them have continued this business along with the present occupation and the majority of them belonged to the non-tribal. Normally the entry of the erstwhile farmers into manufacturing units is not a direct one as the farmers generally leave their occupation, join some new occupations and then take to industrial entrepreneurship. However, in our sample study 14.81 per cent respondent entrepreneurs are directly coming from farmers. Another three entrepreneurs are coming from Government job. The study reveals that around 74.07 per cent of the respondents (100% of tribal respondent entrepreneurs) have informed 'farmers' as the main occupation of their fathers. It implies that all of the tribal entrepreneurs are the first generation entrepreneurs. Only 18.72 per cent have come from business background. There are only two entrepreneurs whose fathers are Government employees. The details are shown in the Table 26.3.

TABLE 26.3: Occupational Mobility—Father's Occupation of the Entrepreneurs Included in the Study

Father's Occupation	Number of Entrepreneurs	Percentage
Farmer	20	74.07
Business	5	18.52
Government Employee	2	7.41
Total	27	100.00

Source: Field Study.

An individual phenomenon is hardly found in the Indian situation entrepreneurship and it has been viewed as an extension of the family aspirations and ambitions which are ultimately realised by an individual. The same situation is found in our sample study which reveals that around 77.77 per cent of the entrepreneurs have admitted that they have received family financial assistance for building up their occupational career as entrepreneurs. Only 22.22 per cent of respondent entrepreneurs have stated that they have received Government loan and most of them are engaged in furniture making and printing etc.

In response to a question the reason for starting career their as entrepreneurs, majority of them (70.37%) have informed that 'no job obtained' and 'to increase the family income' are the major reasons for taking up the profession. Only four of them have started the business for Government encouragement. Regarding the question of 'problems faced', majority (59.25%) of them have stated that financial and transport problems are the major problems which they are facing. Four respondents have revealed that lack of demand is the major problem which they are now facing.

Conclusion

The study shows that the local entrepreneurs have not emerged properly even after twenty years of modern phase of development. The local entrepreneurs are mainly the first generation entrepreneurs. The educational standards of the entrepreneurs are not also good. It appears that graduates and above qualified persons are looking for Government jobs and most of them are absorbed in Government jobs. Majority of persons who are not graduates or who have not got the Government jobs have started their career as entrepreneurs. However, the present study does not adequately explain the process of emergence and growth of entrepreneurial class in entire Arunachal Pradesh. It only includes some small and tiny industries of a newly emerged town and a district headquarters of one of the districts of the state. However the information obtained from the field study regarding the socio-economic background of entrepreneurs will be helpful for the planners and policy makers for the development of entrepreneurs. Finally it can be said that the self-sustained development of the state warrants rapid industrialisation which cannot be achieved without skill formation and entrepreneurial development among the local people of the state. The Government should adopt measures for the ideal process of interaction between entrepreneurial development and industrialisation. However, much will depend on the success of motivating the youths at different levels of education to shake off their fond fascination for Government jobs (where the absorption capacity is limited) and to take up the adventurers career of an independent entrepreneur.

REFERENCES

Das, Gurudas, *Tribes of Arunachal Pradesh in Transition*, Vikash Publishing House, New Delhi, 1995.

Despande Manohar, *Entrepreneurship of Small Scale Industries,* Deep and Deep, Delhi, 1982.

Elwin, V., *A Philosophy of NEFA,* Shillong, 1959.

Furer Haimendorf, C.V., *The Apa Tanis and their Neighbours*, Routledge, London, 1962.

Furer Haimendorf, C.V., *A Himalayan Tribe*, Vikas Publishing House, New Delhi, 1980.

Government of Arunachal Pradesh, *Economic Review of Arunachal Pradesh,* Itanagar, 1993.

North Eastern Council, *Basic Statistics of North Eastern Region,* Shillong, 1992.

27

GROWTH OF ENTREPRENEURSHIP IN ARUNACHAL PRADESH: PROBLEMS AND PROSPECTS—A STUDY WITH REFERENCE TO THE KHAMPTI TRIBE

— M.C. Behera and Helina Mantaw

Studies relating to the growth of entrepreneurship in the tribal areas have assumed greater significance in view of *top-down* policy of the administration to transform their primitive economy into a market oriented diversified economy. A tribal economy, basically self-sufficient in nature, produces for self-consumption and in some cases barters the surplus for goods which have practical use and are either not available or fall short of demand. The Apatanis, expert in weaving, used to barter rice with the neighbouring Nishis for cotton[1] and yarn.

Production in a tribal economy is the totality of operations aimed at procuring its "material means of existence and non-economic social structures may function in the social organisation of production".[2] It is organised at the level of community on the basis of both a technical and a social division of labour based on age and sex and on simple or complex co-operation. The internal organisation of the tribe around specific marriage and kinship relations may vary. Variations at this level govern the precise character of the distribution of the product within the community since that is the result of the intervention of ideological (cultural, religious) social relations."[3]

Distribution in tribal communities, even where individual production is allowed, is also influenced by socio-cultural considerations in the absence of market mechanism. The Khamptis and Apatanis who have been practising wet rice cultivation since long past had to see to the need of the community before any outside transaction. The outside transaction had no commercial motive other than procuring/bartering goods having use-value in the community. The Khamptis, for example, used to sell rice and potato[4] at Sadiya; the sale being organised on a co-operative basis by members tied together with kinship relations which necessarily did not rely on 'blood'.[5] The sale was not organised to earn profit but to procure goods such as yarn, cloths whose utility was conspicuous in the community.[6] Organisation of production for market was not a feature of the Khampti economy though they used to sell their produce.

The economic domain of the tribals within their socio-cultural framework does not generate conditions like the existence of capital accumulation, productive economic conditions and social enforcement for the growth of entrepreneurship, surplus produce of the individual families gets channelised into organising feasts and other pleasure pursuits which used to carry status symbol with it in the community.

The Economic-Culture Type[7] of different ethnic groups living in Arunachal Pradesh was roughly at an identical level of historical development. Mode of appropriation of material means of existence was also identical varying in degree in relation to the nature of economic activities ranging between "food gathering" and "food production". Production was need based and was being organised on communal ways of appropriating resources. Such economies held no ground for the existence of the role of entrepreneur.

But with the introduction of development measures, production relations have been modified and distribution system is being influenced by market forces. Forces of production i.e. the mode of appropriation of nature in the process of combining factors of production has assumed significance in relation to market forces and profit earning has become a motive behind organising productive activities. The economy has been diversified and has generated a change in the relative role of different sectors in the economy of the state.[8] Consequent upon this, the entrepreneurial activities are growing up in the territory.

Growth of entrepreneurship is a function of socio-cultural factors and is a feature of market economy. The term entrepreneurship, though has different interpretation, atleast includes "a part of the administrative function of making decisions for the conduct of some type of organisation".[9] The difference arises largely from the characteristics of the sector of the economy that chiefly attracted the attention of the economists. Economists interested in the government saw the entrepreneur as contractor or architect,[10] the specialists on agriculture as a farmer and the proponents of industry as a risk-taker.[11] Cantillon's[12] entrepreneur is anybody who is engaged in economic activity and bears uncertainty while Say's[13] one is the agent who combines all means of production. Hawley writing in 1982 saw risk taking as the distinguishing attribute of the entrepreneur, and ranked this as a factor in production on a par with land, labour and capital.[14] To Schumpeter[15] entrepreneurship is a new way of doing things or doing new things i.e. innovation while to Cole[16] it is the purposeful activity of an individual or group of associated individuals, undertaken to initiate, maintain or aggrandize a profit oriented business unit for the production or distribution of economic goods and services.

Entrepreneur as a quality may be original or acquired through education and training and the entrepreneurs' function may relate to industrial or non-industrial activities. Initiating any economic activity in a novel way or initiating a novel economic activity on the face of typical uncertainties in the present business world needs as much capability as in industrial activities. So, entrepreneur as an innovator, initiator and uncertainty bearer plays significant role both in the context of industrial and non-industrial activities.

With this backdrop this chapter aims at studying the growth of entrepreneurship in the Khampti community, both in industrial and non-industrial activities, after the introduction of development measures in the community in particular and in the state in general.

Objectives of the Study

The study is based on the following objectives:

(i) To discuss the industrial activities that are being undertaken in Arunachal Pradesh,

(ii) To identify entrepreneurial activities, both in industrial and non-industrial activities in Khampti community,

(iii) To study the trend of entrepreneurial activities among the Khamptis in their cultural perspective and identify problems detrimental to entrepreneurship growth, and

(iv) To generalise plan implications in the state for the growth of entrepreneurship in cultural perspective.

Methodology

The study is based on both primary and secondary sources. For secondary source data, reference had been made to earlier works on Khamptis and other works related to the topic. Data from primary source were collected from internal records of concerned departments and from the field study which was undertaken aiming at qualitative perception of the culture of the Khamptis. Field study was undertaken for the purpose during the period from December 25, to January 31, 1996, though the authors have had long association with the community.

II

Industrialisation as an indicator of economic development is in a poor state in Arunachal Pradesh in view of 20.82 per cent share of secondary sector in net state domestic product (NSDP) at constant prices during 1993-94. The secondary sector activities simply comprise unregistered manufacturing activities, construction activities and electricity, gas and water supply.[17] Workforce participation in this sector also presents a dismal picture. About 8.66 per cent of main workers were recorded in secondary sector activities in 1991 census report and this was almost same (8.62%) as in 1981. Among the tribal population in the state, this work force constitutes 2.98 per cent of tribal main workers in 1991.

The secondary sector activities include activities in private sector, public sector and co-operative sector undertakings. A cement plant at Tezu with the capacity of 30 TDP, citronella distillation plant and light roofing sheet factory at Pasighat, food processing unit at Nigmoi (Along), muga seed plant at Jia, TV and Walkman sterio assembling unit at Itanagar, sericulture rearing centre at Nongkhon are public sector undertakings. Activities of 81 craft/weaving/knitting centres, 13 emporia, 28 sericulture demonstration centres, 12 district industry centres (DICs)[18] etc. come under this sector along with electricity, gas and water supply.

For providing infrastructural facilities, the government has developed 13 industrial estates in the state. In Naharlagun industrial estate, there are 23 sheds out of which seven were found closed down. The activities of remaining sheds comprise three printing press units, five steel fabrication/wire product units, two furniture units, one flour milling-cum-oil expelling unit, one handloom production unit, one cigarettes manufacturing unit and one tyre retarding unit.

The industrial activities, in private, public and co-operative sectors are confined to 18 medium and 3,306 village and small scale industries[19] and include activities of forest and agro-based industries, bakery, weaving, knitting units, candle making, flour and oil mills, rice mills, steel and iron fabrication units, handlooms and handicrafts, etc. The number of wood based industries for which licenses have been issued is noted 217 and out of this 130 are functioning including Nocte Timber Co. Ltd., M/s. Narrottam Co-operatives Industries (Pvt.) Ltd., M/s Borduria Timber Products (Pvt.) Ltd. under public and co-operative management.[20] The SSI units had generated employment to 10,465 youth upto 1994. During 1995-96, employment generated and entrepreneurs trained are recorded 1893 and 625 respectively.

The above analysis throws light on limited industrial activities in the state and more so in private sector. Increase in the share of tertiary sector in NSDP from 20.48 per cent in 1971 to 33.83 per cent in 1993-94 and almost unchanged contribution of secondary sector during the period (it was 20.33% in 1971 and rose to 20.82% in 1933-94) manifests the stagnant nature of secondary sector. Manufacturing activities, confined to unregistered units only, contribute 29.61 per cent to NSDP while construction activities contribute 80.54 per cent. The contribution of electricity, gas and water supply is 10.15 per cent. The magnitude of manufacturing activities in relation to its share in NSDP is low as compared to that of construction activities. The Report[21] of the Group on Industrial Development of the North-Eastern Region has also identified industrial backwardness in the region in general and Arunachal Pradesh in particular. The first ever industrial policy which came into effect from 1st April, 1994 has the provision for 17 packages of state incentives to gear up industrialisation process in the state[22] and these incentives are almost the same as extended earlier.[23] This suggests that industrial activities promoted earlier did not come up to the desired level and so same policy has been adopted in the industrial policy of the state As per the available information from the Department of Industries, 7,801 entrepreneurs were trained in different crafts during the period 1954 to 1982. But 3,306 number of SSI units upto 1996 shows that the scope in the field is still under-utilised.

Internalisation of external forces of change in the process of industrialisation could not be achieved because of the nature of socio-economic transformation that generated scope for easy money through contract works and political involvement. Besides, there are conventional constraints like inadequate infrastructure., financial resource. Above, all, there is the lack of a general attitude and motivation for undertaking industrial activities, in spite of the state's endeavour to gear up such activities. The chapter attempts to analyse the psycho-social constraints in cultural perspectives which are related to the emergence of entrepreneurial class with Khamptis as the case study.

III

The Khamptis living in about 30 major villages of Chowkham and Namsai circles of Lohit district of Arunachal Pradesh are of Shan descent and practise wet rice cultivation. Besides agriculture, they were also engaged in non-farm activities before independence[24] but such activities were compatible with the features of tribal economy. Their trade relation with the plains of Assam could not bring about any perceptible change in their socio-economic forces in existence.[25] The traditional economy, like other tribals, had more cultural elements in its domain than economic factors. Excess of production over sustenance was channelised into feasts, festivals and donations which were supposed to earn religious merit. Though they are Buddhists of Theraveda cult and observe all ceremonial pieties, they still follow 'animism'. The two opposing faiths have been internalised into their system in such a way as to give them a distinct cultural identity. They believe in animism for material gain and worldly happiness and at the same time use these material wealth to earn religious merit and afterlife happiness.[26]

Land tenure system of the Khamptis was communal in nature and individual right as subject to land utilization within the framework of community ownership. Though land was free gift of nature and carried status symbol with it, the general attitude for land ownership was not for 'acquisition for accumulation' but for satisfaction of needs as perceived by their socio-cultural outlook. The Khamptis had a chieftainship type of society and the *Chaufa* and *Chauman* had command over community resource base. Still, the attitude behind land acquisition was need based and therefore no exclusive individual right on land ownership was recognised in the community.

After independence, the Khampti economy has been diversified[27] and the Khamptis have been identified as emerging entrepreneurs.[28] So, for present study, 50 entrepreneurs were selected on purpose. On the basis of field study following observations were made:

1. The entrepreneurial activities were confined to wood-based industry, plantation, backery, knitting units, bricks manufacturing, trunk manufacturing, handlooms, establishment of schools, contract works, rice and flour mills, oil mills etc.
2. Out of 10 wood based factories, six bebonged to chief's families and four to others and all had command over traditional resource base. These families were found having kinship relations and involved in active state politics. One saw mill owner was reported to be a surrendered ULVA who was rehabilitated by the government and another had received the saw mill as a gift from the Khampti Chief *(Chaufa)* after his matrimonial alliance with the chief's family.
3. All the five residential schools noted were run by women entrepreneurs, four of whose male counterparts own wood based industries.
4. Of 10 entrepreneurs engaged in wood based industries, five had channelised their investible surplus to plantation industries and one to an agro-based industry.
5. Two cases of entrepreneurs who invested in petrol depot were recorded and they belonged to two of the above 10 entrepreneurial families.
6. Out of fifty entrepreneurs 10 women entrepreneurs were recorded who also came from above 10 families. Five of them ran weaving/knitting units.
7. Forty entrepreneurs were noted who had invested on housing which they had rented for commercial and residential purposes.
8. Two entrepreneurs interested in investing on paper mills were reported to have restrained from undertaking the venture because of their inaccessibility to information on technical matters.
9. Other units such as bakery, furniture making and trunk making units were rented to outside businessmen as all of local entrepreneurs were engaged in contract works.
10. Except wood based industries. income generated from other activities was spent on consumer durables, tours, feasts and festivals and on gambling. Though quantitative income figure was not available, level of income from wood based industries was quite high. The expenditure of such entrepreneurs on

luxuries, religious ceremonies and on pleasure pursuits along with investment on other productive activities gives an idea of a quite high level of income.

11. Of fifty entrepreneurs, eight were reported to be graduates, ten with higher secondary education and others below secondary level. Even women entrepreneurs running schools were reported below higher secondary level of education.

IV

Entrepreneurial activities among the Khamptis have been concentrated in a few families. Industrial entrepreneurs are mostly from chief's families and these families had outside contact due to historical reasons. The nature of industrial activities show that such activities have been undertaken which are comparatively more profit yielding and which have a place in their socio-cultural life. The Khamptis were involved in forest and agricultural activities and this might be attributed to the growth of wood based and plantation industries. It was found during field study that entrepreneurs did not have any knowledge or had little knowledge about activities in the field of chemical, plastic and electronic goods industries. The level of education is not quite high among the entrepreneurs. It was brought to the notice of the researchers that those who get higher education opt for government jobs. The entrepreneurs are found to have emerged from families with command over traditional resource base and political connection. The traditional socio-cultural hold in the way of life of the people channelises surplus into unproductive activities. The demonstration effect has become so powerful that people spend their surplus on conspicuous consumption. The hedonistic attitude of the Khamptis is observed to be adversely affecting the risk bearing quality which is very much essential for the growth of entrepreneurial activities. The few cases of industrial entrepreneurs among the Khamptis are the result of their attitudinal difference due to historical factors which developed the quality of adaptability to external thrust with compatibility to their socio-cultural and environmental sense of appreciation.

Industrial policy should be directed to identify cultural dynamics of the people, generate awareness and impart vigorous training by touching every aspect of entrepreneurial activities so that motivation for risk taking in entrepreneurial activities is created. Consequent upon this a class of entrepreneurs with proper motivation, awareness will emerge.

The tribal way of life and their interaction with nature have given them natural quality to bear uncertainty and undertake risk. Such qualities need to be tuned with the requirements of entrepreneurship. As a result, the process of economic transformation will be smooth, and balanced in a state with multiethnic groups as Arunachal Pradesh and the development will be sustainable.

REFERENCES

Shukla, B.K. (1959): *The Daflas of the Subansiri Region*, Reprint 1965, NEFA, Shillong, 25.

Mathew, T. (1980): *Tribal Economy of North Eastern Region* (ed.); Spectrum Publications, Guwahati, p. 7.

Ibid., p. 14

Cooper, T.T. (1873): *The Mishmi Hills*. Reproduced in 1995, Mital Publications. New Delhi, p. 150.

For kinship relation other than 'blood'. see Sills, D.L., (1972): *International Encylopaedia of the Social Sciences*, Vol. 7 & 8, The Macmillan Company of the Free Press, New York, pp. 408-413. During field study villagers of Monong supplied the information that group of individuals with no blood relation used to go to Sadiya to sell rice, boat etc.

Information collected during field study.

Alexeev, P.V. (1986): *The Origin of Human Race*, Progress Publishers, Moscow, p. 287.

Das, Gurudas (1992): Structural Change in the Economy of Arunachal Pradesh in the *Journal of NEICSSR*, (16:2) Oct., 1992 Shillong, pp. 37-46.

Sills, D.L. *op. cit.*, p. 87.

Hoselitz, Bert F. (1951): The early History of Entrepreneurial Theory, Explorations in *Entrepreneurial History*: 3, p. 195.

Ibid, pp. 205-12.

Cantillon, Richard (1755): 1952: *Essai Sur la nature du' commerce en general*. Paris, Institute National d 'E' tudes Demographiques.

Say, J.B. (1815-16): Catechim of Political Economy: Or, Familiar conversations on the Manner in which Wealth is Produced, Distributed and Consumed by society, Sherwood, London.

Dorfman, Joseph, (1946-59): *The Economic Mind in American Civilization*, 5 Vols. (especially Vol. 3 & 4), Viking, New York.

Schumpeter, J.A. (1947): *The Creative Response in Economic History*: 7, pp. 149-59.

Cole, A.H. (1959): *Business Enterprise in its Social Setting*, Harvard University Press.

Economic Review of Arunachal Pradesh, 1994. Directorate of Economics and Statistics, Govt. of Arunachal Pradesh, Itanagar, pp. 9-13.

Directorate of Industries, Govt. of Arunachal Pradesh, Itanagar.

Ibid.

The Annual Administration Report, 1993-94, The Department of Environment and Forest, Govt. of Arunachal Pradesh, Itanagar.

The Report of the Group on Industrial Development of the North-Eastern Region including Sikkim and the Andaman and Nicobar Islands (1995); Ministry of Finance, Dept. of Economic Affairs.

Industrial Policy of Arunachal Pradesh, Dept. of Industries, Govt. of Arunachal Pradesh, Itangar.

Das, Gurudas (1995): *Tribes of Arunachal Pradesh in Transition,* Vikas Publishing House, Pvt. Ltd., New Delhi, pp. 98-109.

Behera, M.C., (1994): *Planning and Socio-Economic Development of the Tribals,* Common Wealth Publishers, New Delhi, pp. 67-72.

Ibid., p. 91,

Ibid., p. 35,

Ibid., pp. 86-89.

Das, Gurudas, *op. cit.,* p. 225.

28

STATUS OF AND SOCIOLOGICAL CONSTRAINTS TO INDUSTRIAL DEVELOPMENT IN ARUNACHAL PRADESH

— B. Panda

The Economy of the land of the rising sun i.e. Arunachal Pradesh is in a transitional stage today. Centuries long isolation of the North-Eastern region in general and the hilly state of Arunachal in particular from the national mainstream had made its economy inward looking and quiet like the mute hills of the region. Subsequently, the end of the British raj, the dynamics of population growth and the imperatives of strategic location have all ensured a new era of development though interaction and administrative impetus. As a result of the unleashed forces of change, the relatively static structure of the economy became dynamic, first horizontally and of the late vertically.

It is the slow Sanskritisation of the structure of the economy from a near cent per cent agrarian one to one with some elements of industry, that has of late necessitated all concerned to have a close look on the state of industrial development in the state along with the sociological constraints in its way so as to formulate suitable policies and programmes of development and employment generation. This chapter is a modest attempt in this direction based largely on secondary data and personal observation.

Industrial Backwardness

Arunachal is industrially backward and has been declared as category

'A' region in terms of industrial backwardness. This backwardness is evident when one looks at the (i) share of the secondary sector in the composition of its state domestic product (SDP) at factor cost, (ii) share of the manufacturing sector in SDP at factor cost, (iii) percentage share of manufacturing sector employment in total employment. Data reveal that in 1991-92 the share of the secondary sector in the NSDP at factor cost in constant prices was 19.90 per cent whereas the all-India average was 25.8 per cent. Further the share of the manufacturing sector in NSDP was 5.74 per cent whereas the corresponding national average was 19.8 per cent. Manufacturing employment forms only 2.68 per cent of the total employment in the state in 1991. On the otherhand, the share of the primary sector in net state domestic product (NSDP) was 47.60 per cent in Arunachal in 1991-92 and the share of the agricultural employment in total gainful employment was 67.26 per cent in 1991. This indicates that the economy is primarily agriculture dominated and industrial development is at a very low level. The share of the different sectors from 1980-81 to 1991-92 has also not shown any radical change. The share of the primary sector has not shown any amount of appreciable change rather almost remained stagnant. The share of the secondary sector has marginally increased during early eighties but after 1986-87 it has almost remained stagnant.

History of Industrialization

A modest beginning in industrialization was made after independence especially during the year 1953-54. Because of various socio-physical and socio-economic constraints the state initially concentrated to consolidate, develop and strengthen the existing traditional cottage and handloom units along with village industries. Subsequently, from the Fourth Five Year Plan onwards a beginning was made to build up small scale units and village industries that depended mostly on locally available resources. Correspondingly the role of the state expanded from providing capital, upgrading technology and ensuring of marketing of products of existing cottage, handloom and village industrial units to setting up training and financial institutions. Establishment of craft centres to train and upgrade technology, to provide subsidies and marketing facilities was a logical step in this direction. It was during the Sixth Five Year Plan period that efforts were vigorously made to encourage setting up village and small scale industries. Thus, followed measures to establish district industries centres in 1978, to solve problems of industrialization and to promote further industrialization in an integrated manner. Initially five DICs were established at Bomdilla, Ziro, Along, Tezu and Khonsa which were soon followed by six sub-district industries centres at Tawang, Seppa, Daparijo, Pasighat, Roing and Changlong. Industrial estates were established in 1978-79 in West-Kameng and East-Kameng districts. By 1987-88, 12 industrial estates came into being. Establishment of supporting institutions like Small Industries Service Institute (1973), Arunachal Pradesh Industrial Development and Finance Corporation (APDFC 1978-79), introduction of the scheme of Growth Centres, upgradation of the Industries Department to a major department during July 1980 etc. paved the way for planned industrial development in the state.

Status of Industrial Development

Industrial development is a wider concept and includes in its ambit the growth *per se* in industrial units of all sizes, their structure and output, growth in supporting infrastructure having direct and immediate bearing on the industrial units. It also encompasses in its scope, industrial outlay, spread of Industries, industrial policy and industrial relations. However, paucity of space and time makes it necessary to confine the discussion to growth in industrial units, structure and output and spread of industries.

Growth in Industrial Units

Growth in Industrial units is depicted in Table 28.1

Structure and Output

The small scale and village industries front consists of cane furniture units, wood-craft units, wood furniture units, wood veneer units, sawn timber units (all forest based); agro-industries, Carpentry, Black-smithy, Silver Simithy, Bee- keeping, Hullers/oil mills, Steel furnitures, Printing Press etc. Out of the total number of medium scale industries, one is a mini-cement plant (Sick these days), One fruit processing plant, and one tea Industries. Rest of the medium scale Industries are wood based.

TABLE 28.1: Number of Cottage, Village, Small Scale and Medium Scale Industrial Units in A.P. as on 31.3.94

Districts	Industries				
	Craft centre	Weaving units	SSI Units	Medium Industries	Sericulture Demonos-tration centre
Tawang	2	2	74	-	-
West Kameng	3	3	204	-	3
East Kameng	7	7	74	-	1
Lower Subansiri	7	7	467	-	-
Upper Subansiri	6	6	138	-	1
West Siang	10	9	331	1	1
East Siang	10	-	297	1	7
Dibang valley	4	4	299	3	2
Lohit	6	6	403	3	2
Tirap	16	16	229	3	1
Changlang	5	4	107	4	6
Papum Pare	4	4	35	1	4
Total	80	78	2660	16	28

Source: Statistical Abstract of Arunachal Pradesh, 1994.

The growth in industrial output is depicted below in Table 28.2.

TABLE 28.2: Movement of Industrial Output (Current Prices) Contribution

(in lakhs of Rs.)

Year	Mining and Quarrying	Reqd. mfg.	Unreqd. mfg.	Total	Percentage Annual growth of total
1984-85	677	-	444	1121	-
1985-86	764	-	515	1279	14.09
1986-87	780	-	594	1374	7.42
1987-88	608	-	679	1287	(-)6.33
1988-89	564	-	770	1334	6.76
1991-92	291	-	2567	2858	-
1992-93 (P)	668	-	4601	5269	84.35
1993-94 (Q)	598	-	5808	6406	21.58

Source : State domestic Product till 1988-89, Directorate of Economics & Statistics, Govt. of A.P.

Spread of Industries

The spread of small scale and medium-scale industrial units is uneven in the state. Table 28.3, 28.4 and 28.5 better explaint it for small scale, medium-scale and craft-centres respectively. Data for number of small-scale, medium scale units and craft centres, total population and percentage of population of various districts are given. Let us take the hypothesis that the spread of population and industrial units in the various districts is in the same proportion or does not differ significantly to each other. Let us also assume the percentage share of Industrial units in each district as "*O*" and the Percentage Share in Population as "*E*" then $X^2 = (O–E)^2/E = 51.47$ for small scale industries. Number of degree of freedom = $(n–1) = 12–1=11$. For II degree of freedom at 5 per cent level of significance the table value of $X^2 = 19.75$. The calculated value of $X^2 = 51.47$. This sugests that the difference in the spread of small scale industries is significant. The spread of small scale industries is not in proportion to population in various districts rather is skewed in favour of a few districts. The districts of Tawang, East Kameng, Upper Subansiri, Dibang Valley, Tirap, Changlang and Papumpare (seven in number) are having lesser proportional share in SSI industrial units than that of their percentage share in population. Only the districts of West Kameng, Lower Subansiri, West Siang, East Siang and Lohit (5 in numbers) are having more than the proportional share in SSI industrial units than that of their percentage share in population. These five districts account for 64 per cent of the total SSI industrial units of the state.

In case of medium scale units $X^2 = 99.77$ which signifies that the difference in spread of industries is highly significant.

In case of craft centre, $X^2 = 22.00$ which is slightly more than the table value of X^2 i.e. 19.75. This suggests the fact that the spread of difference is although significant is not very high.

Constraints to Industrial Development

Industrial Development in a tribal economy like Arunachal Pradesh is a function of its socio-cultural, economic, political, geographical and institutional variables. The state has considerable amount of forest, mineral and water resources. It has provided a stable government for the last twenty years or so. Capital is aplenty as reflected in very low credit-deposit ratios of all most all the commercial banks operating in the state.

TABLE 28.3: Position of S.S.I. in the Districts of Arunachal Pradesh

Name of the district	Population	S.S.I. Sector No. of Units	Percentage share in S.S.I. Units (O)	Population (E)	$\frac{(O-E)^2}{E}$
Tawang	28287	74	2.78	3.27	0.07
West Kameng	56421	204	7.67	6.53	0.20
East Kameng	50395	74	2.78	5.83	1.60
Lower Subansiri	83167	469	17.63	9.62	6.67
Upper Subansiri	72811	138	5.19	8.42	1.24
West Siang	50086	331	12.44	5.79	7.64
East Siang	89936	297	11.17	10.40	0.06
Dibang Valley	99643	299	11.24	11.53	0.01
Lohit	43068	403	15.15	4.98	20.77
Tirap	109706	229	8.16	12.69	1.31
Changlang	95530	107	4.02	11.05	4.47
Papum Pare	85508	35	1.32	9.89	7.43
Arunachal Pradesh	864558	2660	100.0	100.0	51.47

TABLE 28.4: Position of Medium Scale Units in the Different Districts of Arunachal Pradesh

Name of the district	Medium Scale Sector No. of Units	Percentage share in Units (O)	Population (E)	$\frac{(O-E)^2}{E}$
Tawang	0	0	3.27	3.27
West Kameng	0	0	6.53	6.53
East Kameng	0	0	5.83	5.83
Lower Subansiri	0	0	9.62	9.62
Upper Subansiri	0	0	8.42	8.42
West Siang	1	6.25	5.79	0.04
East Siang	1	6.25	10.40	1.66
Dibang Valley	3	18.75	11.53	4.52
Lohit	3	18.75	4.98	38.04
Tirap	3	18.75	12.69	2.89
Changlang	4	25.00	11.05	17.61
Papum Pare	1	6.25	9.89	1.34
Arunachal Pradesh	16	100.0	100.0	99.77

TABLE 28.5 : Position of Craft Centres in Different Districts of Arunachal Pradesh

Name of the district	Craft Centre			
	No. of Units	Percentage share in		
		Units (O)	Population (E)	$\frac{(O-E)^2}{E}$
Tawang	2	2.50	3.27	0.18
West Kameng	3	3.75	6.53	1.18
East Kameng	7	8.75	5.83	1.46
Lower Subansiri	7	8.75	9.62	0.08
Upper Subansiri	6	7.50	8.42	0.10
West Siang	10	12.50	5.79	7.78
East Siang	10	12.50	10.40	0.42
Dibang Valley	4	5.00	11.53	3.70
Lohit	6	7.50	7.50	1.28
Tirap	16	20.00	12.69	4.21
Changlang	5	6.25	11.05	2.09
Papum Pare	4	5.00	9.80	2.42
Arunachal Pradesh	80	100.0	100.0	22.00

Supporting institutions for providing training, consultancy, capital have come up in recent years because of state initiative. There is sufficient demand for a number of products such as food items, furnitures, electronic goods, stationery articles, construction materials and other household and kitchen durables and non-durables etc. The environment is dust free and pollution free. Education and literacy have first developed significantly over the past two decades. Pressure on land has started increasing as reflected in the continuous decline in average size of land holding because of a high decadal population growth requiring theoretically a shift in occupational structure. However, in spite of all these positive developments and existing resources and factors, the state has remained one of the industrially most backward states in the country. Why? This is a very vital question which needs to be addressed immediately and logically.

There is no denying of the fact that poor core-infrastructures especially communication, transport and power are important reasons for the industrial backwardness of the state. Much has been written on this aspect and it need not has to be emphasised here. The same is also the case so far as its difficult topography is concerned.

Apart from these genuine limitations, the most important constraint to industrial development in the state is the dearth of entrepreneurs and entrepreneurial skills in the natives for lack of pre-existing conditions and present exigencies. Genuine entrepreneurship growth is as much dependent on psychological and socio-cultural factors as on economic and technical factors. It is as much conditioned by the Psychol-Socio-Cultural, socio economic factors and material prerequisites as it conditions them. Over the last few years there has been a tremendous improvement in the provisions of social, economic and institutional infrastructure but it has not resulted in any notable development of genuine entrepreneurship. In my private discussion with the high level officers of industries department, concerned officers of the State Bank of India, political leaders and student leaders here in Lohit district, a fact which is common in their deliberations is that a high percentage of the number of native entrepreneurs shown in Government and bank records are not *de facto* entrepreneurs. A survey undertaken by me on 25 SSI units (the universe is also 25) recorded by D.I.C. Lohit district in 1994 reveal that 80 per cent of the units are managed and run by nonlocal proxy entrepreneurs. The *de jure* native entrepreneurs simply get licenses in their names and lend them to proxy entrepreneurs on monthly/yearly payment agreement. Such a practice strikes at the very root of entrepreneurship development.

The prevailing social arrangement provides ample opportunities for the natives to earn easy money without taking up any risk. For example in districts such as Lohit, Lower Subansiri, East Siang, West Kameng etc. geting a trade licence for timber business is a craze with the natives especially the educated and social elite. After procurement of the licence they lend it to non-locals. The agreed rate of return in this case is high in comparision to the same in other types of trades.

Besides timber licence it is a common practice in entire Arunachal to procure trade licence for other types of business such as merchandise and service trades and lend it to proxy businessmen on contract against monthly/yearly handsome payments. Again the expanding construction sector has provided ample opportunities to the semi-educated and educated youths to work as full contractors, petty contractors and sub-contractors in various construction activities undertaken by the state P.W.D. and R.W.D. and thus earn huge amounts of money facing practically no risk. These opportunities of earning easy money without investing a single pie and without putting on any labour, is responsible for discouraging the neo-social elite and educated youths to opt for setting up Industries/Industrial concerns where the initial ground work is comparatively difficult and the returns are not so much promising. In a recent survey undertaken by this author on native students of I.G. Government College, it is found that 70 per cent of them want to graduate to a career of *de jure* business involving easy money, 10 per cent want to enter into active politics, 15 per cent want employment in public and private sectors and only 5 per cent want to enter into industrial ventures.

In the prevailing social system in Arunachal the dignity of Industrial enterprise and the dignity of labour are not the factors for social elevation and prestige rather it is one's stock of money resources, assets and the frequency and degree of lavish entertainment of the members of one's clan and enlarged community that is the index of one's vertical ranking in social hierarchy and passport to political ascendency. In such social milieu growth of entrepreneurship,therefore,takes a back seat.

It is a well-known fact that entrepreneurship growth is a positive function of strong will power and spirit of hardwork which to some extent can be created through motivation and other state incentives. Assuming ever-increasing state incentives, it is motivation that counts. But in the prevaling social milieu neither the political bosses nor the bureaucrats seem to be genuinely interested to motivate the people at large for taking up industrial activities. Unemployment magnitude is not so high that it would warrant a sort of compulsion in bringing a significant change in occupational structure in favour of industrialisation.

Further the typical habit of the native males to take to country liqour (in case of rural masses) and country plus foreign liquors (in case of the social elite) undermines their spirit and capacity to undertake genuine mental and physical work so fundamental to entrepreneurial growth.

Certain existing social institutions and customs such as joint and extended family systems (through polygamy) practised among a number of tribes such as Mishmis, Tanqsas, Wanchois, Noctes, Nishis; community ownership of land etc. breed lethargy and dependency which is not conducive for material development and thus for entrepreneurship development. The system of community ascendency over individual supremacy kills private intiative so vital for industrial development and for entrepreneurship growth.

Industrial entrepreneurship in large number of cases is a family culture if one goes by the background of successful entrepreneurs in India. All but all the existing few *de facto* native entrepreneurs in Arunachal Pradesh are first generation ones and those who are going to be the entrepreneurs in near future would also mostly going to be first generation ones. And it is doubtless to say that the odds are too heavy atleast psychologically for them. Hence these psychological odds and lack of basic entrepreneurial skill come in the way of faster entrepreneurial growth in the state.

However so far as the cottage and village industries are concerned it is observed that most of the native entrepreneurs of these tiny units suffer from marketing deficiency and product redundancy. A centralized marketing agency is the need of the hour which will go a long way in solving their most serious constraint. Product upgradation can be realized through pioneering efforts of the technical personnels of the industries department and other specialized institutions operating in this field.

Finally it is an industrial culture that begets entrepreneurship and entrepreneurs. Such a culture is lacking in Arunachal Pradesh. Thus more the industrialization more is the chances of birth of entrepreneurs. To have more industries, the state should in initial periods invite industrialists from outside to have industries established or to have joint ventures undertaken with native private entrepreneurs or state entrepreneur. This humble beginning will expose the future native entrepreneurs to an industrial culture so that through diffusion of it, more innovator and immitator entrepreneurs shall appear in coming years and would devise their plan and programmes of industrialisation in the light of the prevailing resource endowments and social requirements. Suitable modifications of the inner line permit and land ownership laws therefore would be the necessities.

Conclusion

Arunachal Pradesh is one of the industrially most bckward states of the union. Its economy is agriculture dominated as reflected in the predominant share of primary sector in the net state domestic product and a very high percentage (67%) of employment in the primary sector. It is after independence and more particularly after Fourth Five Year Plan that industrial development received the attention of the planners and policy makers. In the very beginning the state concentrated on the development of existing handloom, handicrafts and village industries. In the seventies it started attending to the establishment of SSI units mostly based on locally available raw materials. From the eighties onwards it is trying to diversify its industrial units especially village and SSI units. With the adoption of the industrial policy resolution in 1994, a clear message has emanated from the policy makers in the field of industrialisation.

However analysis of data suggests that in the field of SSI and medium scale units, the spread of industries is not in proportion to the population in various districts. The rate of growth of industrialization is not at all in proportion to the availability of pre-requisites of industrial growth. Poor infrastructure (power, transport and communication) and lack of proper marketing network, no doubt are two of the important constraints to industrial development. Nonetheless, industrial development has much to do with healthy entrepreneurship development. It is in this regard that Arunachal finds the greatest constraint to industrial growth. Dearth of genuine entrepreneurs is largely because of certain existing socio-cultural value systems and arrangements in Arunachal society. Availability of easy money against lending of trade and industrial licences to proxy non-local businessmen and industrialists, distorted version of social heirarchy, extended family, liquor addiction, community based life and community ownership of land and asset etc. dampen private initiative so crucial for entrepreneurship development. Existence of an inward looking and corrupt bureaucracy adds to the problem.

If this vicious circle of poor industrialization and poor entrepreneurship development is to be broken, motivation and partnership with outside entrepreneurs in the initial period are the only viable means (along with infrastructure and marketing network improvement) needed to be adopted in this young state. Once the first generation entrepreneurs stand firm on their own foot, industrial development can be smooth thereafter.

REFERENCES

Gopalakrishnan R.: *Arunachal Pradesh--Land and People*, 1994, Omsons Publications, New Delhi.

Economic Review of Arunachal Pradesh, 1994. Directorate of Economics and Statistics, Govt of A.P.

Melo de Martha, Ofer Gur and Sandler Olga—"Pioneers for Profit: St. Peters burg Entrepreneurs in services", *The World Bank Economic Review*, Vol-9, number 3, Sept. 1995.

Mali D.D. and R. Bandopadhyay: *Small Industry Development in North-East India*, 1993, Omsons Publications, New Delhi.

Statistical Abstract of Arunachal Pradesh, 1994. Directorate of Economics and Statistics, Govt. of Arunachal Pradesh.

29

SOCIOLOGICAL CONSTRAINTS OF TRIBALS ON INDUSTRIALISATION IN TRIPURA

-- Sankha Subhara Devbarman

The North-East India which was introduced as Kirat Bhumi in the mythological texts, added different colours and shape in the Indian social fabric. Risley writes "no one who is acquainted with the population of the lower Himalayas can have failed to observe that in the West there have been a substantial intermixture of Indo-Aryan elements, while in the east the prevailing type down to the verge of the plain is exclusively Mongoloid." So "An appraisement of the role of the Mongoloid people in the development of composite Hindu or Indian culture, the North-Eastern and Eastern India through Mongoloid contact or participation would be looked upon as an important line of enquiring in tracing the history of Indian civilization."[1] Thus we see frequent description of Kirat Bhumi and its people in world renowned two of our all time great epices "the Ramayana" and "the Mahabharata."

India was repeatedly attacked by the mighty foreign aggressors since time immemorial. But the foreign power never dared to invade the densely forested and topographically inaccessible North-East India. Even during the British rule in India subcontinent most of the parts of North-East were out of jurisdiction of the British Empire. Either most of the princely states of this region came into friendly pact with the Imperial Government or violently protested against the latter--if there was any attempt to dominate them. The Imperial Government too did not show much interest to widen its direct supremacy in this region.

After the departure of the British Government, economic measures had to be taken up by the independent Indian Government to revamp its dwindling economic condition. Its economic resources were indiscriminately plundered for two hundred years. Hence it was an urgent task to rebuild its broken economic infrastructure. This was the beginning of planned economy. Perhaps in accordance with the time it was the most viable means to re-construct the devasted Indian economic condition. But so far as the structure of our economy is concerned, after more then 30 years of planning we are there where we were. "Economic transformation is really a difficult task and is extremely slow process, but it (process) cannot be done without due consideration for the basic parameters which should be clearly identified so that the planning can become realistic. The same holds for the tribal economy where the task is much more complex and difficult"[2] The economic condition of tribal inhabited North-East also could not get the momentum due to number of factors.

Tripura being the part of North-East India has to face the innumerable hurdles for industrialisation. "Tripura is a relic of once a powerful kingdom of the name in the great Sanskrit epic *Mahabharata* and coming down to the historic period in the *Ain-i-Akbari.* The dialect of these people belong to the same big family of the Tibeto-Burman language. Ethnologically most of the tribes are the same non-Aryan stock."[3] This princely state was integrated into the Republic of India on 15th October, 1949. During the time of merger with India, it had Asiatic feudal economic structure like any other state of North-East India. There was no organised industrial growth in the state, except some tea gardens. Basic infrastructural aspects like power, communication, transport were almost absent. The present situation has not improved upto the mark of expectation till to-day. Moreover, in comparison to other states in North East India, Tripura suffers more from acute locational problem.

Tripura is located at the south west extremity of Assam and it is surrounded on three sides by Bangaladesh. To the north-east are the states of Assam and Mizoram. The area is 10,491 sq. kms. About 60 per cent of the land area is hilly, while remaining 40 per cent constitutes plain land. The state has 839 kms of long bonder with Bangladesh. Ironically the state has only a token presence in the Rail map of India. NH-44, Tripura's life line which connects Agartala with Shillong through Badarpur is neither reliable nor effective. It is subjected to inundation and land slides while not meeting even the basic specification of a National highway. Air links, especially with the North-East is tenous and highly expensive. Consequently a sense of alienation has gripped the mind of people in Tripura.

The population of the state according to the latest census is 27 lakhs 57 thousands and 205. The tribals, who are the original inhabitant of the state, constitute nearly 31 per cent of the total population. Earlier the tribals constituted the major portion of the population. But the partition completely changed the demographic scenario of the state.

"The influx of Hindus from Pakistan to Tripura began mainly from the middle of February 1950 and this number began to increase rapidly."[4] After partition and settlement of refugee "the population composition and demographic aspect of Tripura have entirely changed. As compared to 6,46,000 in 1951 the estimated population for the year 1957 was 9,21,000. The refugee outnumbered the original inhabitant."[5] From the very beginning the peculiar geographical condition of the state kept the people isolated from mainland India. The tribals were never exposed to the modern industrial development. Moreover, on account of influx from erstwhile East Pakistan, the original inhabitant had to sacrifice huge landed areas to the new settlers. It should be noted here that the tribal society entirely depends on the natural resources for their livelihood. But the settlement policy changed the gamut of socio-economic condition of tribal life. During the kingdom, tribals were badly neglected. They were neither encouraged to improve their condition nor were inspired to go for education. So tribals failed to maintain their pace with the demand of time. The new settlers outsmarted the original inhabitants of the state with their superior technological skill. Education, and financial wise the new settlers were more developed than the tribals. The tribals did not have any specific economic system. The *jhuming* cultivation and various handloom and handicrafts used to form the simplistic economic infrastructure. Further the rehabilitation policy pursued by the State Government for refugees led the decrease of *jhumia* field and forest. When the forest was there the tribal had enough to live on. Now this development has begun to hurt their stomach. These new developments had tremendous impact on socio-economic condition of tribals.

The tribals were incredibly good at handloom and handicrafts products. They showed remarkable efficiency in their handmade products. But no efforts were made to expand their craftsmanship. The commercialisation of the products were never in their mind. They used to produce their goods to meet their own demand. Apparently it seems that the industries which were not directly related with their lives never attracted them. That is why tea being one of the oldest industries in the state, which were set up by some private entrepreneurs in the mid of this century, failed to draw attention of tribals. The number of tribal labourers working in the total 55 tea gardens in the state, is very less in number. Less than 600 tribals have been working in the tea garden till today. The figure does not only indicate the small presence of tribals in the tea gardens, it also shows their apathy to get involve in the industrial sector of the states. The same phenomenon can be noticed in the Rubber and Gas-based industries in the state. Like any other state in North-

East India, the tribals in Tripura are also orthodox, highly ritualistic, inward lookings, complacent and have limited needs and takes time to conceive/adopt to modern concepts/instruments. These attitudes have become a great obstacle to make congenial atmosphere for industrialisation in the state. Everywhere it has been noticed that the participation of tribals in Industrial Sectors are miserably low. The State Government despite its earnest endeavour to improve the lot of aboriginal people, could not succeed much to convince them about the yielding good results of industrialisation.

In the above context one can presume that the awareness about industrialisation among the tribals depend on the spread of mass education. Although literacy rate (60.44%) in Tripura is quite high (In Indian context, Tripura secured 15th place in literacy rate), but the literacy compaign initiated by the Government and N.G.O. could not yield any fruitful result among the tribals. The curse of illiteracy looms large on the aboriginal people. The number of school dropout among tribal boys and girls is very high (91.56%) and the rate of dropout has been increasing. The recent development in the tribals society aggravated the situation from bad to worse. This development not only deteriorated the tribal plight, it also vitiated the communal harmony in the state. Some discontent tribal youth have been blaming the pact by which Tripura was annexed with India.

Further, they have been claiming that due to large number of influx from erstwhile East Pakistan, tribals of this state have turned into microscopic minority in their own land. So they raised the demand to oust the "foreigners" who came to the state after the partition. Ironically separatist forces in the state are also some time being assisted by some political parties for suppression of their political opponents. All these led great uncertainty in the State. So called separatist movement, also has been causing great hindrance towards all kinds of development. Investors are getting scared to invest in the Industrial Sectors. Diverting the huge money which could have been utilised for the overall development of the state, the Government has been trying to neutralise the separatist movement. The process of industrialisation has almost broken down. Now it has become the responsibility of the Government to call back the misguided youth so that by throwing the arms and ammunitions they can play an important role in the industrial development of the state. Without the cooperation of tribal population the pace of industrialisation is bound to be thwarted.

The next thing we must say that the tribals have great deal of misunderstanding about the industrialisation. Infact they are worried about the juggernut of the industrialisation. Off and on the tribals have witnessed the devastating impact of industrialization in the state. They just take it for granted that they are being uprooted from their own land under the so called process of industrialisation.

Though adequate compensation and rehabilitation for the effected families are being promised, these are never kept. "Take the example of the victim of the Gomti Hydel Power Project in Tripura two decades ago, then 10 MW Gomti Project took off, the then Chief Minister declared that the ousted families would be economically rehabilitated. At least 2,558 families mostly tribals were uprooted from their ancestral land which were submerged by the damned water. State rehabilitation officials say during the last two decades, only about 500 families were compensated while the rest of them are yet to receive any help from the Government. Over Rs. 2 crores would be required to economically resettle the ousted people. Meanwhile, the dillydallying over compensation shattered many homes. Deprived of land, which would offer shelter and livelihood, they were forced to take up work as rickshaw pullers or as daily labourers. Some of them could not even manage that and turned to beggary, uncommon to tribal people."[6]

In India whenever the Government made any attempt to set up industries the first casuality was the local tribals. Since Independence, the juggernut of development--ambitious dams, mines and power plants--has displaced 30 million people from their homes. Tripura is no exception to this process. But no effective measures are being taken up by the Government for the proper rehabilitation of tribals who are the worst victims of industrialisation. The astounding fact is that despite the magnitude of displacement, there is no national policy to cope with it. "If the overall figures of major projects are analysed, certain little known but disturbing facts emerge. 20 per cent of the country's tribal population had been displaced; the single largest group to be effected by development."[7]

Another disturbing sign is that the industrialisation might be in its nascent stage in Tripura, but its process has already cast aspersed evils effect on tribal society. Gradually the new generation of tribals are becoming money-oriented, self centered and consumerist. It is seen, a sort of social unrest has been started to fumigate. The incident of rampant crime and dowry is no more a new phenomenon to the tribal society. Sometimes various assistance and offers are being given to tribals as compensation packages for industrialisation by the Government. Often this is more than what many of them had been in their lives. The money is splurged on irrelevant amusement like transistors and brassware. Liquor and *gambling dance* opened.

Till now the situation might not be out of control, but the older generation is anxious and making allegation to the process of industrialisation for the recent social discord. The causes of growing tribal discontent should have been looked into the indiscriminate process of industrialisation in the state. It is a process where tribals do not have any role to play, but only pain to suffer. The sociological constraint to the industrial development in Tripura should be analysed in the contexts which are mentioned here above.

To remove the fear about industrialisation from the mind of tribals, the Central and State Government have taken various steps. "The Government is aware of the constraints to industrial development in Tripura. To help the entrepreneurs to overcome these difficulties, the Government provide large number of liberal incentives. The Government of India have also declared all Districts of Tripura No Industry Districts and announced special incentives for the existing as well as prospective enterprises."[8]

It goes without saying in accordance with the Government policy, tribals are entitled to get liberal concession for setting up industries. Even the State Government has come forward with a scheme which is being called "Tripura State Scheme for Incentives to Industrial Units." The objective of the scheme is to extend financial incentive, technical assistance and relief in the form of subsidies and grant to all industries in order to encourage and promote the growth of Tripura. Here also special incentive are being given to the tribals. Tribals manufacturers are being encouraged to sell their products to Government at profitable rate.

Indeed "the development of tribals should be along the line of genius of their community and that there should be no imposition on them. Their own traditional art and culture should be encouraged. It would also provide for integration of tribals with the rest of the society in a manner that their own tradition and culture remain undisturbed and there is no loss of identity of tribals--the rights of the tribals on land and forest should be preserved and they should themselves be prepared and trained for Administration and Development."[9] Many experts have suggested that the tribals be made partners in the process of industrialisation. Part of cash compensation could go towards making them shareholders in power stations and other enterprises to ensure a constant source of income to them. But far more important is the establishment of a national policy on resettlement and rehabilitation.

The tribals of Tripura are neither idle nor less innovative. In fact these people are highly energetic, innovative, imaginative and industrious. We have got ample evidences of their efficiency from their beautiful crafted handicraft and handloom products. They might be producing these small articles to cater their frugal demand but these products bear the evidence of delicate artistic work. It shows that the tribals are also adequately efficient to go for painstaking undaunted work. If any effort is made to create a congenial atmosphere for industrialisation in the state the inspired tribals will be the part of process. For this it needs to convince them that industrialisation does not mean the destruction of their livelihood, the massive deforestation and unbound miseries.

REFERENCES

S.K. Chatterjee: *Kirat-Jana-Kriti*, pp. 18-19.

B.D. Sharma: *Basic Issue in Tribal Development:* TUI (1995), (A quarterly Research Journal on Tribal folk & culture), Vol. IV, p. 10.

The Tribes of Tripura (Introduction): Directorate of Tribal Research, Government of Tripura.

Census of India, Vol. XII Assam, Manipur and Tripura, Part 1, p. 361.

Techno-Economic Survey of Tripura, National Council of Applied Economic Research.

Chakraborty, Sanaat K. (ed.): *Grass root Options* (September, 1995), p. 5.

Refugees of Progress: *India Today,* September 30, 1993.

Tripura Industries, Government Policy and Incentives, Directorate of Industries, Govt. of Tripura, Agartala (Second Edition: March, 1992), p. 10.

D. K. Tyagi: *Redefining the Role of the Extension Agencies in Tribal Development:* TUI (A quarterly research journal on tribal life and culture), Vol. IV., 1995, p. 35.

30

SOCIOLOGICAL CONSTRAINTS TO INDUSTRIAL DEVELOPMENT IN MIZORAM

-- A.K. Agarwal

Rapid industrial growth itself is a potent dynamic factor which contributes to the process of accelerated economic growth. Further, industry tends to exercise profound influence on the other sectors of the economy including agriculture. That is why industrialisation is generally considered synonymous with economic progress and hence the developing countries give the highest priority to industrial development.

In India, by and large industrial locations have been influenced either by the availability of raw materials or political decisions. Pure economic considerations were seldom given weightage in the location of industry. The industrial development in India has remained concentrated in a few states like Maharashtra, Gujarat, West Bengal and Tamilnadu (Anuradha and Rao : 1995). The north-eastern region despite its vast natural resources is one of the industrially backward region of the country. The Working Group on the Development of the North-Eastern Region (1985) reported categorically that the location and growth of industries are largely the result of a long process of historical evolution of market forces and deliberate public policies. These coupled with lack of investment climate, absence of alert entrepreneurship and strong pressure group to lobby for various forms of Government interventions have left the resource-rich north-east region industrially backward. Further the regional industrial scene is heavily influenced by the tea and petroleum with almost absence of engineering industry. There are few paper mills, cement plants, plywood industries, rubber and plastics, spinning mills, jute mills, khandsari and sugar mills, chemical industries and other miscellaneous industries, etc. under the large and medium industries and, that too, majority of them are located in Assam alone. Existence of very few large and medium industries in other states of the North-East and complete absence of such industries in Mizoram shows that other states of this region are at the very nascent stage of industrialisation.

The existing medium and large industries in the region operate much below the average productivity level of the industry in the country (Yogi : 1991). This points towards our attention needed to improve the productivity levels in the existing industrial units alongwith the programmes of speedier industrialisation of the North-East. The number of SSI units has increased considerably in the region. Majority of them are local resource based producing large number of products but lack diversification in the field of modern SSI units. Further, relative high incidence of sickness among these units has resulted in retarding progress in this sector.

Land-use and Population in Mizoram

Out of total geographical area of 2108 thousand hectares, the area reporting for land utilisation in Mizoram is as high as 2102 thousand hectares. About 74.6 thousand hectares is the gross cropped area with nett irrigated area of 19.2 thousand hectares. The area under fruits is 9.1 thousand hectares with production of 38.2 thousand tonnes in 1993-94. Some of the major agricultural commercial produce include chillies, ginger, oranges, banana, pineapple, and sugarcane. The prevalence of shifting cultivation on a wide scale in the hilly areas is one of the major constraint responsible for agricultural backwardness. Despite the state government efforts made under New Land-Use Policy (NLUP) and the North-Eastern Council (NEC) during the last so many years to control *jhumming,* the area operated under *jhum* rice alone is 43.2 thousand hectares producing 56.7 thousand tonnes of rice in 1993-94. Further in absence of a well knit communication system and market network it is not possible and certain that the farmers are reaping the benefits of new technology and the available inputs. The fastly growing population together with synchronising job opportunities in the government sector, growing number of educated youths entering in the job market every year make it a crying need for speeding up the industrialisation process and, that too, of medium and small scale units to absorb the future expanding labour force (Agarwal : 1988). The unorganised traditional village and small industries which include khadi and village industries, handloom, sericulture, handicrafts and coir are mostly rural and semi-urban in character. These industries sustain and create employment opportunities either partially or full employment to the people mainly agricultural labourers and artisans. Besides, increasing the income of poor artisans, these traditional industries preserve craftsmanship and art heritage. Such SSI units enable a large number of people to earn a descent income and thus pave the way for social justice.

Government Efforts

Mizo district was one of the most industrially backward districts of Mizoram. A few industrial units found in the district were the traditional cottage and village industries like weaving (loin-loom), carpentry, etc. In 1961, 0.28 per cent of the industrial units in the district were run on electricity but there was no registered factory. Rural Industries Project (RIP) set up in 1962 was resposible for looking after industrial activities. The Directorate of Industries was created in 1972 and the RIP was made responsible to look after the centrally sponsored schemes.

The Industrial Policy of Mizoram, 1989 was declared for an all-round development and gainful employment to the local people and to create self employment opportunities in the industry and allied sectors. Priority industries in the Industrial Policy include agro and forest based industries, handloom and handicrafts, sericulture, electronic, village and cottage industries, etc. The policy *inter-alia,* lay stress on even development of all sectors by extending various types of supports including institutional, organisational, marketing, infrastructural, manpower training apart from initiation to attract prospective entrepreneurs.

The Mizoram Khadi and Village Industries Board established in 1982 provides financial assistance to the village industrial units and create self employment opportunities to the people. Various schemes operated by the Board include carpentry works, blacksmithy, soap making, bakery, sugarcane crushing, spinning and weaving, etc. For the promotion of sericulture activities a separate Directorate started functioning since 1985. The Sericulture Training Institute, Zemabawk is extending technical and various other facilities to the farmers co-operative and rural development department for the promotion of sericulture in the state. The Mizoram Handloom and Handicrafts Development Corporation Limited (ZOHANDCO) was incorporated in 1988 to promote, develop and protect the interest of the concerned handloom and handicrafts units apart from extending assistance in procurement and sale of quality raw material at reasonable rates. The Mizoram Food and Allied Industries Corporation Limited (MIFCO) was set up in 1989 with the objectives to develop promote and improve processing and preservation of food, milk, fish, fruits, vegetables, etc. The Corporation is looking after food preservation factory at Vairengte, ginger oil and oleoresin plant at Sairang, maize milling plant at Khawzawl and food processing plant at Sairang. Other coming up projects under its supervision and control include fruit juice concentrate at Chhingchhip, mushroom cultivation, processing, pork and poultry processing plants etc. To promote electronic and allied industry in the state the Mizoram Electronics Development Corporation (ZENICS) was set up in 1991. A separate Directorate of Geology and Mining was established to take up geological investigations and mapping by seeking cooperation with the GSI and the ONGC. Shell limestone has been identified at several places to be utilised for polishing slabs and limestone industry. A cement clinker grinding unit is being set up by the Cement Corporation of India at Kolasib.

There were 2,447 small scale units in the state, 29 government sericulture farms and 909 private sericulture farms in 1993-94. The total production of cocoons is 112 quintals, mulberry 106.58 quintals and muga 21 kgs in the same year. The Zoram Industrial Development Corporation (ZIDCO) disbursed loan to the extent of Rs.149.71 lakhs to 112 SSI units in 1993-94. of which 104 units are in Aizawl district alone with sanction loan of Rs. 141.78 lakhs. This indicate the immediate need to eradicate the menace through district distribution of industrial activity so that the benefits of earning higher income can be shared by all including a rural area. For the promotion of village and small industries Industrial Estates at Kolasib, Zuangtui (Zemabawk), Luangmual, and factory sheds at Lunglei and Saiha have been set up. There are many weaver's service centres, craft training centres and raw material depot for the entrepreneur's assistance. It may be noted here that a small scale sector of traditional pattern can be favoured from view point of scarce capital, low level of technical know-how, inadequate managerial experience, and absence of huge mineral reserves. However, in the long run the small scale sector would be helpful in forging a competitive idustrial structure through establishment of both functional and spatial ancillary relationship. It is high time that the nature of hard work and ambitions to raise the living standard of a common Mizo can be cashed in by providing suitable facilities for setting up new industrial units in the state.

Constraints

Mizos are passing through a phase with two extremes from socio-cultural point of view. The extremes are traditional and western. But the latter has more influence. In dress, dance and music, festivals, the Mizos, especially the younger generation, are more fond of western culture (Hluna : 1995). However, the induction of modern components into their traditional indigenous structure has failed to expand sufficiently to a forward shift of an agriculture economy towards industrialisation.

Social System

The indigenous or native social system is characterised by low levels of techniques, precapitalists and limited markets due to limited needs and wants. Such a society is plagued by religious dogmas without any will for material progress. The people are fatalists and have no initiative to invest and take risks. They indulge more in speculative activities. Labour is unskilled and unorganised and willing to suffer or live in whatever poor conditions that exists. People in the indigenous sector are unwilling to leave their village communities. There are immobilities of resources in this sector. The indigenous social sector is almost non-commercialised. High prices do not induce them to produce more, and high wages do not make the labour to work more. With the emergence of capitalism imported from the west, another sector westernised social sector has emerged. The wants of the people in this sector are influenced by economic considerations rather than social and religious considerations. This capitalists sector is characterised by common sense, adventurism and rationality. It is more advanced, more modern and more amenable to modern development.

Primitive Techniques of Food Production and the Question of Surplus

The age-old attachment to primitive and unscientific methods of cultivation in the large indigenous rural sector may be due to some compulsions, need based like geographical location, topography and psychological fatalist attitudes of the people. Absence of capital, low level of technology do not allow some of the progressive farmers to go for improvement in land and application of scientific methods of farming. Those who are close to administration and around seat of power, have managed to grab vast area of land in the name of permanent cultivation and plantation. The limited number of such absentee landlords, emerged recently, has not influenced much to the common villagers--cultivating village common land to reap the benefits of modern and scientific method of cultivation. There is hardly any surplus available with the *jhumias* to invest in improvement of land productivity.

It is more important when the land is not owned privately by the village farmers. The declining land : man ratio due to natural growth of population and in addition influx of immigrants from Burma and to some extent Bangladeshi has affected the carrying capacity of land in an adverse manner. The old-dated social ideas and dire poverty of the masses has compelled the rural people to live a very low standard of living with limited wants. It may be mentioned here that many big land owners prefer to go for cultivation and sale the produce for purchase of a car or gypsy--a status symbol amongst the Mizos.

Handloom and Infrastructure

It is true that in spite of the region having a long heritage in weaving, every inch of mill made modern fabric and every item of hosiery product is imported from outside the state. One possible explanation lies in the adoption of western dress by and large by the people which cannot be produced by the local handloom sector. Moreover it is not possible to install and promote modern textile mills in the hills in absence of adequate infrastructural facilities, remoteness of the market, non-availability of required number of indigenous skilled labour, hostile attitude towards the immigrant labour coming from neighbouring parts of the country, bad shape of road network and communication system. It is difficult to introduce high capital intensive methods of production due to inferiority complex and economic backwardness. It may be noted here that the attempts to apply western techniques and methodology for industrial development has met with limited success and destroyed small and village industries thereby replacing labour and increasing unemployment.

Emergence of Neo Rich Mizo Capitalists Class

Since the last 25 years or so the central government has pumped huge amount of money for a planned development of the region--including improvement in agriculture and industrial production. The income generation is an outcome of planned developmental expenditure by the government and growing consumerism due to increase in population size have resulted in market expansion for consumer goods essential for modern living. The emergence of neo-rich class--successful in cornering a major chunk of government developmental money in the form of contracts and supply against the development projects and departmental schemes, growing dependence on the government for a white collar job by the educated youth as a safest way of earning livelihood have further added to the demand of factory made goods in the state. In absence of taxation and accountability of hoarding black money by the government officials and business class people--this neo-rich class of Mizos prefer to spend on luxury items, motor vehicles and construction of multistoreyed building for rental purposes to the government departments and offices, and residential complexes fitted with latest amenities and comforts of life and electronic goods to maintain a high standard of living in the society. They lack enthusiasm to come forward to take up new ventures risky in nature and of low profit margins.

Absence of Entrepreneurship

The entrepreneurs lack in accepting management risks involved in capital, skilled manpower, raw material supply, quality and marketing of finished products. It is obvious that once you find the ways of earning an easy and quick money either through contracts or supply and develop an antipathy to soil the hands by undertaking new ventures in grain production, manufacturing, trade and commerce, the people fail miserably in accepting the challenges of life and thereby increase dependence on government to come to their rescue always through sponsored programmes from above--which, of course, remain confined within very narrow limits.

Preference to Government Secured Jobs

High literacy coupled with essential carpentry and mechanical skill and the nature of hard work could not do much in creating industrial climate in the state. The youth even possessing requisite technical education prefer to go for government jobs and in absence of such opportunities available immediately prefer to wait for. There are many engineering graduates unemployed insisting the government to create jobs to them even as a graduate teacher, the reasons may be so many behind this proposal but it is certain that they hesitate to start new enterprise of their own. The easy going traditional life style and the desirability of earning quick and easy money has failed to break the vicious circle of non-industrialisation. The prevalent high prices of commodities in general and high profit margins charged by the traders as usual in the hills and backward remote areas have failed to generate demand for indigenously produced goods.

Though there exist a capitalist class but lack talented enterepreneurs with ability and motivation to undertake long term productive investment. This class also prefer to go for wholesale trade, distributors of well known companies produce, medicines, etc. The poor loan recovery by the financial institutions hamper the process of sanctioning fresh loans.

The shortage of skilled labour can be overcome by providing facilities for training but this involves a time lag. The extension of essential infrastructural facilities, promotion of entrepreneurship among the talented hard working Mizos, maintenance of harmony and peace in the region are some of the preconditions for undertaking new ventures and reaping the benefits of sustained growth. Provision of adedquate resources to raise productive investment can be made through mobilisation of savings of well-to-do section with emphasis on middle income group of the state. Adoption of technology suited to the local needs will be helpful in creating the necessary social and psychological climate which will make social and industrial development strategy a success.

Concluding Remarks

It has been proved that given the opportunities, powerful incentives do work in underdeveloped countries and create a desire for development. People do have shown willingness to work to satisfy new wants without compulsions. Under the present circumstances the urge for development has to come from the habitants themselves, for which a gradual approach is necessary instead of any radical approach based on the western economic theory. The available vast potential of agriculture, horticulture and forest in the state calls for adopting a vigorous approach for creating a suitable industrial climate which would ultimately bring large income to the government and the people as well.

REFERENCES

Agarwal A. K. (1988); "Industrialisation in Mizoram: Problems and Prospects," *Commerce*, Vol. 157: 4024, July 9-15, pp. 22-24.

Anuradha A. and AVVSK. Rao (1995): "An Analysis of Inter-State Industrial Disparities in India, 1970-71 to 1985-86", *Indian Journal of Regional Science*. Vol. XXVII: 1&2, p. 33.

Hluna J.V. (1995); "A Note on the Socio-Economic and Political Situation in Mizoram", in Prasad R. N. and A. K. Agarwal (eds.), *A Study of Public Administration in Mizoram*, IIPA, Aizawl, p. 102.

Report of the Working Group on Development of N-E Region for the Seventh Five Year Plan, NEC, March 1985, p. 92.

Yogi A.K. (1991): *Development of the North-East Region: Problems and Prospects*, Spectrum Publications, Guwahati, p. 175.

31

SOCIOLOGICAL CONSTRAINTS IN THE ECONOMIC DEVELOPMENT OF MANIPUR

-- A. Rajmani Singh and Bibhuti B. Pradhan

Introduction

Economic Development is directly associated with development of underdeveloped countries/states through a process of transformation. It is directly dependent upon the natural resources, human resources, capital resources, enterprises and technological development etc. Economic development is "the process of increasing the degree of utilisation and improving the productivity of the available resources of a country which leads to an increase of the economic welfare of the community by stimulating the growth of national income."[1]

The economic development of a state is directly measured in terms of an increasingly economy's real national income over a long period of time or in terms of increasing per capita real income or a set of social indicator. The development of economy moves through a set of environmental variable like Socio-cultural environment, Economic environment and Politico-legal environment.

The available resources and prevailing environment is balanced by an entrepreneur to convert into productive capacity of the people through a process of innovation and risk. The entrepreneur lives in a social system and is a highly respectable in the society as he/she produce and distribute the goods and services to the public in one hand and strengthen the capital base of the nation on the other. "The set of attributes the entrepreneur possesses is called entrepreneurship. Entrepreneurship plays a premium mobile role in promoting industrial development of an effect for which entrepreneurship is the cause."[2] The entrepreneur is an important change agent in every society. Yet he is one of the most enigmatic characters in the drama of economic development particularly in the less developed or developing countries. Entrepreneurial capacity can be able to bring modern economic growth by changing the per capita product with productivity in a process of structural transformation and organisation by competing with the international flows of men, goods and capital.

Growth of Small Scale Industries (SSI) in Manipur: A Comparative Analysis

The growth of SSI in the North-Eastern Region is very slow. The slow growth in the region appears to be a paradox, when we consider that the region has two well developed labour intensive industry of Tea and capital intensive industry of Oil. Furthermore, the first plywood factory in the country was set up in the region and this industry is still one of the most important industries in the private sector. The ninth finance commission measured the backwardness of this region and seems to be too backward as the weighted combined relative share of 0.1459, 1.5656, 0.1525, 0.3901, 0.1491, 0.2063 and 0.4101 in the states of Arunachal Pradesh, Assam, Manipur, Meghalaya, Mizoram, Nagaland and Tripura respectively (1981). The trend of development of SSI in the North-Eastern Region is given in the Table 31.1. Manipur occupies the third place in terms of contribution to the total number of units in the region next to Assam and Tripura and sixth in terms of growth rate from 1988 to 1992 which is only 10.51 per cent below the average growth rate of the region, i.e. 11.38 per cent. Assam stands at the top in terms of number of units contribution and fifth in terms of growth over the period of 1988 to 1992. The growth rate of Meghalaya is very high, i.e. 12.68 per cent compared to other states of the region eventhough the size of SSI units is very small. Out of seven states, only two states i.e. Manipur and Nagaland are below the average rate of the region.

Industrial Profile of Manipur

Small scale industries occupy an important role in the contribution of state's economy by providing employment and income generation, next to agriculture. The government of India have declared the state as industrially backward since its state-hood, the growth of industrial sector is more or less stagnant in public sector industries and medium and large scale industries. Manipur is having 16 state enterprises, comprising of one statutory corporation (MSRTC), one deemed company (NECON)

TABLE 31.1: Statement showing cumulative number of SIDO units registered on permanent basis and its growth rate in different states of North Eastern Region

Sl.	States	Cumulative Number of SIDO units as on 31st December					Growth rate %
		1988	1989	1990	1991	1992	
1.	Arunachal	365	451	474	525	571	
	Pradesh	(1.89)	(1.92)	(1.94)	(1.96)	(1.92)	11.80
2.	Assam	9,374	11,510	11,366	12,805	14,354	
		(48.42)	(49.02)	(46.47)	(47.76)	(48.17)	11.24
3.	Manipur	2,890	3,719	4,152	4,059	4,310E	
		(14.93)	(15.84)	(16.97)	(15.14)	(14.46)	10.51
4.	Meghalaya	1,003	1,114	1,233	1,360	1,617E	
		(5.18)	(4.74)	(5.04)	(5.08)	(5.43)	12.68
5.	Mizoram	1,694	2,087	2,245	2,478	2,638	
		(8.75)	(8.89)	(9.18)	(9.24)	(8.85)	11.71
6.	Nagaland	509	547	580	615	642	
		(2.63)	(2.33)	(2.37)	(2.29)	(2.15)	06.00
7.	Tripura	3,523	4,054	4,411	4,967	5,665	
		(18.20)	(17.26)	(18.03)	(18.53)	(19.02)	12.61
All states of		19,358	23,482	24,461	26,809	29,797	
North Eastern Region		(100.00)	(100.00)	(100.00)	(100.00)	(100.00)	11.38

Source: Report on Functions & Activities of Small Industries Development Organisation (SIDO) 1992-93. Government of India.

Note: E=Estimated.

and 14 government companies such as MSMC, MANIDCO, MANITRON etc. and in SSI sector 5,351 units of Small Industries Development Organisation (SIDO) group and 2,990 units of Non-SIDO have been registered as on March 1995. Both the SIDO and of Non-SIDO units in the state generated an employment of 42,720 persons directly with an investment of Rs. 27.37 lakhs which can be seen from the Table 31.2. Imphal district have occupied an important place in distribution of SSI units among the eight districts. Likewise, out of 8,341 SIDO and Non-SIDO units in the state, more than 50 per cent units are located in Imphal district and rest all are spread in seven districts. It clearly indicates the imbalance of distribution of industries in the state. As a landlocked state, the state's SSI sector lies on the craftsmanship of entrepreneurs in a concept of self sufficiency, which lead for one way of changing the living standard of the people. For women, the handloom and handicraft sector give a chance of

TABLE 31.2: Registered Industrial Units, Employment, Investment and Production by Districts of Manipur State in 1994-95.

(Rs. in lakhs)

Sl. No.	Districts	SIDO	NON SIDO	Total	Employ-ment	Invest-ment	Produc-tion
1.	Imphal	2774	2161	4935	25,375	16.17	72.12
2.	Ukhrul	715	88	803	4,134	2.62	12.56
3.	Bishenpur	420	160	580	2,516	1.90	8.35
4.	Churachandpur	429	104	533	2,781	1.76	8.68
5.	Tamenglong	248	203	451	2,371	1.49	6.49
6.	Thoubal	305	96	401	2,121	1.32	5.77
7.	Chandel	209	129	338	1,806	1.12	4.87
8.	Senapati	251	49	300	1,616	0.99	4.32
	Total	5351	2990	8341	42,720	27.37	123.16

Source: NUCLEUS CELL, Industries Department, Government of Manipur, 1994-95.

employment and income generation for the economic development of the State. "About 5,00,000 or 28 per cent of the total population of the state are employed both full time and part time on about 3,50,000 looms. More than 80 per cent of women in the state are engaged in this industry to fulfil their domestic requirement."[3]

Indicators of Economic Development

The present study highlights a few selected indicators for economic development such as, Per Capita Net State Domestic Product and Sectoral Contribution to State income of Manipur.

(a) *Per Capita Net State Domestic Product:* Per capita net state domestic product is one of the most important indicators for economic development. Per capita net state domestic product (PCNSDP) is calculated dividing the total state domestic product by the total number of population. SDP is the overall contribution of primary sector, secondary sector and tertiary sector to the state. Table 31.3 shows the PCNSDP from 1980-81 to 1993-94 with their percentage of indices at constant (1980-81) prices. The state has increased more than 35 per cent from 1980-81 to 1993-94 against all-India rate of 40 per cent during the same year. It was Rs. 1,419 per capita net state domestic product in 1980-81 but it rose to Rs. 1,921 in 1993-94. SDP per capita of the state is very low as compared to all

India NDP per capita of Rs. 2,282 at constant price in 1993-94. Increase in PCNSDP implies increase in all the sectors viz., primary, secondary and tertiary. In Manipur the maximum contribution is from the primary sector in comparison to others, which is not a sound indicator of economic development. Economic growth requires transformation from a state of dominance of agricultural sector to that of industrial sector. Structural transformation in favour of industrial sector (secondary sector) and diminution in the agricultural sector (primary sector) in terms of output and employment is considered the *sine-qua-non* of the economic growth.

TABLE 31.3: Per Capita Net State Domestic Product (PCNSDP) at Constant (1980-81) Prices

YEAR	All India		Manipur	
	Per capita increase in rupees	% change 1980-81 =100	Per capita increase Rs.	% change 1980-81 =100
1980-81	1,630	100.00	1,419	100.00
1985-86	1,844	113.13	1,598	112.61
1986-87	1,871	114.78	1,588	111.91
1987-88	1,901	116.63	1,669	117.62
1988-89	2,059	126.32	1,707	120.29
1989-90	2,160	132.52	1,687	118.89
1990-91	2,213	135.77	1,739	122.55
1991-92	2,167	132.94	1,842	129.81
1992-93	2,226	136.56	1,890	138.19
1993-94Q	2,282	140.00	1,921	135.38

Note : Q = Quick estimate.

Source : State Domestic Product of Manipur (New Series Revised), 1993-94, p. 15.

(b) *Sectoral Contributions to the State Income:* Manipur is dominated by the agricultural sector and has an impact on economic life of the people of state. It may be measured by their contribution to the State income. In the economically developed countries/states, the contribution of primary sector to the state income is relatively less than of the secondary and tertiary sector and vice versa in developing/underdeveloped countries. Table 31.4 represents the Net State Domestic Product (NSDP) at factor cost by sectors at constant (1980-81) prices for Manipur from 1980-81 to 1993-94.

The primary sector includes the agriculture (including livestocks), forest, fishing, mining and quarrying. The contribution of primary sector to NSDP in 1980-81 was Rs. 9,800 lakhs (49.11%) of the total sectoral contribution, which has gradually decline to 35.64 per cent in the subsequent years except 1993-95. It is a symptom of economic development with a very slow pace of growth.

The secondary sector to NSDP is the contribution given by manufacturing, construction, electricity, gas and water supply. It is an important sector for economic development as it generate maximum capital formation of the country. The contribution of this sector is very poor in Manipur than other sectors on account of slow growth in industrial/development scenario. It was only 7.65 per cent or Rs. 1,526 lakhs in 1980-81, rose to 10.52 per cent in 1993-94 with an increasing trend. It is a favourable indicator of economic development of state.

The tertiary sector includes the contribution given by (a) transport, trade, storage and communication; (b) banking, insurance and business services; and (c) public administration and other services. Since 1980-81 the contribution from this sector is gradually increased till 1989-90 and it has slightly decline to 51.78 per cent in 1990-91 from 52.26 per cent in 1989-90. There is some fluctuation in growth from 1991-92 onwards till 1993-94, it is due to provisional and quick estimate of NSDP. It is also a favourable indicator of economic development in the state, with a slow pace of economic development.

Constraints in Growth of Entrepreneurship in the State

It is clear that the state's domestic product growth rate is very slow. It may be result of slow growth of tertiary and secondary sector, and has an impact on the growth of entrepreneurship development. The causes of slow growth of entrepreneurship development can be broadly classified into: Social, Economic and Environmental factors, which has a direct consequences on the development of the state in particular and the region in general. These factors particularly identified as sociological constraints of entrepreneurs for the economic development of Manipur.

I. Social Factor

The following are the social factors which cause the constraints in the entrepreneurial development:

(a) *Family Background:* Almost all the families of Manipur are having unfavourable family background. The place of individual entrepreneur was very clearly defined in the social hierarchy of the

TABLE 31.4: Net State Domestic Product (NSDP) at Factor Cost by Sectors at Constant (1980-81) Prices

(Rs. in Lakhs)

Sl. No	Sector	1980-81	1985-86	1986-87	1987-88	1988-89	1989-90	1990-91	1991-92	1992-93	1993-94
1.	Primary	9.800	11,214	10,933	11,505	11,452	11,453	12,023	12,976	12,839	13,560
		(49.11)	(43.78)	(41.85)	(40.85)	(38.79)	(38.26)	(38.02)	(37.84)	(35.64)	(36.20)
2.	Secondary	1,526	2,316	2,300	2,457	2,881	2.839	3,226	3,423	3,703	3,942
		(7.65)	(9.04)	(8.80)	(8.72)	(9.76)	(9.48)	(10.20)	(9.98)	(10.28)	(10.52)
3.	Tertiary	8,630	12,087	12,892	14,204	15,193	15,642	16,373	17,893	19,479	19,956
		(43.24)	(47.18)	(49.35)	(50.43)	(51.46)	(52.26)	(51.78)	(52.18)	(54.08)	(53.28)
Total		19,956	25,617	26,125	28,166	29,526	29,934	31,622	34,292	36,021	37,458
		(100.00)	(100.00)	(100.00)	(100.00)	(100.00)	(100.00)	(100.00)	(100.00)	(100.00)	(100.00)

Source : State Domestic Product of Manipur (New series revised) 1993-94, pp. 11-13.

Note : P = Provisional, Q = Quick estimate. Figure in brackets indicate percentage of sectoral contribution to all sectors.

joint family system, where decision making was centralised in the hand of the head of a family, who commanded respect by way of age and experience. The position of women and children was very poor while taking decision of the business.

There is slow pace of entrepreneurial growth in Manipur due to women's dual role. Unlike men, they are entrepreneur in one side and housewives in another. Women play the active role in household work in addition to the activities of being an entrepreneur. There is no restriction in the demarcation of work between men and women from the household work to economic activities but they work in a collective strength base on co-operative and mutual dependence for self reliance and economic activity.

(b) *Education and Work Culture:* Most of the entrepreneur have come up without having the basic knowledge of business education such as effective management, right project report, feasibility report, proper maintenance of records and accounts etc. They have developed or started their enterprises in hereditary. The emerging entrepreneurs lack proper education. Work culture among the entrepreneurs and workers is almost negligible, in an average an educated youth opted for white collar job. It is due to the fact that the entrepreneurs and workers do not want to take risk by undertaking business establishment may be due to their easy goingness in life.

(c) *Social Values and Ethics:* Today, most of these old age social institutions are dying fast. It is because, the social values and ethics are changing very fast. The western values of individualism have caught up our imagination. Our women do not any longer remain satisfied as housewives. Business does not remain confined any more within a given community or caste, customs, traditions and conventions are no longer rigid, but flexible. The society's view towards authorities, responsibility, delegation, business as a profession, view towards achievement and work--all have very definite implications for sociological constraints of business.

The development of an enterprise lies on social responsibility concept with the external world with ethical reasoning like values, right and duties, morale rules and relationship towards the views of the society. The entrepreneur must aware of and avoid the temptation of naive relativism the idea that human beings are themselves the standard by which they should judge--and cultural relativism--the idea that morality is relative to a particular culture. Worker should be treated as partner, not as a worker.

(d) *Recognising Barriers to Entry:* The organisation never stands an isolation. It require proper cooperation with a work culture within the organisation. At the same time the inter linkage with the supplementary/complementary enterprises are desirable for the growth of the unit with competition. The enterprises should not run away from this concept but encourage for competition, forward and backward integration in the line of business. The entrepreneurs of the state do not recognise the entry of supplementary and complementary competitors.

(e) *Social Group and Movement:* Social tension originates in groups composed of frustrated individuals. In a society, individual form groups on the basis of caste, creed, religion, language, trade and profession. Some of these groups nave direct business interests. Thus, Consumerism, Trade Unionism, Co-operative movement; all pose challenges for business operation. But in Manipur such social movement to foster the industrial growth/economic growth had not seen like other states/regions of the country.

(f) *Lack of Freedom to Choose a Job according to Ability:* Present day is days of specialisation and cut throat competition. Without keeping weightage on their ability and specialisation, most of the entrepreneur in the state are choosing a project by looking the success of others which require specialisation in that particular area. As such the potential entrepreneur never look the enterprising concept of risk, innovation and opportunities.

(g) *Aptitudes and Training:* Training facilities undertaken by the different government agencies like SISI, NECON and ICM in the state is very negligible. To conduct a few programme of entrepreneurship development once in a blue moon will not improve aptitude and knowledge of the entrepreneurs. It requires their interest to learn, observed and diagnose the study packages with utmost care. It is also observed that entrepreneurs are not willing to participate any such training programme on payment basis.

All these retarding causes are due to the unfavourable socio-economic conditions and tradition bound society.

II. Economic Factor

In Manipur, almost all the enterprises were borne and established with sick. It is due to lack of infrastructural facilities from all directions which are outcome of various economical factors like shortage of capital, shortage of technical know-how, lack of transport and communication, absence of quality raw material, shortage of cheaper and regular supply of power. A brief discussion of above factors is given below:

(a) *Shortage of Capital:* Finance is the backbone of any enterprise irrespective of big and small. Without proper sources and management of finance, none of the enterprise can survive and grow, the source of capital are generally comes from entrepreneurs own investment and term loans from financial institutions like MANIDCO, SIDBI, NABARD, NCDC and scheduled commercial banks besides working capital finance from financial institutions and commercial banks. The mass people in general and entrepreneurs in particular in the state do not have savings and investment habit in banks. The repayment ethics are absent among the people. This has caused difficulty for recycling of funds and hence reduction and capital base." As on 31-3-94 the average recovery of the loan in the state was about 8 per cent of the total demand."[4] For instance, two major banking institutions viz., MSCB and MRB are faced with severe liquidity crisis which has forced these banks to stop lending for the last couple of years. The average populations per branch of CBs and RRBs is over 21,000 population (1995-96).

(b) *Shortage of Technical Know How:* The state is situated far flung from the capital and remote corner of the country. Whenever. any technical know-how want to import from abroad, it is a very difficult task for the small entrepreneurs in the state. On the other hand government agencies and political leaders of the state are also not extending their support to prospective entrepreneurs of the state, in spite of the facilities given in various industrial policy resolution. It is due to lack of initiative and competitiveness among the entrepreneurs.

(c) *Lack of Transport and Communication*: Transport and communication plays a significant role in economic development of a state/country. The state is landlock in the north-eastern region sorrounded by hills. The state has negligible railways track to the extent of 0.06 km per lakhs of population by 1995-96. The only transport network is feasible through surface road in the valley as the state covers 90 per cent of the total area by dense forest and hills. The total road length is 6,765 kms or 3.70 kms per 1,000 population as on 31-3-92. Air transport also found irregular due to wheather and climatic condition of the state.

The communication network can be strengthened along with the transport network and availability of better Post & Telegraph facilities. The state has 660 post offices with a coverage of 2,727 persons per post office along with 9,503 working telephone connections as on December 1992.

(d) *Shortage of Cheaper and Regular Supply of Power:* In any modern small scale industry, power plays the significant role for turning the wheel of the industry to convert raw materials into finished products. Such important factor of production in modern small scale industry is totally lacking in the state. The state has its own power generation of

2.80 MW Hydro and 7.41 MW Diesel and 105 MW generation capacity of Loktak Hydro Electric Project financed by North Eastern Council. Maximum output of Loktak Hydro is supplied to neighbouring states without fulfil the demand required by the state. The present per head consumption has increased manifolds from 70s and 80s without increasing the state's own power generation, i.e. 140.4 KWH in 1992-93 against 5 KWH and 6 KWH in 70s and 80s respectively. Eventhough the state's per head consumption has increased manifolds but it is far behind the all India average per head consumption of 330.6 KWH in 1992-93. In spite of the availability of power and power subsidy provided by the Government of Manipur the growth of the enterprises in the state is not satisfactory.

(e) *Absence of Quality Raw Materials:* Another important economic factor for slow growth of entrepreneurial development in the state is absence of quality, required quantity and imported raw materials with reasonable price. A few living example in the state is Manipur Spinning Mill Corporation Ltd. and Khandsari Sugar Factory, both of them have started without proper base of raw materials availability of cotton and sugarcane, consequence the prices of respective product goes up as the handloom sector has to depend external market for procurement of raw yarn and at the same time few horticultural sector depends on supply of sugar outside the state.

Manipur government is providing a transport subsidy for procurement of required raw material for the MH&HDC/MANIDCO/ MSHWCS upto 100 per cent by surface and 75 per cent by Air subject to a ceiling of Rs. 1 lakh in respect of Air Cargo. The state's transport subsidy cannot benefit all the entrepreneurs as the claiming of subsidy is associated with the value addition on the raw material.

III. Environmental Factors

This is the external factor which is beyond the control of enterprises. The following are the important environmental factors which causes the constraints in the entrepreneurial development:

(a) *Unstable State Government:* Very often the state government is used to change. Many new emerging policies have come and gone along with the government. Therefore, implementation part is almost negligible. Government of Manipur is not in a position to change the Industrial Policy since 1990 in spite of the liberalisation package initiated by the Government of India. Political pressure, red tapism and bureaucracy are prevailing from the very moments of registration of SSI units and various stages of sanction of grants in aid, technical know-how, training subsidy from the government side towards the entrepreneurs.

(b) *Lack of Security and Legal Protection:* The present law and order situation in the state is another obstacle encountered by the entrepreneurs in the process of development. Frequent bandh call by the various organisation, curfew imposed by the government, and conflict between two major groups in the state creates severe problems and hindrance in smooth functioning of the enterprises. Low productivity is the outcome of these problems and which leads to slow growth of economic development.

(c) *Absence of Adequate Market Place and Business Education*: There is no adequate market place where entrepreneurs can sell their finished products. Consumer awareness about the products within and outside the state is also lacking far behind. For selling their products entrepreneurs has to depend on so called *Mayang* traders (traders who came from outside the state) who exploit the poor but potential entrepreneurs.

Basic knowledge on business and technical education is very low. As on September 1992, there were 1,052 students took enrolment their name in Polytechnics and Technical and Industrial Schools. Without having proper background of business education an entrepreneur can never come out from the problems faced while operating modern SSI units.

(d) *Corruption in Administration:* Nowadays, any office or department irrespective of high and low rank of portfolio, big or small it is hardly to find there is no corruption. Corruption is anywhere and spreading like an epidemic. It pave the way for delay in payment, diversion of scheme or project from one person to another, which spoiled/destroyed the work culture of skilled entrepreneurs and root causes for industrial unrest. The state has no exception from this incurable disease of corruption.

Consequences

As a result of various constraints prevailing in the state and more specifically socio-economic constraints will lead for lack of entrepreneurial spirit among the people of the state. These constraints have direct impact on the economic life of the people. More specifically the following two major consequences emerged:

(i) Industrial Sickness; and
(ii) Social Disturbance.

Over the period of time the prevailing constraints forced the existing enterprise fail to increase the productivity or maintain the productivity of their respective units. Later on their units became sick. As per the CMIE, Bombay, basic statistics relating to Indian Economy-state 1992, the number of sick units in the state is 669 and 1540 as on December 1985 and September 1990 respectively, out of 6,758 of December 1985 and 13,669 of September 1990 in sickness of SSI units in North-Eastern Region. This sickness of Small Scale Sector resulted in closing down of units. As per NISIET Guwahati, 7.5 per cent of the working units has been closed by the end of 1990s. As a consequence the capital formation of the state resume a slow growth, hence resulting in cripling growth in secondary sector and economy growth of the state.

In spite of high literacy rate the percentage technical education holder were very few, which defy the educated mass for self employment. The unemployment of the state increases with an alarming rate than the growth of population which causes for social disturbances. The social taboo and cultural beliefs forced the unemployment youth to go for unproductive exercises. It resulted slow pace of economic development of the state.

Suggestion

Keeping in view the importance of entrepreneurial development, the following strategies may be suggested:

1. There is need to develop business education and industrial training. In modern times, business education is being viewed as an effective supplement to the development of entrepreneurship. Besides, industrial training programmes should be organised frequently. It necessitates the setting up of scientific, technological, managerial, research and training institutes. Education and training will very much help in developing and augmenting the supply of new entrepreneurs which is very much needed to utilise fully the scarce resources of economic development.

2. Financial institutions and scheduled commercial banks should provide adequate and timely credit and technical assistance, especially to the small and medium sized enterprises. Delay in payment, long time taken for grants and subsidy should be abolished and prompt payment in loan, grants and subsidy is highly needed.

3. Being an industrially backward states, Public entrepreneurship should remain confined only to those industries and sectors where

private enterprise, individual and corporate, are generally not attracted. It will make balance regional development of the state.

4. A good climate of work culture should be developed among the entrepreneurs and youth. Government cannot provide job to all unemployed youths. Self employment scheme should be encouraged. Self employment scheme may provide job to the concern person by solving the problems of unemployment.

5. Entrepreneurs should see the prospect of backward and forward integration along with the existing enterprise in the same line of business. This will pave the way for expansion and growth of enterprises.

6. Improvement in business climate by state through well designed economic policies in the area of fiscal, commercial, industrial or agricultural will benefit the humble entrepreneur in a changing society and would facilitate healthy development of entrepreneurship.

7. Entrepreneur should avail the facilities of transport subsidies provided by the state and central government. At present 100 per cent surface transport subsidies and 75 per cent Air transport subsidies is provided only to few sectors. It should be made available to all units established in the state and should not be associated with value addition on the raw material. With this restriction all the units may not get these facilities.

8. This is a vital aspect of a SSI unit, and the governmental agencies like raw materials servicing centres must be able to plan free flow of raw material so that a SSI unit need not invest more money than necessary for stocking raw materials. Care should be taken for better planning of normal flow of raw materials and the SSI units must be able to purchase raw materials. It can also solve the problem of shortage of working capital.

9. Strict quality control measures must be implemented on the outgoing product to keep up the prestige of the enterprises and to avoid the back bouncing of the product. In this regard state government should set up a Quality Control Board as a branch of Bureau of Indian Standard. It can find and strengthen competition not only within the state but also outside the state.

10. Power is a major constraint today for entrepreneurship development. It is very unfortunate that a SSI units is to suffer for power eventhough the state has Loktak Hydro Project with a generating capacity of 105 MW under the North-Eastern Council as centrally sponsored project. State government should try to convert the said project into state owned project in consultation with the NEC and the Central Government, otherwise, the state government should make necessary arrangement to ensure the supply of power on demand.

11. Entrepreneur is a risk taker but not a risk averter. In state like Manipur entrepreneur plays the crucial role from the very idea of establishing an enterprise till becoming a sound enterprise. The entrepreneur should be systematic in planning and implementation his/her idea cautiously to help the economic development of the state.

12. The present law and order situation in the state in particular and in the region in general is not suitable climate for any business enterprises. In this regard a tripartite talk should bring a peace in the state as well as in the region.

Conclusion

Development of a state lies on increase in the per capita income of people. The manufacturing sector has great contribution to reveal the economic growth of the state. Most specifically the contribution given by entrepreneurs remain unique. To nurture the entrepreneurship development from the grass-root level is a must and inevitable. But due to sociological constraints prevailed in the state, leads to slow pace of development in secondary and tertiary sector, as a consequence almost all the enterprises in the state become sick and some have already out from the market. Government of India, State governments, various agencies and entrepreneurs should join together for solving the problem and constraints faced by the entrepreneurs in time, if not it is very difficult to overcome when the problems and constraints become critical.

REFERENCES

Emprime Eshag, *Fiscal and Monetary Policies and Problems in Developing Countries.* (Cambridge University Press 1981), p. 2.

Khanka S.S.: Key note address of one day seminar on Dynamic of Entrepreneurship Development in Manipur; Organised by Department of Commerce, Manipur University on 17th April 1996.

Singh Rajmani, Management in Handloom Industry; A study of the Production and Marketing of handloom for exports. Unpublished Ph.d. Thesis, Manipur University 1992 p. 166.

NABARD, State Credit Plan Manipur 1995-96, p. 19.

Desai Vasant, *Dynamics of Entrepreneurial Development and Management,* Himalaya Publishing House 1992.

Adhikary M. *Economic Environment of Business,* Sultan Chand & Co. New Delhi. p.6.

Jhingan M.L. *The Economics of Development & Planning,* Konark Publication, Delhi. 1992.

North Eastern Council, Basic Statistics of North Eastern Region 1995.

Economic Survey 1994-95, Government of India, Ministry of Finance, Economic Division.

Report on Functions & Activities of Small Industries Development Organisation (SIDO) 1992-93, Development Commissioner, Ministry of Industry, Government of India, New Delhi-11.

Statistical Abstract of Manipur 1992, Directorate of Economics and Statistics, Government of Manipur.

State Domestic Product of Manipur 1993-94, Directorate of Economics and Statistics, Government of Manipur.

INDEX